The Wit and Wisdom of
Father George Rutler

Books by Father George Rutler

Grace and Truth

Calm in Chaos

He Spoke to Us

Hints of Heaven

A Year with Fr. Rutler (4 volumes)

Powers and Principalities

The Stories of Hymns

Coincidentally

Cloud of Witnesses

Christ and Reason

The Seven Wonders of the World

The Seven Ages of Man

A Crisis of Saints

Beyond Modernity

The Four Last Things

Adam Danced

The Impatience of Job

The Curé d'Ars Today

Priests of the Gospel

George William Rutler

The Wit and Wisdom
of Father George Rutler

❧

Edited and introduced by
Edward Short

With a foreword by
Anthony Esolen

SOPHIA INSTITUTE PRESS
Manchester, New Hampshire

Sophia Institute Press
Box 5284, Manchester, NH 03108
1-800-888-9344

www.SophiaInstitute.com

Sophia Institute Press® is a registered trademark of Sophia Institute.

Library of Congress Cataloging-in-Publication Data

Names: Rutler, George W. (George William), author. | Short, Edward, editor.
| Esolen, Anthony M., writer of foreword.
Title: The wit and wisdom of Father George Rutler / edited and introduced
by Edward Short ; with a foreword by Anthony Esolen.
Description: Manchester, New Hampshire : Sophia Institute Press, [2020] |
Includes bibliographical references and index. | Summary: "A collection
of excerpts from Father George Rutler's writings, organized
alphabetically by topic"— Provided by publisher.
Identifiers: LCCN 2020002904 | ISBN 9781622828524 (paperback) | ISBN
9781622828531 (ebook)
Subjects: LCSH: Rutler, George W. (George William)—Quotations. | Catholic
wit and humor. | Christian life—Miscellanea. | Catholic
Church—Miscellanea. | Christianity—Miscellanea. | Civilization,
Modern—21st century—Miscellanea.
Classification: LCC BX4705.R778 A25 2020 | DDC 282.092—dc23
LC record available at https://lccn.loc.gov/2020002904

First printing

For Carolynn Lucca Black
Brave, Faithful, Indomitable Friend

Practically my whole life as a priest has been spent in parishes. . . .
A well-known, but uncomprehending scholar told me once
that too much pastoral work would be a waste
of certain of my abilities, but I have not found it so.
— Father George Rutler

Lord, I will enter thy house. I will give thanks to thee
in thy temple. And I will give glory to thy name.
— Psalm 138:2

It is the peculiar and grave responsibility especially of
pastors of souls to see to the catechetical instruction
of the Christian people.
— Code of Canon Law, canon 1329

A teacher affects eternity;
he can never tell where his influence stops.
— Henry Adams, *The Education of Henry Adams* (1907)

Contents

Foreword. xi

Introduction. xv

The Wit and Wisdom of Father George Rutler. 1

Acknowledgments 283

Index. 285

About the Author 317

About the Editor 317

Foreword
by Anthony Esolen

*O taste and see that the Lord is good: blessed
is the man that trusteth in Him.*

—Psalm 34:8, KJV

When I was young and foolish, though growing old and feeble in sin, I happened upon the work of a theologian, a celebrity, who asked whether it was reasonable to believe in the existence of God. After many hundreds of pages and a survey of philosophers and theologians, he answered that question in the affirmative, much to this reader's relief. I owe him, therefore, a debt of gratitude. But he also said that he would trade all the words of Mary from every one of her apparitions for a single additional verse from St. Paul. That was ironic, given that he and his like have spent many years tossing away whole letters by St. Paul, calling them spurious, because they do not agree with the theology of St. Paul, which is, I see now, not Paul's but theirs. And that was much to this readers' harm. He added that much of the Bible was garbage. That was poison, and I ingested it.

A long time ago it was, and God has brought me from that far country of scholars, proud of what they take to be knowledge, back into the real world of grace and humility and truth. Many friends await those who return. Among the brightest and truest is Father George Rutler. He has read all those authors that the other fellow read, and taken their measure; and he has read more, far more, in authors that the other fellow would not deign to touch, such as Chesterton and Belloc, Ronald Knox and Robert Hugh Benson; and he has known and shepherded thousands of people and done many things to build up the kingdom of God, specific things, rooted in this place or that, as did his model and the model for all priests, the Curé of Ars, St. John Vianney, about whom he has written so wisely and well.

That Father Rutler can turn a phrase, everyone who has read a single one of his essays will readily see. But cynics and atheists can do as much. H. L. Mencken could turn a phrase and be none the wiser for it. George Bernard Shaw could turn a phrase. They are well-wrought pewter ashtrays in a newspaper office or a gentleman's club. For all their art, what do they contain? They miss something: the universe and its Creator. Suppose Father Rutler had been no better a craftsman of the English language than a cabbie or a paperboy. Supposing he were no deeper than a puddle in the street — and who can confidently claim more for himself? Still, for his love of God and his devotion to the Church founded by the Lord, he would, like that puddle, reflect the stars above, and in him, though not by him, one might peer into unfathomable depths. "Except ye be converted," says the Lord, "and become as little children, ye shall not enter into the kingdom of heaven" (Matt. 18:3, KJV).

Father Rutler is a first-rate scholar. No one ever accused St. John Vianney of being one of those. But if we change the word a little bit, maybe we can see something that brings them together with all those who sit at the feet of the Lord to hear His words. They are *discipuli*, from the Latin: *schoolboys*, we might say. They are *leornungcnihtas*, from Anglo-Saxon: *knights in training*. They are *Jungen*, from German: *youngsters*, observing and obeying the Master. And they are not ashamed to be so. There always was a frolic youthfulness about the Curé of Ars, despite his fasts, his watching through the night, and the physical exertions to which he subjected his body. There is that same youthfulness, I find, in the words of Father Rutler, as if everyone he meets — he is a wonderful teller of human stories — is an adventure, the adventure of sin and grace.

That is the pastor in him, too. He is the lad with the far-seeing eyes and the shepherd's crook, ready at hand to swing against wolves. Many a serious man of the cloth prefers to chat with those wolves over a supper of lamb curry and wine. Father Rutler is not of age for that. But he is young enough to minister to everyone who comes his way, the fools who are fools and the wise who are bigger fools, the high-stakes financier and the maid who cleans his office at night, the drunk and the man who would be better off drunk. The reader can see this care for them shining out in all that he says. It is not a sentimental care. The shepherd is not sentimental about wolves. He wants them gone, or dead. The surgeon is not sentimental about cancer. He wants it out. The fire of love burns hot, and woe to the creature that would lay an evil hand upon one of the sheep. For Christ suffered the agony of the Cross for each of those little ones and rose triumphant from the dead.

Read then these words of Father Rutler. They speak of Christ, first and last. They do not miss the universe, or the God who made it.

Introduction

Father Rutler is a teacher, not an entertainer, though he often entertains to teach. The extracts from his books gathered here will show readers what an exceptionally good teacher he is, not only because the wit he deploys to impart his wisdom is often brilliant but also because the wisdom itself is so timely and so timeless.

What sort of wisdom does the teacher in Father Rutler impart? To answer that, I shall quote something from one of his favorite saints. "Wisdom," St. John Henry Cardinal Newman wrote in his *Oxford University Sermons* (1843), "is the clear, calm, accurate vision, and comprehension of the whole course, the whole work of God; and though there is none who has it in its fulness but He who 'searcheth all things, yea, the deep things of' the Creator, yet 'by that Spirit' they are, in a measure, 'revealed unto us.'" They have certainly been revealed unto Father Rutler. The "deep things of the Creator" imbue every fibre of his being. Yet it is his wit that enables him to share this wisdom with others—a wit that may be whimsical, paradoxical, droll, or ironic, as the occasion warrants, but is always rapier-like in defending the truth of the "whole work of God."

"Ancient salt is best packing," the good traditional poet in William Butler Yeats said. For Father Rutler, there is no ancient salt like Roman salt, and it is with that incomparable preservative that he seasons all of the fare he sets before his readers. My charge has been to give readers a sampling of that fare. In this introduction, I am tempted simply to say, "Bon appétit" and leave my readers to see for themselves the fare's sumptuousness. Good food, after all, like good wine, needs no bush. Yet it might be helpful to share with my readers how I came to choose the extracts I chose and what I think, together, they say of my subject's apologetical achievement.

In poring over Father Rutler's various books in preparation for this project, I decided early on that I would not simply cull "quotes" from the various books in the sense of *bons mots* or aphorisms. I do not know how my readers feel about such things, but books of quotes have always struck me as deadly dull. La Rochefoucauld has much to answer for in this line, though even the epigrammatical Duc did not restrict himself to mere aphorisms in his *Maxims* (1665). Consequently, I resolved to include longer extracts that would give my readers a better sense of the depth, acuity, and appeal of my subject's thinking, without excluding the odd apothegm here and there.

Father Rutler is a rather good aphorist. His definition of "relativism" nicely shows this. "Relativism," he says, "is the attempt to realize unreality." Elsewhere, he observes how "Lent is not for the fey." In still another case, he makes a distinction that should give pause to those quick to censure: "Perfectionists are easily scandalized by what is not good. Saints are only scandalized by what is not glorious." As good as these aphorisms are, to have limited the anthology to exhibiting aphorisms would have been to do scant justice to my subject's work overall. It would certainly have robbed the collection of longer extracts such as the following, which are more redolent of Father Rutler's critical incisiveness.

> In 1940, a refugee from the horrors of the Nazis wrote a letter that was published in *Time* magazine. He said that he had seen the universities collapse before three ego- isms — the self, the state, and the body. He saw the media collapse; the journalists surrender; the courts cave in; and the government institutionalize the roots of discord. Only one voice clearly and serenely spoke out telling the truth, and that was the voice of the Catholic Church. He admitted that he had not thought much about the Church while growing up, and when he did, he did not think very much of her. But now he wanted to say that he had a profound respect for the Church as the one voice of peace in a world torn apart. The man was Albert Einstein. The great scientist was not anti-intellectual, of course, but he once warned that we shouldn't expect intellectu- als to show courage in times of crisis. Certainly, there have been great thinkers who have heroically offered their voices, their minds, and their bodies in defense of truth. But collectively, Einstein knew the temptation of pride that haunts the intellectual and that tells us that the ego is god, that our institutions can be god, that our flesh can be god.

As for editorial principles, I have included only what I thought worth including, in accordance with my set purpose of compil- ing a book that would at once instruct and amuse. I have not aimed at producing a collection that would be representative of all of Father Rutler's books, some of which simply do not lend themselves to extracts. Instead, I have sought to produce a collection representative of his thinking. As for the marvelous unity of his thinking, my readers will see this plainly in the detailed index that follows the extracts. With respect to the arrangement of the extracts, I have opted mostly for an alphabetical, rather than categorical ordering, convinced that this would make for more surprising juxtapositions. Since capturing the surprise of revelation, the surprise of truth and the discernment of truth, is of the essence of Father Rutler's wit, arranging the extracts to highlight this surprise was critical.

Looking at the compiling of the collection in retrospect, I can see now that what the extracts I chose called for most was an anthology that would show how the overall effect of Father Rutler's writing is *to edify*, an unjustly disesteemed word (from the Latin *aedificare*, "to make") which entered the language in the fourteenth century meaning "to build, to construct." Since the eighteenth century, it has often been used ironically, especially by impious sophisticates. Edward Gibbon uses it in this way when he says in his *Decline and Fall*: "The complaints and mutual accusations which assailed the throne of Constantine were ill adapted to edify an imperfect proselyte." This may be a clever use of the word, but it is not the sense in which I am applying it to Father Rutler's work, which is: "To build up [the Church, the soul] in faith and holiness; to benefit spiritually; to strengthen, support."

This gets at the heart of what the teacher in Father Rutler does in all of his work. He addresses his readers not as members of a gallery or mob but as individual souls. The charge he sets himself is to build up, to construct souls in the truths of the Faith; and he does this by familiarizing them with Our Lord and Savior and His one, holy, catholic, and apostolic Church. At every turn, he shows his readers what genuine solicitude he has for their spiritual well-being. To illustrate this, I could point to any number of extracts, but here is as good an example as any:

> Human love opens to eternal joy when it is lived as a type of God's perfect and unfailing love. For instance, marriages lived as images of Christ's love for his Church will be faithful and sacrificing, but by being indissoluble they will also be eternal. To say "Catholics can't get divorced" is a stuttering way of saying that love is given and never withdrawn. Of course, it is possible to think that love is given by humans, when in fact it is only given to them. It is a deliberate act of God; if you deny that, you lapse into strange and vague language about "falling in love." And in the next breath those who fall in love speak of "falling out of love." It is a strange object, indeed, that we can both fall in and fall out of. It is in fact a fiction. And the Cross of Christ stands as the perpetual sign that love is nothing unless it is what you have to climb up to, through every obstacle that pride puts in the way.

One of the revelations in editing *The Wit and Wisdom of Father George Rutler* has been how consistent, coherent, and, indeed, prophetic my subject's thinking is. Although prolific, Father Rutler has never been merely topical. He might write on the news of the day, but he always does so *sub specie aeternitatis*. He has also pursued themes over the years that show his keen understanding of history. If he recognizes that the nineteenth century was bedeviled by the slave trade, he also recognizes that the twentieth and twenty-first centuries have been bedeviled by the abortion trade. Indeed, an entirely separate collection could be put together highlighting Father Rutler's unstinting defense of the unborn. More than many Catholic apologists, he has never been mum about the calamity that would be brought upon our social order and, indeed, our Church by our abandoning the home truths of *Humanae Vitae*. The extracts included here reaffirming the sanctity of life are some of the book's best.

Father Rutler also understands that many of our contemporary woes stem from the same rationalism that animated the French Revolution, whose *philosophes*, in tearing down the civilization of Christendom and seeking to supplant it with their "Temple of Reason," still inspire enemies of the Faith today.[1] There is certainly something apt in Father Rutler's having written a biography of St. John Mary Vianney, the Curé d'Ars (1786–1859), the patron saint of priests, who figures in many of the extracts here as the salutary antithesis of those ruinous *philosophes* and

---

[1]   How should we define the rationalism that Father Rutler opposes? As the trusty *Catholic Encyclopedia* defines it: "Rationalism, in ... the popular meaning of the term, is used to designate any mode of thought in which human reason holds the place of supreme criterion of truth; in this sense, it is especially applied to such modes of thought as contrasted with faith. Thus Atheism, Materialism, Naturalism, Pantheism, Scepticism, etc., fall under the head of rationalistic systems. As such, the rationalistic tendency has always existed in philosophy, and has generally shown itself powerful in all the critical schools.... German Rationalism had strong affinities with English Deism and French Materialism, two historic forms in which the tendency has manifested itself. But with the vulgarization of the ideas contained in the various systems that composed these movements, Rationalism has degenerated. It has become connected in the popular mind with the shallow and misleading philosophy frequently put forward in the name of science, so that a double confusion has arisen, in which questionable philosophical speculations are taken for scientific facts, and science is falsely supposed to be in opposition to religion."

their twenty-first-century legatees. If Vianney came to the rescue of postrevolutionary France by preaching the Risen Christ over against the aridity of rationalism, Father Rutler comes to the rescue of our postmodernist society by preaching the Risen Christ over against our infinitely more pathological rationalism.

There is another striking parallel between the Curé d'Ars and Father Rutler. "Vianney," Father Rutler says, "did not mind quoting reams from the saints." For him, "the treasury of merit ... was meant to be plundered. And with the sonorous ridicule of his old professors still loud in his ears, it seemed the safer course." It is unlikely that Father Rutler's professors at Dartmouth, Johns Hopkins, Rome, or Oxford ever ridiculed him — by all accounts, he was an unobjectionable student — but he certainly has spent a good deal of his pastoral life "quoting reams from the saints." Readers of the present volume will welcome his quoting something St. John Paul II said in Philadelphia in 1976, the uncanny foresight of which clarifies a good deal of the distress that afflicts our contemporary Church:

> We are now standing in the face of the greatest historical confrontation humanity has gone through. I do not think that wide circles of the American society or wide circles of the Christian community realize this fully. We are now facing the final confrontation between the Church and the anti-Church, of the Gospel versus the anti-Gospel. This confrontation lies within the plans of divine Providence; it is a trial which the whole Church ... must take up. It is a trial of not only ... the Church, but, in a sense, a test of 2,000 years of culture and Christian civilization with all of its consequences for human dignity, individual rights, human rights and the rights of nations.

Precisely because of Vianney's devotion to the saints, he was no party man. As Father Rutler points out in his biography, the great evangelist might have become the legendary confessor he became at a time "when liberals and ultramontanists in the Church were closing their ranks, but the abstruse concerns of both signified little to Vianney.... In retrospect, it might be tempting to pin a party label on him, but such would have been implausible: his one party was Catholicism." Now, when so many preen themselves on being "liberal" or "conservative" Catholics, Father Rutler's having deplored such unreal terms as early as the 1980s proves his prescience.

While Father Rutler turns his attention again and again in these selections to questions of faith and reason, the world and the devout life, nature and grace, sin and redemption, truth and error, and illusion and reality, what most preoccupies him is the love of God—both God's love for us and what ought to be our love for Him. In choosing the various extracts that make up the book, I frequently thought of St. Augustine, so much does my subject's faithful witness to this love recall that of the great Doctor of the Church. "Though we are born and die here," St. Augustine told his readers, "let us not love this world; let us ever, through love of God, pass on hence; let us by charity dwell among the heights, by that charity wherewith we love God. Let us during this our earthly pilgrimage be ever occupied with the thoughts that we shall not always be here, and then, by leading good lives, we shall be preparing for ourselves a place whence we shall never pass on." This could easily have been written by Father Rutler. Indeed, my readers should keep this passage in mind when they read the collection, for they will hear variations on it in page after page of the extracts that follow.

They might also find themselves recalling another rather more famous passage from St. Augustine in which the convert addresses his Maker directly: "Late have I loved thee, O Beauty so ancient and so new; late have I loved Thee! For behold Thou wert within me, and I outside; and I sought thee outside and in my unloveliness fell upon those things that Thou has made. Thou wert within me and I was not with Thee." Since no one knows better than Father Rutler what an arduous process of conversion the Catholic must undergo to embrace this "Beauty so ancient and so new," many of the extracts included in this collection could serve as a gloss on this one profound passage alone. Here is one of them from perhaps his best book, the four-volume *A Year with Fr. Rutler* (2017):

> Conversion of unbelievers starts with a daily conversion of believers themselves to more genuine and mature practice of the Faith. This Epiphany is a time to commit ourselves to that great project. Our parish church is dedicated to Our Saviour. It is a reminder that we have a special responsibility in the heart of this great metropolis to announce why Christ has come into the world: not just to edify or inspire or console, but to save souls. Christians must "comfort the afflicted and afflict the comfortable," and they do this by starting with themselves.

Mulling this passage over, my readers will better understand why Father Rutler was moved to compose one of his more memorable epigrams. "A parish is not a family heirloom," he says in one of his weekly parish bulletins, "but a military base."

What the extracts of this collection preeminently show is what a good shepherd Father Rutler is. As all of his many parishioners, past and present, know, he is the personification of the good faithful dutiful evangelizing parish priest. In light of the apostasy and antinomianism that now disgrace the Church, it is imperative that the faithful be reminded of the Church's exemplary priests, and no one fulfills this role more admirably than Father Rutler. We often hear of what a crisis of catechetical learning the Church now faces. Well, readers will find in this anthology an excellent companion to the *Catechism of the Catholic Church* authoritatively promulgated by Pope John Paul II in 1992, one that will help not only catechumens obtain a richer, firmer, truer understanding of our doctrinal Faith, but catechists as well—indeed all Catholics, whether they happen to be convert, cradle, or stray Catholics.

For example, regarding Advent, the *Catechism* says: "When the Church celebrates the liturgy of Advent each year, she makes present this ancient expectancy of the Messiah, for by sharing in the long preparation for the Savior's first coming, the faithful renew their ardent desire for his second coming (cf. Rev. 22:17). By celebrating the precursor's birth and martyrdom, the Church unites herself to his desire: 'He must increase, but I must decrease' (John 3:30)" (524). Here is Father Rutler on the same topic:

> If confession has become the lost sacrament of our age, Advent has become its lost season. These absences are the unholy hollows of the Culture of Death: if man does not confess his sins, he cannot live eternally; and if he has no promise to await, he will find no reason to confess. As a nocturne indicates beauty in what coarse perception registers only as an absence of day, so Advent is the sign that our present life is greater than incidental existence. The season of anticipating the coming of the Savior who is also our Judge is the calendar's tribute to the Beatitude of Purity. The pure in heart are blessed for they shall see God; and the heart's purity consists in moral focus on God

as the purpose of all living. Dead men keep no Advent. Secularized Christians have let themselves be swept into this swirl of obscurity and denial by "rushing" Christmas at the expense of Advent — which is like rushing birth by eliminating pregnancy.

Here we have the teacher in Father Rutler at his best, living out his pastoral vocation by transmitting the Faith to his far-flung flocks, whether in New York or around the world, though passages like this also show that if he has made the Catholic tradition his own, he also renews it.

Still another commendable aspect about Father Rutler is that he has dedicated himself not only to the teaching of the Faith but to *cura animarum*, the salvation of souls, and it is this that gives all of his writing its missionary force. Indeed, Father Rutler has shown himself to be an indefatigable missionary, whether serving as a pastor at the Church of Saint Michael the Archangel in Hell's Kitchen or as a commentator on the television and the Internet, and nothing confirms this better than Pope John Paul II's encyclical *Redemptoris Missio* (1990), a passage from which could almost serve as a kind of job description for my subject.

In proclaiming Christ to non-Christians, the missionary is convinced that, through the working of the Spirit, there already exists in individuals and peoples an expectation, even if an unconscious one, of knowing the truth about God, about man, and about how we are to be set free from sin and death. The missionary's enthusiasm in proclaiming Christ comes from the conviction that he is responding to that expectation, and so he does not become discouraged or cease his witness even when he is called to manifest his faith in an environment that is hostile or indifferent. He knows that the Spirit of the Father is speaking through him (cf. Matt. 10:17-20; Luke 12:11–12) and he can say with the apostles: "We are witnesses to these things, and so is the Holy Spirit" (Acts 5:32). He knows that he is not proclaiming a human truth, but the "word of God," which has an intrinsic and mysterious power of its own (cf. Rom. 1:16).

Now, one might quibble with this and say that Father Rutler proclaims Christ primarily to Christians, not non-Christians. That may be so, but in a world in which so many Christians know so little of the doctrinal Faith, and practice it even more negligently, in a Catholic world, as I have noted, riddled with apostasy, he might as well be addressing a largely non-Christian audience, or, at least, a pitiably uncatechized one. In all events, in the passages that follow, my readers will be able to hear the Spirit of the Father speaking through Father Rutler as through few others.

How to conclude? Father Rutler has always been amusingly dismissive of those who would eulogize him prematurely. This anthology, although a distillation of a lifetime's writing, is only the first installment of what I am sure will swell to be a larger collection as he continues to publish. If not a eulogy, it can serve as a welcome *Festschrift* for a most endearing teacher, one whose wise and witty meditations on the Faith will continue to edify the faithful, the unfaithful, and the would-be faithful for many years to come.

—Edward Short
Astoria, New York
23 November 2019
Feast of Saint Amphilocus

The Wit and Wisdom of
Father George Rutler

.

Absolution and 9/11

On September 11, policemen and firemen came to priests to be absolved of sin. And even as metal was falling, they would take their helmets off for blessings. There were so many that eventually the priests were giving general absolution the way one does on a battlefield—and this was a battlefield. Seeing that scene, smelling the acrid smoke—which was not just chemical smoke, but the smoke of burning flesh redolent of all the acrid smoke of the modern age, which has consumed men and women, body and soul—the priest was able to say in the Name of Christ, "I absolve you from your sins, in the Name of the Father and of the Son and of the Holy Spirit." Those rescue workers were not going through a formality. They knew what they were getting into, and they knew how to get out of it—not how to get out of earthly death, but how to get out of eternal death. One can ask for absolution only if one knows that there is a True God who will absolve sin. One can speak of sin only if one knows virtue. And one can know virtue only if one knows the ultimate truth that there is a God in whose image we are made. In other words, we have an intellect and a will that can reflect the offering of God, who, in a gratuitous act, said, "Let there be life." All virtue is a participation in that life.

Grace and Truth (2019)

Acts

The Gospel issues in a Book of Acts, not a Book of Ideas.

He Spoke to Us (2016)

John Adams, John Quincy Adams, and Islam

It is fair to read John Adams's sense of Islam in his son John Quincy Adams's distillation of it:

> The precept of the Koran is perpetual war against all who deny that Mahomet is the prophet of God. The vanquished may purchase their lives by the payment of tribute; the victorious may be appeased by a false and delusive promise of peace; and the faithful follower of the prophet may submit to the imperious necessities of defeat: but the command to propagate the Moslem creed by the sword is always obligatory, when it can be made effective. The commands of the prophet may be performed alike, by fraud, or by force.[2]

Adams was aware not only that Islam promoted history's largest slave system, including over a million Europeans and tens of millions of Africans, but that it had even nibbled at New Englanders. In 1625, Governor William Bradford lamented that one of the Massachusetts Bay Colony's ships, in the English Channel within view of Plymouth, had been boarded by Turks who took the captain and crew as slaves to Morocco. The sultan there, Moulay Ismail, pride of the Alaouite dynasty, kept twenty-five

---

[2]   *The American Annual Register for the Years 1827-8-9* (New York: E. and G. W Blunt, 1830), 274.

thousand white slaves. He was known to test his latest axes and knives on slaves, but for that purpose he used Africans.

He Spoke to Us (2016)

Adoration

As a parish, as an archdiocese, and as members of the Universal Church, we may convert a troubled world and reconvert our own souls by making adoration the first motion of our day and the constant motive of our lives.

A Year with Fr. Rutler (2017)

Advent

Advent became widely observed by the seventh century in Spain and has a longer history and length in the Eastern Church. While its penitential nature is less pronounced than that of Lent, its tone and liturgical customs are clear about its sobriety. I recall the folded chasubles of Advent and Lent, symbols of austerity like draping statues and covering altar paintings. If a soul sorely tried does not yield to cynicism out of pride, it can return to anticipation out of humility.

The Stories of Hymns (2014)

The Aesthetics of Worship

Neglect of the aesthetics of worship is not remedied by the worship of aesthetics.

Calm in Chaos (2018)

Albert Einstein

In 1940, a refugee from the horrors of the Nazis wrote a letter that was published in *Time* magazine. He said that he had seen the universities collapse before three egoisms—the self, the state, and the body. He saw the media collapse; the journalists surrender; the courts cave in; and the government institutionalize the roots of discord. Only one voice clearly and serenely spoke out telling the truth, and that was the voice of the Catholic Church. He admitted that he had not thought much about the Church while growing up, and when he did, he did not think very much of her. But now he wanted to say that he had a profound respect for the Church as the one voice of peace in a world torn apart. The man was Albert Einstein. The great scientist was not anti-intellectual, of course, but he once warned that we shouldn't expect intellectuals to show courage in times of crisis. Certainly, there have been great thinkers who have heroically offered their voices, their minds, and their bodies in defense of truth. But collectively, Einstein knew the temptation of pride that haunts the intellectual and that tells us that the ego is god, that our institutions can be god, that our flesh can be god.

Grace and Truth (2019)

All History

All history is the Emmaus Road.

He Spoke to Us (2016)

No Almsgiving, No Heaven

The gates of heaven will not open to those who shut their own gates in this world.

Hints of Heaven (2014)

A Dreadful Amnesia

The clarion message of Ars is this: there is a more perilous impediment to holiness than misdeeds, and it is tepidity. The human soul can share, above even angelic knowledge and love, in the intelligence and nature of God Himself, but only through divine union. Goodness is a fruit of the Christian life; it is not the tree itself. Thus, the symbol of salvation is the Cross and not the holy Commandments, for holiness as a state more profound than conformity to moral precept requires identity with the salvific sacrifice of Christ: "Father, I desire that they also, whom thou hast given me, may be with me where I am" (John 17:24).

The Calvinist moral tradition had been uprooted from the unitive vision of the natural law; consequently, the common environment of much Western culture has a deontological morality, aware of legal precepts but unaware of holiness as their end. It festers even among nominal Catholics, who become indigenized to its cultural matrix. People then can ask in perfect seriousness, "Is such-and-such still a sin?" and they can think that if a mortal sin is legalized by the civil courts, then it is not a sin at all. The lukewarm spirit lacks the resolve to investigate the inconsistencies of these errors; certainly, it lacks the courage for sacrificial worship. A veritable hallmark of the tendency, in fact, is the decline of the high concept of the Eucharist as a sacrifice; it is easier for tepidity to find expression in ritual fellowship meals and the like when it has not yet slid out of religious customs altogether. The Saint of Ars stands as a refutation of the mediocrity of both the old deists and their new counterparts, who have celebrated life in ways that have forgotten how to celebrate death and Resurrection. By a dreadful amnesia of all that makes the soul breathe, the blood of Calvary and the white of Easter have been blended through the alchemy of reductionism into a sentimental pink.

The Curé d'Ars Today (1988)

Amoris Laetitia

As with the ancient Roman shrines, liberal Protestantism decayed as a result of denuding ritual of dogma and giving primacy to manners over morals. The tendency now also threatens the Holy Church herself. Consider how the apostolic exhortation *Amoris Laetitia* quotes Aquinas in treating of mercy: "Every human being is bound to live agreeably with those around him." That is one of its thirteen salutary citations of the Angelic Doctor, and it represents the best of pagan comity, but the second part is omitted: "For the sake of some good that will result, or in order to avoid some evil, the virtuous man will sometimes not shrink from bringing sorrow to those among whom he lives." To neglect that virile Christian admonition, to melt prophecy into sentimentality, to cherry-pick the *Summa*, is like treating the word "not" as an interpolation in some of the Ten Commandments.

Calm in Chaos (2018)

Angels

As angels have no bodies, they have no size, and so they care for everyone equally, regardless of size or age or worldly importance. Jesus said that the littlest human body has a guardian angel in heaven (Matt. 18:10). In each of us the guardian angels see their Lord and Our Lord.... St. Pius of Pietrelcina (Padre Pio) wrote to a young girl: "Never say you are alone in sustaining the battle against your enemies. Never say you have nobody to whom you can open up and confide. You would do this heavenly messenger a grave wrong."

A Year with Fr. Rutler (2017)

Elizabeth Anscombe

Elizabeth Anscombe was too Catholic to be patient with third-rate feminism, outward appearance notwithstanding. Elizabeth always wore trousers. Entering the apostolic palace to see the pope, she approached the gate in trousers and pulled a string, lowering her skirt like a parachute. Her last conscious act on her deathbed was to kiss her husband, but she abjured her married name. Telephoning her in Cambridge from Oxford, which is possibly the world's longest long-distance call, I asked to speak with Mrs. Geach. "There is no such person," said the voice before hanging up. A second call to "Professor Anscombe" initiated a friendly conversation with no allusion to the faux pas. She had been diligent in securing an academic posting for me in Oxford, but she could also be absentminded. Her young children wandered along the canal with signs pinned to them: "Do not feed me, I am a Geach." She was, nevertheless, an utterly devoted mother.

Cloud of Witnesses (2009)

The Apostolic Faith Has No Secrets

The Apostolic Faith has no secrets, no inner light reserved for a brightened few; the last book of the Scriptures is Revelation, with all its seven seals open. The God of Abraham manifests Himself in outer light to the darkened, but not blinded, intellect. "Remember where you stand: not before the palpable, blazing fire of Sinai, with the darkness, gloom and whirlwind, the trumpet blast and the oracular voice, which they heard and begged to hear no more No, you stand before Mount Zion and the city of the living God, heavenly Jerusalem, before myriads of angels, the full concourse and assembly of the first-born citizens of heaven, and God the judge of all, and the spirits of good men made perfect" (Heb. 12:18–23).

The Curé d'Ars Today (1988)

No Bored Apostles

It is hardly a tribute to the glory of God's creative power to be bored with what He has made and to be a bore to others. Christ excited many different reactions in those who encountered Him. He attracted crowds and delighted them, for He was not like the pedantic scribes. He frightened many, including His closest followers, who, on at least two occasions, thought He must be a ghost. He confused His neighbors, who could not reconcile His domesticity with His transcendent speech. When He passed by, some cheered and others bowed before Him. He scandalized those who had a miniature sense of life and angered those who resented the way He threatened their moral myopia. There were those who were willing to die for Him, and there were those who made Him die. But there is no record of anyone saying that He bored them. He showed how extraordinary it is to be ordinary, and He sanctified Ordinary Time so that the days between feasts are feasts themselves.

A Year with Fr. Rutler (2017)

Arrogance

Arrogance, the opposite of meekness, is spiritual arthritis. Get rid of that moral stiffness, and then "the Counselor, the Holy Spirit, whom the Father will send in my name,... will teach you all things, and bring to your remembrance all that I have said to you" (John 14:26).

Calm in Chaos (2018)

Art, Science, and Grace

In arts and in literature, the Catholic voice has manifested to the world the right use of the mind and of matter: for the glory of God. Cézanne and Bernini, two artists, very dissimilar in style, went to Mass every day recognizing the sacred vocation God had given them with paintbrush and chisel. Similarly, we can look to the music of Palestrina, Monteverdi, Vivaldi, Corelli, Haydn, Mozart, Bach, Beethoven, Bruckner, and so on. Just as a saint cannot be explained without the grace of God, neither can these high achievements of civilization. And even if the artist, even if the musician, even if the scientist does not fully articulate or explicitly acknowledge the source of his inspiration, it is still there. And the more one lives the life of grace, the more invention and art and science literally become full of grace.

Grace and Truth (2019)

The Ascension

Watching the Ascension, frail human eyes had a hard time processing that glory.... The Apostle grasps for words to describe what is beyond familiar physical formulas: "He was lifted up, and a cloud took him from their sight" (Acts 1:9). Christ's departure would make Him more vividly present. It was not like people on the dock waving wistfully to passengers on a departing ship while the band plays "Now Is the Hour." I remember that scene from the days when the great ocean liners pulled out from the piers down the street from our church. Christ is no longer limited by space, so His Church can be everywhere, with Him present on every altar. There is then a paradox of glory: as Christ leaves, He says, "I am with you always, until the end of the age" (Matt. 28:20). This is the treasure and confidence of the Church at times when the presence of Christ seems obscured by tragic events and vain people.

A Year with Fr. Rutler (2017)

Ashes to Ashes

A curate presiding at a funeral might toss soil onto the coffin and say, "Dust to dust, ash to ash." This is an amen to the parable of the Sower. Christ told the parable so that each of us might let Him make of our graves what He made of His own borrowed tomb: a gateway to Heaven.

Hints of Heaven (2014)

Ash Wednesday

I live in the middle of Manhattan, where Ash Wednesday is perhaps the most popular religious day of the year, albeit confused with Mardi Gras, the day before, and being quickly surpassed in popularity by Halloween. Thousands come to the Catholic churches for ashes, many without full knowledge of what the ritual really is but at least palpably aware that we are dust. Even the bulimic syntax of the English translation of the rite cannot rob our sense of mortality of a pathetic majesty. We are an Easter people, and, as St. Augustine was wont to say, Alleluia is our song. But without confession of our many morbid betrayals of the living God, the song becomes a ditty, and instead of the scarred bishops calling the people to repentance, as at Nicaea, the Paschal landscape is festooned with harmless adults dressed as rabbits hiding eggs from bewildered children.

He Spoke to Us (2016)

Atheists

Atheists, who are politely called "secularists," are different from the saints who are "in this world but not of it" because they are "of the world but not in it." This explains why their solutions to the world's ills are so wrong.

A Year with Fr. Rutler (2017)

Auden in New York

Auden admired Kierkegaard for making Christianity seem Bohemian. He was looking in a mirror. His Oxford College finally agreed to place a small portrait of him in its great hall, but in the most Bohemian corner next to the kitchen. Much of him is still in New York, and when the smoke was twirling so cruelly above the city in the days after September 11, 2001, there were those who remembered verses some veiled prophet inspired him to write in 1939: "The unmentionable odour of death/ Offends the September night."

Cloud of Witnesses (2009)

Baptismal Vows

As Christ reaches out His hand, we are free to accept it or go our own way. In the fourth century, St. Gregory Nazianzen studied at the Athenian academy under the tutors Himerius and Proaeresius. One of his fellow students, Basil, also became a saint. A third class-mate, Julian, became the last Roman emperor of the Constantinian dynasty and renounced Christ. This is a good time to renew our baptismal vows and go safely into the unknown. St. Gregory wrote:

> Today let us do honor to Christ's baptism and celebrate this feast in holiness.... He wants you to become a living force for all mankind, lights shining in the world. You are to be radiant lights as you stand beside Christ, the great light, bathed in the glory of him who is the light of heaven. You are to enjoy more and more the pure and dazzling light of the Trinity, as now you have received—though not in its fullness—a ray of its splendour, proceeding from the one God, in Christ Jesus Our Lord, to whom be glory and power for ever and ever. Amen.

A Year with Fr. Rutler (2017)

Baptism and the First Amendment

On the day the First Amendment was passed, Washington invoked "prayer" and "Almighty God" in proclaiming a national day of thanksgiving. None of the Founding Fathers would have countenanced the recent abuse of the First Amendment to ban the Ten Commandments from civil discourse or to prohibit state-supported celebrations of Christmas and Easter. The national elections in November will test our religious integrity. Baptism disenfranchises no one. The baptismal renunciations of Satan and all his evil works and all his empty promises are the surest safeguard of our civic integrity.

A Year with Fr. Rutler (2017)

Barbarians

Cultural progress is not inevitable, and it is possible to regress to a barbaric state. Theocratic legal systems that do not recognize Christian justice as we know it allow rights for nonbelievers only as a privilege that can be withdrawn. We need only look back on the Marxist and National Socialist empires to see the consequences of blocking the gates of civilization to the Messiah. Barbarians are always milling about, and civilization admits them at its own peril.

A Year with Fr. Rutler (2017)

Behold, Your Mother

Among the things hidden from the learned and the clever are the glories of Heaven. There are glories of human intelligence and design on this earth, but the eternal glories of Heaven are revealed to children, who have no desire to outwit God. The child expects God to be God. God's Heaven is no stranger than God's earth. To a child, gates of wood and gates of pearl are equally wonderful, and a sea of water and a sea of crystal are both remarkable only in that they are seas. Our Lord says, "Unless you turn and become like children, you will never enter the kingdom of heaven" (Matt. 18:3).

Our first ancestors did not have childhoods, being born fully formed from the dust of the ground and the side of man. So great was their intelligence that they could delight God by reason as happily as children can delight God by lack of reason. Yet intelligence is no vaccine against pride. Adam and Eve did not want to be like children, for the cleverness of evil had persuaded them to want to be like gods. They could not be like gods, but they did stop being like children. Those who will not be childlike will be childish. Adam hid behind a tree because he was ashamed of himself. To be childlike is to love God. To be childish is to envy God.

Our God could have come to us any way He wanted two thousand years ago. He willed to come down from Heaven through a human mother because we can only go to Heaven through a human mother. The heavenly Jerusalem is mother of us all who have received the gift of life in the womb of a woman. St. John, writing the book of Revelation, saw "a great multitude which no man could number, from every nation, from all tribes and peoples and tongues ... before the throne and before the Lamb, clothed in white robes, with palm branches in their hands" (Rev 7:9).

Our Lord offers the same gracious greatness to every generation by giving all of us the same mother. From the Cross in unspeakable pain, covered with blood, He said to you and me: "Behold, your mother."

He Spoke to Us (2016)

Bernard Basset, S.J.

After eight years as a parish priest in the Isles of Scilly, Bernard Basset, S.J., moved near Newman's old haunts in Littlemore. There he lived in the long shadows of the Oxford spires, where in bright youth he had finished a brilliant degree. Overlong illness encumbered his twilight but was no burden to his ebullience while in the Catholic nursing home on Oxford's Cowley Road. Both legs had been amputated, and he related this with sparkling and unaffected cheerfulness. Several months after the first leg, the doctors advised removing the second, and this relieved him of the fuss of being fitted for an artificial limb. I saw him days before he died, and his parting words were: "I have loved St. Ignatius and Newman. All my life I have studied them. But had I to do it over again, I'd have read nothing but St. Paul. Yes. St. Paul. It's all there."

Cloud of Witnesses (2009)

The Battle of Lepanto

The Battle of Lepanto ranks as one of the greatest sea battles of all time, and in one sense it was the most important. There never would have been a Trafalgar or a Jutland or a Leyte Gulf without it, and as a matter of fact, it is likely that it made possible the survival of everything we know as civilization. Had the Christian fleets sunk off western Greece on October 7, 1571, we would not be here now, these words would not be written in English, and there would be no universities, human rights, holy Matrimony, advanced science, enfranchised women, fair justice, and morality as it was carved on the tablets of Moses and enfleshed in Christ.

Calm in Chaos (2018)

Background Music

I have never been able to play background music since the time Auden came in carpet slippers to a black-tie sherry party I gave for him and he bellowed over my Victrola: "Do you want to listen to me or to that?"

Cloud of Witnesses (2009)

Hans Urs von Balthasar and Mozart

The twentieth-century Swiss theologian Hans Urs von Balthasar wrote much about music and all the mysteries of beauty in God's creation. He was a good friend of the Calvinist theologian Karl Barth. While they didn't agree on all religious doctrines, they did agree about Mozart; in fact, they regularly got together to listen to his music. Balthasar had one of the most phenomenal minds of the modern age. He memorized Mozart's corpus so thoroughly that he threw out his Victrola turntable and listened to whatever he wanted in his head, playing it in his mind. It was extraordinary. He once said rather whimsically that he supposed that the angels play Bach when they are performing for God—but amongst themselves, they sing Mozart.

Grace and Truth (2019)

Being a New Yorker

Being a New Yorker, I go to the top of the Empire State Building only about once every thirty-five years, and I have been to the Statue of Liberty just twice. Merely once in my life have I welcomed the New Year in Times Square, and I had the impression that I was the only New Yorker in the crowd. As for the opera, people who live here boycott it under its present management, and I have never shopped in Macy's, even though it is practically next door. Only once, as a child, did I see the Easter show at Radio City Music Hall, and even then the spectacle of a rabbit and a lily dancing to Rubinstein's "Kamennoi Ostrow" played on the mighty Wurlitzer was a shattering experience never repeated. By way of reaction, it may have been an impetus for my choice of theology as a career.

Calm in Chaos (2018)

The Best Schools

While I have spent a lot of time in schools, the lives of people themselves are the best schools.

Cloud of Witnesses (2009)

The Bible

There are no throwaway lines in the Bible.

A Year with Fr. Rutler (2017)

Biography and the Lives of Saints

Christ prayed in the presence of his apostles: "I am remaining in the world no longer, but they remain in the world, while I am on my way to thee. Holy Father, keep them true to thy name, thy gift to me, that they may be one, as we are one" (John 17:11). The "oneness" is the character of holiness, the effective coopera-tion of the human intellect and will with the intellect and will of God. When human thought and desire wander off on their own, they begin the meander called sin. This is a plain fact of history. A sinner is evidence of Christ by default, as someone lost is a sign of a place where one is not lost. But a saint is particular evidence of Christ by example. "The saints have not all started well,", said the Curé d'Ars, "but they have all finished well." The sinner and the saint may have the same name; a saint, after all, is a sinner who has perfectly accepted forgiveness. A biography of a saint should ... do justice to the acceptance.

The Curé d'Ars Today (1988)

The Biography of Every Soul Risen Up

Surrounded by so much ruined honesty, the faithful heart can feel like Esau, whose brother has taken away his birthright by guile. If there is to be a consolation before the final consolation of all, it is this: Jacob lied in a big and vicious way and took his spoils, but when he abandoned fraud, he became Israel. Then began a great race and a great history, and when all hours and days came to the right moment, Christ called to Nathanael: "Behold, an Israelite indeed, in whom is no guile!" (John 1:47). That chronicle of a nation is the biography of every soul that has risen up from deceit and confessed to the Lord, who "is the Amen, the faithful and true witness" (Rev. 3:14). Jesus the Christ is not Diogenes the Cynic, searching the streets with a little lamp to find an honest man. He is the Light of the World, and in His presence, every human being either lies and dies or tells the truth and lives.

Calm in Chaos (2018)

The Birthplace of Our Savior

A Boston acquaintance of James Whistler did not approve of Lowell, Massachusetts, where Whistler had been born. "Whatever possessed you to be born in a place like that?" The artist replied, "I wished to be near my mother." There are various reasons why Christ was born in Bethlehem, but the most obvious one was because His Mother happened to be there.

A Year with Fr. Rutler (2017)

Blessed Are the Meek

The concept of sacrifice, alien to a culture of self-assertion, is the foundation of moral strength. Friedrich Nietzsche, the philosopher of power, mocked Christ's willing submission to suffering for others and thought that the beatitude delivered on the Mount—"Blessed are the meek"—constituted a "slave mentality." He did not realize that "meek," as used here, is rooted in the Greek word *paos* and means the kind of discipline that tames a wild animal and makes it able to put its strength to useful purpose, which is why the meek, so disciplined, inherit the earth. The priest must be tamed by the Holy Spirit so that his holy meekness will also strengthen the faithful.

A Year with Fr. Rutler (2017)

Blessing the Sick

Vianney blessed the sick frequently, but with reluctance. He was no more of a professional healer than was his Master. Healing of the sick had the urgency of compassion in counterpoint to the salvific mystery of suffering, but not as an end in itself; the crookedest bodies often seemed to him to have the most upright souls. It would be an awful thing, he thought, to seek release from pain while remaining captive to pride. "The worst cross is not to have a cross."

The Curé d'Ars Today (1988)

The Body and Blood of the Messiah No Theory

Living an abstraction by bearing false witness against the truth inevitably causes an emptiness in the soul. We know that there is something wrong with emptiness; there is an instinct in everyone to fill a void. Some time ago, Leonardo da Vinci's *Mona Lisa* was stolen from the Louvre. In the weeks between the theft and the painting's recovery, when the wall was blank, more people went to the Louvre Museum to see the empty space than went when the painting was there. I suppose we could make that an analogy with the philosophical conceits of our modern age. The philosophy of existentialism really was a fascination with emptiness, the creation of a myth that said that life is not really alive, that there is no purpose, that there is no dignity in the human condition apart from the simple fact of our existence. More dramatically, nihilism and anarchism were (and are) forms of fascination with emptiness. Our Lord fills our emptiness with His own Body and His own Blood. He says in the Eucharistic dialogue in John's Gospel: "Unless you eat the flesh of the Son of man and drink his blood, you have no life in you" (John 6:53). His disciples, used to theory rather than fact, accustomed to abstract ceremonies instead of something so basic as the Body and Blood of the Messiah, responded: "This is a hard saying" (John 6:60). Jesus then asserted, "But there are some of you that do not believe," which the Gospel writer comments is in reference to the one who would betray Him (John 6:64). This man, Judas, followed Our Lord as though He were a theory. Judas confected his own mental image of what the Messiah should be: a humanitarian, yes; a reformer, yes; a political liberator, yes—but not the Son of God, the Word Made Flesh, the Redeemer crucified on a Cross for the wiping away of sins and the reconciliation between man and God. And so he walked away.

Grace and Truth (2019)

Borrowing Glory

"The saints are like so many mirrors in which Christ contemplates himself." The Curé d'Ars's language was Pauline; the saints are able "to catch the glory of the Lord as in a mirror, with faces unveiled, and we have become transfigured into the same likeness, borrowing glory from that glory, as the Spirit of the Lord enables us" (2 Cor. 3:18). When Vianney's face looked incandescent in later years, the light still was from within a common-looking face; the combination, in the words of one witness "was enough to turn crowds to salutary thoughts." Churchill called himself a worm, but a glowworm. That has to be truer of the saints, who have moved from mortal glory into the expanse of holy freedom itself. The saints not only shine; they can shine the light.[3]

The Curé d'Ars Today (1988)

---

[3] The way the saints "shine the light" of the Church is nicely captured by that repository of good sense, the *Catholic Encyclopedia* (1917), which states in its entry on "sanctity":

"To show that the Church possesses the note of holiness it suffices to establish that her teaching is holy: that she is endowed with the means of producing supernatural holiness in her children: that, notwithstanding the unfaithfulness of many members, a vast number do in fact cultivate a sanctity beyond anything that can be found elsewhere: and that in certain cases this sanctity attains so high a degree that God honors it with miraculous powers.

"It is not difficult to show that the Catholic and Roman Church, and she alone, fulfills these conditions. In regard to her doctrines, it is manifest that the moral law which she proposes as of Divine obligation, is more lofty and more exacting than that which any of the sects has ventured to require. Her vindication of the indissolubility of marriage in the face of a licentious world affords the most conspicuous instance of this. She alone maintains in its integrity her Master's teaching on marriage. Every other religious body without exception has given place to the demands of human passion. In regard to the means of holiness, she, through her seven sacraments, applies to her members the fruits of the Atonement. She pardons the guilt of sin, and nourishes the faithful on the Body and Blood of Christ. Nor is the justice of her claims less manifest when we consider the result of her work. In the Catholic Church is found a marvelous succession of saints whose lives are as beacon-lights in the history of mankind. In sanctity the supremacy of Bernard, of Dominic, of Francis, of Ignatius, of Theresa, is as

William F. Buckley

In his circle William F. Buckley was Newman's prototypical gentleman, who "makes light of favours while he does them, and seems to be receiving when he is conferring" and who does not slander or gossip, treats his enemy as a potential friend, and is "merciful towards the absurd." His mercy was even extravagant, as when he told a *Firing Line* guest: "I would like to take you seriously, but to do so would affront your intelligence."

He Spoke to Us (2016)

Caesar's Chronic Itch

In every age and in every culture, Caesar has a chronic itch to sit on the altar.

He Spoke to Us (2106)

Catholic Schools and State Education

It is astonishing that so many Catholic school systems, neglecting the Church's social tenet of subsidiarity, have displayed such mindless acquiescence in the federalization of education. We may not be Parisian enough to cry "*Aux barricades!*" But we can profit from the counsel of Chesterton on the virtue of classical

---

unquestioned as is that of Alexander and of Caesar in the art of war. Outside the Catholic Church the world has nothing to show which can in any degree compare with them. Within the Church the succession never fails."

education over ideology: "Without education, we are in the horrible and deadly danger of taking educated people seriously."

Calm in Chaos (2018)

A Celebration of Littleness

The parable of the Mustard Seed takes account of the apparent insignificance of the early Church and declares that same Church's vitality. As the seed grows into the greatest of all the bushes, so does the Church grow from her beginnings into her full glory. This makes sense only in the light of Heaven, for the Church's glory will always be brightest as a celebration of littleness. It is glorious when a million people gather to hear the pope, but only because the pope himself knows that he would never be more like Christ than if the whole crowd were to walk away, leaving him alone.

Hints of Heaven (2014)

Choices

Society is free to redefine reality, to contracept life, to redefine marriage, and to justify the killing of the innocent as a "personal choice." Choices have consequences, and bad choices have bad consequences. When the equivalent of the media in Old Jerusalem, "the council and all the senate of Israel," ordered Peter and the apostles to be silent, they replied, "We must obey God rather than men" (Acts 5:29).

A Year with Fr. Rutler (2017)

The Church and the Making of Great Art

The Church is not faithful to her prophetic, priestly, and kingly offices if she does not inspire great art.

The Stories of Hymns (2016)

Church Bells after Snowfall

New York City became a quiet village during this past week's snowstorm. The snowdrifts seemed much higher when I was a child, but I remember my father telling me the same thing. The fact remains: this technological marvel of a metropolis can be brought to a halt by snowflakes. The more intricate the workings of a social structure, the easier it is to disrupt it. To live in a society requires cooperation, and thus, the word "civilization" means being able to live in a city, which is another way of saying that to be civilized we have to be able to work together. Walking down the middle of Park Avenue all alone, with no traffic, makes the great city seem a very fragile place. Last Monday one could almost hear a pin drop in mid-Manhattan. When other sounds were silenced, our church bells kept ringing. In the stillness they could be heard over an even greater distance, and they had a consoling sound in the storm, like the bell on a buoy in dense fog. *Stat crux dum volvitur orbis.* "As the world turns, the Cross stands." The Cross is like the axle that stabilizes the wheel, and without it we would careen off into oblivion.

A Year with Fr. Rutler (2017)

The Church No Preservation Society

The Church would never have survived had she been a preservation society, and Christ would have been long forgotten had He organized a committee to keep it going.

The Seven Wonders of the World (1993)

Calvin Coolidge

Coolidge became president at the unexpected death of Warren G. Harding, who thought of himself as a significant orator. But that splendid curmudgeon H. L. Mencken said of Harding's rhetoric: "It reminds me of a string of wet sponges, it reminds me of tattered washing on the line; it reminds me of stale bean soup, of college yells, of dogs barking idiotically through endless nights. It is so bad that a sort of grandeur creeps into it." On the other hand, Coolidge spoke very well indeed. He was the last president to write his own speeches. Though the media caricatured him as "Silent Cal," he gave more press conferences than any president before or since. On the 150th anniversary of the Declaration of Independence, Coolidge said that equality, liberty, popular sovereignty, and the rights of man "belong to the unseen world. Unless the faith of the American people in these religious convictions is to endure, the principles of our Declaration will perish."

A Year with Fr. Rutler (2017)

Capital Punishment

The medicinal reason for inflicting capital punishment is not merely to prevent the criminal from repeating his crime and to protect society but to encourage the guilty to repent and die in a state of grace. It also seeks to expiate the disorder caused by the crime in order to lessen the moral debt of the guilty. In the early years of the nineteenth century, St. Vincent Pallotti frequently assisted the condemned to the scaffold, as St. Catherine had done in Siena. He was edified by the many holy deaths he saw while helping the confraternity of San Giovanni, under the patronage of his friend the English cardinal Acton. Headquartered in the Church of San Giovanni Decollato (St. John the Beheaded), their rule was to urge the condemned to a good confession, followed by an exhortation, Holy Communion, and the grant of a plenary indulgence. The whole population of Rome was instructed to fast and pray for the intention of the criminal's soul.

He Spoke to Us (2016)

Cardinal Kasper and the African Church

During the Synod on the Family, Walter Cardinal Kasper expressed frustration with African bishops for opposing more conciliatory attitudes toward homosexuality, which he called their "taboo," and said that Africans "should not tell us too much what we have to do." Although Cardinal Kasper denied having said this, he managed an awkward apology when a recording of what he said was presented as evidence. The cardinal's remarks echoed those of the poorly tutored John Shelby Spong of the Episcopal Church, who said of Africans in 1998: "They've moved out of animism into a very superstitious kind of Christianity. They've yet to face the intellectual revolution of Copernicus and Einstein that we've had to face in the developing world. That's just not on their radar screen."[4] After the close of the synod, the official website of the German bishops' conference said that the exponential growth of the "romantic, poor Church" in Africa is due to the lamentable fact that "the educational situation there is on average at a rather low level and the people accept simple answers to difficult questions." The number of Christians in Africa has grown from about eight million in 1900 to over half a billion today. By contrast, according to a survey published in April 2015 by the German bishops' own conference, only 54 percent of priests in Germany go to confession, and only a bare majority of them pray daily, while 60 percent of the German laity do not believe in life after death.

Calm in Chaos (2018)

Carpe Diem

Lent is such a brief time that it seems to end almost as soon as it begins, but such also is life itself, and the purpose of Lent is to make precisely that point. The ashes yield quickly to Alleluias for those who outgrow themselves.

A Year with Fr. Rutler (2017)

---

[4]   "Spong was infuriated by Africans overriding his politically correct position on sexuality. He said of the African bishops: 'They've moved out of animism into a very superstitious kind of Christianity. They've yet to face the intellectual revolution of Copernicus and Einstein that we've had to face in the developing world. That's just not on their radar screen.' (Of course, Spong never explained—because it is unexplainable—how heliocentricity and general relativity could possibly affect traditional Christian beliefs regarding sexuality.)" J. Stuart Buck, "Ignoring W. B Noble's Spirit," *Harvard Crimson* (March 6, 2000).

A Case against the Cause of Thomas à Kempis

A case against the canonization of Thomas à Kempis was once made on the basis of an exhumation of his body. The poor man, it seems, had been buried alive, and scratch marks were found on the inside of his coffin. The evidence of panic on the part of Kempis was taken by some as token that he lacked the virtue of hope. It was rather, I should think, proof of right reason. Wanting to get out of your coffin when you should not be in it is the mark of the sensible mystic who wants to get to the Celestial Salem — in due time.

The Stories of Hymns (2016)

Catholic Journalists

John Richard Neuhaus was a social philosopher, who, like Chesterton, influenced religion in his capacity as a journalist. Chesterton's only lapse into false modesty was his description of journalism as the art of writing badly. Neither GKC nor RJN could write badly, and I was not the only one to start reading *First Things* at the end, for Father Neuhaus's ruminations were like the prize at the bottom of the Cracker Jack box, which normal children have always opened upside down. Our age's abandonment of reason and literacy has left us with a burlesque journalism, and it is poignant that Father Neuhaus's last column was an explanation of why the *New York Times* is no longer even worth satirizing.

Cloud of Witnesses (2009)

Catholic-Lite

People focused on themselves seek therapy instead of salvation. Religion, or its substitutes in the form of pop psychology and narcissistic culture, is to them just an emotional attempt to re-design nature to fit one's illusions. Therapy replaces grace, and then selfishness inverts natural law. When this infects Catholics, self-absorption replaces the worship of God, and Catholic Light becomes Catholic-Lite.

A Year with Fr. Rutler (2017)

The Greatest Change in History

The greatest change in history was a factual event in a tomb in Jerusalem when Tiberius was emperor. To live as though it did not happen is to inhabit a social illusion. As that anonymous guide to the perplexed, Diognetus said of Christians: "The course of conduct which they follow has not been devised by any speculation or deliberation of inquisitive men; nor do they, like some, proclaim themselves the advocates of any merely human doctrines."

Calm in Chaos (2018)

Charles the Second, Julian of Norwich, and "Our Courteous Lord"

King Charles II said that a gentleman is one who puts those around him at ease. Even on his deathbed he apologized to the courtiers in attendance: "I am sorry, gentlemen, for being such an unconscionable time a-dying." ... One risks glibness if not irreverence to say that Christ was a gentleman in the natural sense, but the graciousness of His human nature was "hypostatic" with the Source of Grace, and one sign of this was His habit of putting those around Him at ease. Julian of Norwich spoke often of this trait refracted in various ways: "Then our courteous Lord sheweth himself to the soul cheerfully with glad countenance, with a friendly welcome." Indeed, the courtly Christ went to great lengths to calm people and care for their comfort, even finding a grassy place for the crowds to sit before He preached and asking that a girl He raised from the dead be given something to eat.

He Spoke to Us (2016)

Cheshire Cats

Those who sit on the sidelines of the age's great debates, grinning knowingly like Cheshire cats, not volunteering a view and faulting those who do, may go through life innocent of criticism, but they are not innocent of the sin of omission. More than one saint has said that Hell is full of closed mouths.

Calm in Chaos (2018)

Choate School

One positive item salvaged by John Kennedy from his Anglo-Saxon formation was a line repeated every year by the headmaster of the Choate School, the Rev. George St. John: "Ask not what your school can do for you, ask what you can do for your school."

He perhaps absorbed the words until he felt free to modify them, as he also did with the Ten Commandments.

He Spoke to Us (2016)

Christ No Robin Hood

Our Lord was not a Robin Hood when He became history's champion of the poor; He did not teach His apostles to be generous with what others have, and he went so far as to say that the lazy servant who hid in the ground what his master had given him was a moral menace (see Matt. 25:14–28).

A Crisis of Saints (1995)

Christ's Athletes

An aphorism says that a priest's pay is not much, but the benefits are out of this world. It is more to the point to say that Christians, clergy and lay, become the most professional athletes by their profession of Faith. The Greek word *asketes*, referring to one who exercises, is also the root for "asceticism," which means getting the soul in shape. Our Lord and His apostles must have been in very good physical shape for the lives they led. St. Paul spent twenty years traveling, well over twenty thousand miles by some estimates; his first missionary journey alone was 1,400 miles. He sailed, but usually walked and suffered many physical tests. One plausible recollection has him short and bowlegged, but wiry. He disciplined a "weakness in the flesh," and it strengthened his humility (2 Cor. 12:7–10). The physically infirm can be better athletes for Christ than the physically strong, and wheelchairs can reach Heaven faster than running shoes.

A Year with Fr. Rutler (2017)

Christ's Authority

The source of Christ's authority was the big question when He healed and forgave sins. He taught "as one with authority and not as the scribes" (Matt. 7:29). When accused of using Satan as the source of His authority over evil spirits, He replied that a house divided against itself cannot stand (Matt. 12:25). And when Pilate invoked his own civil authority, the Lord told Him that he would have no authority at all were it not "given from above" (John 19:11). Conflicted, Pilate on his grand judgment throne suddenly seemed shriveled by Christ's innocence, and he surrendered his authority to the mob. Here was Shakespeare's "Man, proud man, dressed in a little brief authority."

A Year with Fr. Rutler (2017)

A Christmas Present for Father Rutler

The parish is my greatest Christmas present and the only one I need. If I could tell all the wondrous things God does, day in and day out, in the lives of people who come here, it would be a microcosm of all salvation history—for what we call salvation history is human experience since Christ the Living Word came and dwelt among us.

A Year with Fr. Rutler (2017)

The Church's Beauty

It is immensely saddening to see so many elements of the Church, in her capacity as Mother of Western Culture, compliant in the promotion of ugliness. There may be no deterrent more formidable to countless potential converts than the low estate of the Church's liturgical life, for the liturgy is the Church's prime means of evangelism. Gone as into a primeval mist are the days not long ago when apologists regularly had to warn against being distracted by, or superficially attracted to, the beauty of the Church's rites. And the plodding and static nature of the revised rites could not have been more ill-timed for a media culture so attuned to color and form and action. Edification is no substitute for inspiration.

A Crisis of Saints (1995)

Churchill, Harry Lauder, and Destiny

In the Second World War, the entire fate of Europe and, consequently, Western civilization hung in the balance. Winston Churchill was one of those characters in history who are hard to explain apart from divine providence. It's not that he was a mystic or a great confessor of the Faith or a saint raised to the altars, but that he was a man with all the gifts needed for that moment in order to resist the denial of God instituted in a political system. It is said that in some of the darkest days of the Second World War, he would go out into the garden at 10 Downing Street with his cigar and sing in an unmelodious voice a number that had been popularized by the Scottish vaudeville singer Harry Lauder.[5] In

---

[5] A recording of Sir Harry Lauder (1870–1950) singing "Keep Right On to the End of the Road" was made in 1926.

those dark days, Churchill knew that across the Channel there was an evil man and an evil system intriguing against God, and so he walked around the garden singing this simple song: "Keep right on to the end of the road. Keep right on to the end. Though the way be long, let your heart be strong. Keep right on to the end. If you are tired and weary, still journey on till you come to your happy abode, where all you love and you're dreaming will be there at the end of the road." Our Lord told us just that two thousand years ago. He said to the apostle Philip what he says to us now at the end of a long period of intriguing against God by civilization in the West and in the East: "Have I been with you so long, and yet you do not know me?" (John 14:9).

Grace and Truth (2019)

The Church Militant

A parish is not a family heirloom, but a military base.

A Year with Fr. Rutler (2017)

The Church Mortified

As a church, we have been mortified: by neglecting the intellectual case against Christ's cultured despisers; by trusting in bureaucracies and utopian movements; by imputing divine inspiration to private conceits; by slothfulness in the face of infanticide; by complacency about hunger and injustice; by grossly exaggerating the value of entertainers and professional athletes while neglecting spiritual heroes; by confusing tradition and nostalgia; by degrading our artistic patrimony; by banality in the pulpits; by scandals and refusing to speak of them as unspeakable; by the consecration of mediocrity; by voting for degenerate Caesars when we had the political power to dethrone them; by contempt for history; by impatience with God's unfathomable patience; by failing to give God thanks for the grace of living in a time of so many saints and miracles—in short, by softness in hard times.

He Spoke to Us (2016)

Civilization

We take civilization for granted. It seems to have always been. But civilization reached its greatest heights when minds and wills tried to stretch upward to God, literally thrusting buildings up as if they were trying to touch Heaven. We live in a time in which civilization is crumbling. It is a simple fact that many of our institutions and our general perception of the moral order and our willingness to promote and defend human dignity are disintegrating. One reason this is happening so quickly is that people have become so accustomed to civilization that it is hard for them to believe that it can possibly collapse. Moreover, people with good intentions often don't suspect or understand the power of evil. The last century is an open textbook giving us instructions in the power of evil over unsuspecting people. The most civilized nations in the world in the twentieth century succumbed to the most lurid barbarities, all because people thought that civilization is self-perpetuating.

Grace and Truth (2019)

Climate Change Debates

Debates about climate change invoke serious moral responsibilities and require that religion and science not be confused, so that saving souls not be overshadowed by saving the planet, the latter being an ambiguous concept anyway. This point was lost on a crowd of people who prostrated themselves on the floor of a chapel in Paris, praying that the Intergovernmental Panel on Climate Change (IPCC) save Planet Earth—just days after scores of people had been killed in that same city by terrorists. If the IPCC could not save the terrorists' victims from physical harm, saving the whole world might be ambitious.

A Year with Fr. Rutler (2017)

Commencement Addresses

Christ the Living Word condescends to come among us so that we might not be vulgarized, and He allows Himself to be mocked, so that we are not demeaned. That is why, after hearing Jesus, even skeptics said what no one has ever been able to say at the end of a graduation speech, however worthy or ignoble: "Never has a man spoken the way this man speaks" (John 7:46).

A Year with Fr. Rutler (2017)

Communion

The only way to make a worthy Communion is to make a humble confession.

A Year with Fr. Rutler (2017)

Confession

With nothing to offer God that He needs, the best gift we can offer is a humble confession of the various ways our human souls have blocked the will of God.... Sins are forms of selfishness, but, when confessed, they become the greatest gifts, offerings of the heart, and they place us back into God's plan for the human race.

A Year with Fr. Rutler (2017)

Divine anger is not a weakness of God, but a sign of His perfection. It is a sign of God's love for those whom He does not want to lose along the way. Another sign of God's love is His tears, as when He wept for Lazarus and for all Jerusalem that would be gathered to Him. As His sons and daughters, we have the gift of holy anger, which is destructive only when we "lose our temper." The solution is to find it, and that we do when we confess our sins, directing our anger at the prince of lies. Along with this confession comes the gift of tears, which man alone among all creatures can shed, for the human being is not made for this world alone.

A Year with Fr. Rutler (2017)

Sometimes I have to stop hearing confessions to offer a second Mass. Most people understand this. A few say that this is inconvenient for them. This is a distress to me, but unless they have borne sons who now are priests, they have no right to complain. Only saints can bilocate.

A Year with Fr. Rutler (2017)

Why do people even consider doing evil? Well, it's in the blood — not the Blood of Christ, but human nature. It's original sin. When we appropriate that original sin in the form of explicit acts against the good, that's what we call a sin. Our Lord told a parable about the owner of a vineyard who left tenants in charge of the land. The proprietor sent one man to visit the vineyard and collect the rents, and that man was beaten. Another went to the vineyard, and he was gravely wounded. And then finally he said, "Surely, they will not touch my son." He sent his son in, and they killed him. Our Lord is giving us an allegory for sin. The beating of the first servant is venial sin, a lighter kind of offense against the good that can easily be remedied through an Act of Contrition. It does not even require a sacramental confession, though it is recommended. But a venial sin is not to be dismissed lightly, because it lays the groundwork for the more direct affront against God represented by the wounding of the other servant, which represents habitual sin. The ache in the soul that takes away our desire for the good forms a habit of behavior. These habits lead to the gravest offense of all: killing of the Son Himself. This is mortal sin, and every mortal sin is an act of violence against the Lord of Life. St. John Vianney said that when we confess our sins, we take the nails out of Jesus.

Grace and Truth (2019)

Confession is not easy, but it is simple. He who forgives sins is Christ the High Priest — worshipped by the Church when she is Catholic enough to wash Christ's feet with her tears and anoint them with the lustre of His own priesthood.

Hints of Heaven (2014)

Confirmation

In confirmation the Holy Spirit blesses the soul with gifts of wisdom, understanding, counsel, fortitude, knowledge, piety, and fear of the Lord. The seven gifts enliven the intellect and the will, just as the Spirit of God breathed upon creation in seven stages. In speaking of character from the position of a detached philosopher, Aristotle emphasized three qualities of a well-integrated personality: *ethos* (an honest use of talent); *logos* (an honest use of the mind); and *pathos* (an honest involvement with the sufferings of the world). The Holy Spirit shifts this into a supernatural dimension by an ethos that lets God guide human talent, a logos that perceives the ultimate truth of God behind all lesser truths, and a pathos that unites human suffering with the suffering of Christ, turning tragedy into triumph.

A Year with Fr. Rutler (2017)

Richard Conway Casey

In 1999, Pope John Paul II received Judge Richard Conway Casey (1933–2006) when he was awarded the Blessed Hyacinthe Cormier Medal at the Angelicum University for outstanding leadership in the promotion of gospel values in the field of justice and ethics. Casey remembered going to Lourdes when he went blind and being led to the grave of an atheist Italian girl who had been brought against her wishes to the shrine for a cure. She remained blind in eye but was transfigured in spirit. As an old lady, she had asked to be buried near the spot where the Lady had appeared to Bernadette. The epitaph read to him was: "What is important is not to see but to understand."

Cloud of Witnesses (2009)

Corinth

Corinth was a Greek city located south of Athens in the area connecting the Peloponnesus to the mainland. In the arts and sciences, it excelled and it produced some engineering marvels. It was full of energy, much of it uncontrolled, and money was the real god, although everything sensual was extolled. The temple of Aphrodite at one point housed one thousand cultic prostitutes, and every sort of fantastic superstition was tolerated. In very many ways, it was like New York City. Just as we say, "If you can make it in New York, you can make it anywhere," the Romans who took over the city said, "Not for everyone is the journey to Corinth."

St. Paul was a brave man to preach the gospel there, and it is no surprise that he had severe difficulties. Unlike the Galatians, whose caution about doing the wrong thing bordered on scrupulosity, the Corinthians were tempted to think "anything goes." Their lush cosmopolitan environment, symbolized by the third architectural order—which was the most elaborate, in contrast to the Doric and Ionic—tolerated any kind of behavior and philosophy, so long as it was aesthetically satisfying. They were heavily influenced by the Gnostic notion that the spiritual world has nothing to do with the material world. They compartmentalized their existence, thinking that they could engage in high, abstract thoughts while living dissolute lives. A sacramental sense of creation was alien to the Corinthians, like some New Yorkers who prefer to speak of "spirituality" rather than Christianity, who think they can be Catholic without confession, and "do what they want with their own bodies" while ignoring the sacredness of life, fornicating and cohabiting outside the marriage bond, and sanctioning perversions as "alternative lifestyles." After St. Paul established the Church in Corinth in about AD 51, he wrote to them from Ephesus in Turkey, reminding them, sometimes with tears, that the human body is a temple of the Holy Spirit. He knew how hard it was for the Corinthians to be countercultural, as a Christian must be in a pagan environment. He was never discouraged, nor did he "lower the bar" by watering down doctrine like a false evangelist hoping to attract crowds by preaching a nonthreatening, generic gospel. Instead, he blesses the raucous Corinthian flock with a highly developed, Trinitarian theology: "May the grace of the Lord Jesus Christ, and the love of God, and the fellowship of the Holy Spirit be with you all" (2 Cor. 13:13).

A Year with Fr. Rutler (2017)

Courage in War

In the darkest days of the Second World War, Winston Churchill delivered a famous speech in which he referenced—not by name, but in essence—Thomas Aquinas on courage.[6] Courage is the essential quality for the virtues. It takes courage to have faith; it takes courage to have hope; it takes courage to love; it takes courage to

---

[6] "Courage is rightly esteemed the first of human qualities, because, as has been said, it is the quality which guarantees all others." Winston Churchill, "Alfonso XIII," in *Great Contemporaries* (London: Thornton Butterworth, 1937), 218. This nicely tallies with what St. Thomas says in the *Summa*: "Courage can be taken to mean a firmness of spirit, and this is a general virtue or rather a condition of every virtue, or a particular firmness in enduring and repulsing threats in situations fraught with conspicuous difficulty, namely in grave perils, and in this sense courage is a special virtue" (*Summa Theologica*, 2a-2ae, cxxiii, 2). See *St. Thomas Aquinas: Philosophical Texts*, selected and translated by Thomas Gilby (Oxford: Oxford University Press, 1951), 336.

be prudent; it takes courage to act justly; it takes courage to practice temperance; and it takes courage to practice the virtue that itself is the manifestation of courage—fortitude. In that same war, during the Blitz, Queen Elizabeth, wife of King George VI, was asked if the two princesses were going to be evacuated. She famously replied, "The children won't go without me. I won't leave without the king. And the king will never leave." Wars among peoples come and go. We are always, however, engaged in a spiritual warfare between God and the prince of lies. And we have an Eternal King, who is the source of all courage. Christ the King says to us, "Be of good cheer. I AM with you even to the end of the world" (see Matt. 28:20).

Grace and Truth (2019)

The Courage of Sanctity

The annals are replete with the failures of famous figures. Although some accounts are embellished, Abraham Lincoln's setbacks are daunting. He lost his job and was defeated for the state legislature in 1832 and then failed in business. He had a nervous breakdown in 1836 and was defeated for speaker of the Illinois House two years later. In 1843 his nomination for Congress failed, and he was defeated for the U.S. Senate in 1854 and 1858, between which he lost the nomination for the vice presidency. That is only half of the picture. After disappointment in 1832, he was elected captain of the Illinois militia in the Black Hawk War. Following the failure of his business, he was appointed postmaster of New Salem and was twice elected to the state legislature. His law practice grew, and he was admitted to plead before the U.S. Supreme Court. His rejection for land officer in 1849 was followed by the offer of the governorship of the Oregon Territory, which he declined. He dusted himself off and was elected president in 1860.... The point is that if one falls, one can get up again. Churchill said, "Success is not final, failure is not fatal: it is the courage to continue that counts." This counsel is more than the banal "positive thinking" of glib men. It is rooted in a genuine humility that is willing to be helped up by a conviction of Providence, rather than refusing to get up out of crippling pride.

A Year with Fr. Rutler (2017)

The Courtesy of Christ

In the Resurrection, Our Lord kept putting people at ease: "Peace." "Do not be afraid." "Why are you troubled?" He let the Magdalene first think He was a gardener, perhaps so that she might not faint, and when He made Himself known to the men on the Emmaus road, He may have done it with a smile that stirred hearts slow to believe. He went so far as to let the apostles touch His wounds, and He ate a piece of baked fish to domesticate their incredulity. I expect that the only one Our Lord did not have to tell to calm down was Our Lady, who was full of grace.

He Spoke to Us (2016)

The Courtliness of Vianney

Vianney was not a backslapper. One young nobleman was surprised at the unrehearsed courtliness with which he opened the confessional door; no trained footman could have done it more elegantly. His typical greeting was of a lovely cadence: *"Je vous présente bien mon respect."* Only on those occasions when he turned quickly in the pulpit could one detect some concealed discomfiture; he did not admit to wearing the hair shirt.

The Curé d'Ars Today (1988)

Credentials

The greatest confessor possibly in the history of that sacrament and the man who spent three-fourths of his life in the confessional was denied faculties for hearing confessions for several months on account of his problematic academic record.

The Curé d'Ars Today (1988)

Crime and the Glamour of Iniquity

Crime and the glamour of iniquity fascinate the human imagination because all humans inherit the consequences of the first crime against God, the original sin of wanting to be gods.

A Year with Fr. Rutler (2017)

The Cross

The crowd at the foot of the Cross mocked Jesus for not being able to save Himself, though He had saved others. So did the cynical thief hanging next to Him. Even Peter at first said he would not allow Jesus to go to Jerusalem to die, but Our Lord said the voice speaking through him was that of Satan. The prince of lies fears the Cross because it conquers him.

A Year with Fr. Rutler (2017)

Christ on the Cross ... says, "If any man would come after me, let him deny himself and take up his cross daily and follow me" (Luke 9:23). All the voices of antiquity longed to hear ... that voice. Most of them did not hear it, and when the rest of them did, they were confused. But on this side of the Cross and the Resurrection, we have no excuse for being confused by Christ or for rejecting Him.

Grace and Truth (2019)

Crossroads

Wherever there is a crossroads, there is a cross. When the Cross of Christ appeared in the world, civilization truly was at a crossroads. It would seem that God in His infinite wisdom chose that moment in history precisely because of its drama. Consider that the Crucifixion of Christ happened almost equidistant between the capture of Rome by the general Pompey and the destruction of Rome by the emperor Titus. It was at that crossroads of civilization that the Lord of history made Himself known.

Grace and Truth (2019)

The Curé d'Ars

Vianney knew that great teachers pass on teachings, but that Christ passes on himself.[7]

The Curé d'Ars (1988)

---

[7] "For it is no small thing that God is going to give to those who thus yearn; no half-efforts will get them to that goal. What God is going to give them is not something He has made. He is going

The Cure for Anger and Timidity

No saint, naturally placid or aggressive, replaced anger with the opposite extreme of timidity. "God has not given us a spirit of timidity, but a spirit of power and love and self-control" (2 Tim. 1:7). The cure for both sinful anger and sinful timidity is the virtue of courage.

A Year with Fr. Rutler (2017)

Damnation

Adam and Eve remain alive in us. Of course, St. Paul said, "It is no longer I who live, but Christ who lives in me" (Gal. 2:20). But Adam also lives in us in our fallen nature. As in Adam, all die, so in Christ, shall all be made alive. And unless the Adam in us is conquered by the Christ in us, the death of Adam is forever. That is damnation.

Grace and Truth (2019)

Darkest before Dawn

When things seem especially confused in the Church and scandals abound, that is a hint from Heaven and a murmur from Hell that something profoundly blessed is about to happen. Christ prays for Peter when the devil tries to sift him like wheat, so that when Peter survives, he will confirm the brethren in a lively

---

to give them Himself, Himself, Who made all things. Toil, then, to lay hold of God; yearn, long for what you are going to possess forever" (attributed to St. Augustine).

tradition of glory "We did not follow cleverly devised myths when we made known to you the power and coming of our Lord Jesus Christ, but we were eyewitnesses of his majesty We heard this voice borne from heaven, for we were with him on the holy mountain" (2 Pet. 1:16–21).

He Spoke to Us (2016)

Dead Men Keep No Advent

If confession has become the lost sacrament of our age, Advent has become its lost season. These absences are the unholy hollows of the Culture of Death: if man does not confess his sins, he cannot live eternally; and if he has no promise to await, he will find no reason to confess.

As a nocturne indicates beauty in what coarse perception registers only as an absence of day, so Advent is the sign that our present life is greater than incidental existence. The season of anticipating the coming of the Savior who is also our Judge is the calendar's tribute to the Beatitude of Purity. The pure in heart are blessed for they shall see God; and the heart's purity consists in moral focus on God as the purpose of all living. Dead men keep no Advent. Secularized Christians have let themselves be swept into this swirl of obscurity and denial by "rushing" Christmas at the expense of Advent—which is like rushing birth by eliminating pregnancy.

The Stories of Hymns (2016)

Our Debt Terms

All of us are indebted to God; none of us has enough to pay the debt. God is willing to forgive the debt, but the condition of the absolution is that we grant it to those around us.

Hints of Heaven (2014)

Decline and Fall

It is a cliché to compare one's own generation with the decline of the Roman Empire, but clichés become clichés usually by their accuracy. Even the Augustan Age came at the expense of the simple virtues of the remnant republic. Its religion had no moral component.... Power was the practical god, and anyone who could secure it was justified by the securing. The Triumvirate of Octavian, Mark Antony, and Lepidus was achieved by each betraying his closest relatives and friends. All was accomplished through the manipulation of a complex legal system of tribunes, praetors, quaestors, consuls, and aediles. It seemed neat on the exterior.... Then appeared people declaring that a man named Jesus had risen from the dead in a backwater of the empire. Not all of them were slaves and downtrodden—some were relatives of the Flavian emperors and rich families such as the Acilii Glabriones. The politicians accused them of *contemptissima inertia*, by which "contemptible laziness" they meant modesty, contempt for celebrity and public honors, reverence for life, disdain for cruelty, the exaltation of the family, and the indissolubility of marriage.

A Year with Fr. Rutler (2017)

The Defiance of Holy Innocence

How ironic it is that some of the voices most outspoken against executing murderers also promote contraception, abortion, and euthanasia. They are living a contradiction of God's plan; they have defied holy innocence. And that's why shedders of innocent blood have to use the language of deceit — that is, euphemisms. Abortionists are called "health-care providers." Well, that's like calling an ax murderer a cutlery specialist. And people who promote abortion say they are "pro-choice." All that manifests, besides their own guilt, is bad grammar. "To choose" is a transitive verb; it needs an object. The "pro-choice" person must finish the sentence: choice of what?

Grace and Truth (2019)

Descartes and the Khmer Rouge

If the soul is treated as only a sort of doll in the body, or as Descartes's "ghost in a machine," the body learns the hard way that this is the deadliest of misjudgments. During the Pol Pot horrors in Cambodia, for instance, large numbers of women went "psychosomatically blind" when they were forced to watch the atrocities inflicted on their families by the Khmer Rouge troops. Hysteria has traumatic physical consequences, because the soul has a sight that can be destroyed when the material order traumatizes moral good.

The Seven Wonders of the World (1993)

Desire and Dogma

G. K. Chesterton gently slapped his readers back to reality from egoistic comas when he wrote in his *Short History of England*: "To have the right to do a thing is not at all the same as to be right in doing it." So when someone says, "I am free to do what I want with my body," you may be impelled by charity and justice to reply that he is indeed so free, but if he defies the law of gravity, the pavement quickly will be of a different opinion, and if he says there is no difference between a man and a woman, two shades named Adam and Eve will rise up with mocking smiles. Those who have long sipped the intoxicating nectar of false perception may hesitate to draw a line between desire and dogma, fabrication and fact. If reality is nothing more than the visible costume of an impression, impressive tyrants will orchestrate that fantasy from their balconies, with rhetoric to mold malleable minds. The long legacy of demagoguery attests that weak points persuade people if the points are shouted loudly enough to overwhelm reason. Opinion polls shout, and network "talking heads" shout, and Internet pundits shout, but then there is a "still, small voice" that does not fade away: the long and logical echo of *"Fiat Lux"* uttered by the real Creator of the real universe.

A Year with Fr. Rutler (2017)

Deus Absconditus

In the detective story "Silver Blaze," Sherlock Holmes told the Scotland Yard detective Inspector Gregory that the "curious incident of the dog in the night-time" was precisely that the dog did not bark. The silence was as revealing as any sound. This is to be remembered when God seems absent from current events, or distant from us in our daily perplexities. He who never lied said that he would be with us until the end of time. Rather than despair when God seems absent, the solution is to try to figure out why He is hidden. "Seek the Lord and his strength. Seek his face always" (Ps. 105:4). To want Him to be near is already to be near Him.

A Year with Fr. Rutler (2017)

Devilry and Destiny

Satan ... is the great intriguer. All human intrigues pale in comparison with his great intrigue against Christ. The worst crimes humans have ever committed in history are mere play-things compared with the vicious scheming of the prince of lies against the Lord of Truth. And here's the thing: he wants us to become part of his intrigue. In our current generation, he wants us to use all the scientific information and communication technology at our hands to perpetuate his plotting against the divine design. He wants us to think that we have no home but our earthly dwelling. He wants us to think that there is no heavenly purpose to our existence. After Theodore Roosevelt left the White House, he went on a safari in Africa and toured Europe. He was wined and dined, given honorary degrees, and returned to his native city of New York, where he was welcomed with great pageantry. On the ship with him were two missionaries who had spent many years in laborious service for the gospel and the salvation of souls. When they saw all the acclamation given to Roosevelt, one said to the other, "They don't even know we exist." And the other replied, "But we are not yet home." Each one of us has a home with God. And the only way we can make sense of our earthly home, the only way we can properly use our advanced technology, and the only way we can really know what to say and to do with all our means of communication is to understand that we have a heavenly destiny.

Grace and Truth (2019)

The Devil's Greatest Compliment

In his last Angelus address, Benedict XVI said that he was now going up the mountain as did Peter, James, and John, and there he would pray. He knew that at the foot of the mountain are all kinds of noise and foaming, and these are the growls of the prince of darkness paying the Church a tribute he pays no other reality: his hatred. While he mocks men and scorns their pretensions, he reserves his bitterness for the Church, which is the only thing he fears in this world.

He Spoke to Us (2016)

Dickensian Clerks

Even in the Church there are ... Dickensian clerks scratching away at their balance sheets, producing little as they ignore the voice from the shore asking with a certain heavenly whimsy, "Have you caught anything?" (John 21:5).

A Year with Fr. Rutler (2017)

"Dictatorship of Relativism"

Pope Benedict XVI ... spoke of ... a "dictatorship of relativism." To propose that opposite assertions can be true is harshly to cancel out truth. In our grammar, two negatives make a positive, but to say that a negative and a positive make a positive would be to say that nothing is really positive. Then, to say that Christ is and is not the Living Word is to say that the Word is just a word. This "dictatorship" inevitably tries to crush any assertion that there is such a thing as logic at all. This is not a matter just for the philosophy class. It has harsh consequences for justice. The "show trials" of Stalin and Hitler were held in a Humpty Dumpty world where a word means anything the judge wants it to mean. This reduces sense to sentimentality, and there is a fine line between sentimentality and cruelty, because it twists logic and explains why demagogues speak of caring for society even as they destroy every vestige of it, condoning unnatural acts as natural, and even offering to help children by killing them, as "lawmakers" in Brussels have recently done. Milton said, "The mind is its own place and in itself can make a Heaven of Hell, a Hell of Heaven."

A Year with Fr. Rutler (2017)

Discipleship

Socrates, having said that the unexamined life is not worth living, changed the lives of many, who passed on what they had learned. None of his disciples, however, and no disciple of any other teacher, could say with St. Paul, who was chosen after the Master had risen from the dead: "It is no longer I who live but Christ who lives in me" (Gal. 2:20).

A Year with Fr. Rutler (2017)

Door Keys

There are keys that open ordinary doors and unlock earthly knowledge. Only the Church can open the eternal doors.

A Year with Fr. Rutler (2017)

Down in the Depths

As Jesus led Peter and James and John up the mountain, so He leads us up to glory, like the priest about to ascend the altar steps in the older form of the Mass: *Introibo ad altare Dei* (I will go unto the altar of God). That brush with divinity at the Transfiguration, enveloped by a cloud, is a preparation for the conflict between splendor and horror at the foot of the mountain. Pope Leo the Great explains how Our Lord was strengthening the apostles for the Crucifixion to come. The kind of life that forgets God's glory becomes depressed, despite attempts to put on a veneer of happiness — as in Cole Porter's song "Down in the Depths on the Ninetieth Floor."[8] This does not mean that Christ saves us from conflicts. His followers must enter this world's gravest conflicts, but the consolation of His glory saves them from being psychologically conflicted. Having led the three apostles up the mountain, He leads them down. More help is needed going down

---

[8] Porter wrote the song for his musical *Red, Hot and Blue* (1936), which introduced the great Ethel Merman to the stage. "With a million neon rainbows burning below me/ And a million blazing taxis raising a roar/ Here I sit, above the town/ In my pet pailletted gown/ Down in the depths on the ninetieth floor/ While the crowds at El Morocco punish the parquet/ And at 21 the couples clamor for more/ I'm deserted and depressed/ In my regal eagle nest/ Down in the depths on the ninetieth floor."

than going up. This is a fact of mountaineering, and it is a fact of life itself. The same three apostles who witnessed Our Lord's glorious Transfiguration on the mountain attended His agony in the garden. By guiding the apostles down the mountain, Christ was instructing them in the virtue of the faith they would need for the trials ahead.

A Year with Fr. Rutler (2017)

The Drug Culture

The human being has a free will to choose good or evil. But after having plotted evil, when a person begins to commit the act itself, it begins to contradict the human dignity and the conscience in a more poignant way. This is why the most evil people in the world have had to redefine evil, pretending that it was good. Or, when that hasn't worked, they have had to drug themselves, either with intoxicating language—slurs and euphemisms and so on—or with chemical drugs. How paradoxical it is that an age such as ours, which claims to be so committed to reason and realism, should really become a drug culture. But it is no puzzle. If we cooperate with evil, if we plot to do evil, and then if we commit ourselves to evil, the human spirit has to deny that what it is doing is evil. Evil always calls itself good; every vice parades itself as a form of liberation.

Grace and Truth (2019)

Duty and Egotism

A few days after the battle of the Allia River on July 18, 390 B.C., the Senones tribesmen of the Celtic Gauls sacked Rome, this being the first of the six notorious pillagings over more than a millennium. While most of the citizens fled by way of the Janiculum Hill, where the North American College now stands, patricians sat on ivory chairs outside their houses in their senatorial robes to await death. One of Livy's most moving passages describes the scene:

> The houses of the plebeians were barricaded, the halls of the patricians stood open, but they felt greater hesitation about entering the open houses than those which were closed. They gazed with feelings of real veneration upon the men who were seated in the porticoes of their mansions, not only because of the superhuman magnificence of their apparel and their whole bearing and demeanour, but also because of the majestic expression of their countenances, wearing the very aspect of gods. So they stood, gazing at them as if they were statues, till, as it is asserted, one of the patricians, M. Papirius, roused the passion of a Gaul, who began to stroke his beard—which in those days was universally worn long—by smiting him on the head with his ivory staff. He was the first to be killed, the others were butchered in their chairs. After this slaughter of the magnates, no living being was thenceforth spared; the houses were rifled, and then set on fire.[9]

In our reduced culture, when wealthy celebrities go about unshaven, neckties are considered an imposition, form letters from the bank address customers by their first names, and no thought is given to how to dress for church, attention to the

---

[9] Titus Livius, *The History of Rome*, bk. 5, ed. Canon Roberts (New York: E. P. Dutton, 1912), 93–94, 173.

gravity of one's office may seem archaic and indeed affected. But the opposite is the case. The amiably eccentric queen Christina of Sweden, having abdicated her throne to become a Catholic, wrote to a friend: "Dignity does not consist in possessing honors, but in deserving them." Customs and outward forms signal that one's duty is greater than one's self, and neglect of them is an exercise in egotism.

Calm in Chaos (2018)

Easter

A most palpable proof of the power of Easter is the way it transformed lives.... St. Paul writes singularly beautiful words to explain his own conversion (Acts 9:1–19). The transformation of St. Peter ranks first in importance because it was he on whom Christ established the "line of command" in the Church. As with Paul, Peter dramatically denied Our Lord before his total conversion, and surely this was of a divine design, so that we might see the Resurrection power as a radical impact and not just the gradual intensification of a point of view. Peter denied Christ three times. Then, after the Resurrection, Christ elicited from him a threefold affirmation of love and then sent him off eventually to Rome. That was a long way from the fishing village of Capernaum. And likewise, Peter's majestic speech in Jerusalem on Pentecost (Acts 2:14–41) demonstrated an astonishing change in this man whose natural rhetoric was halting and rough. When Peter hung upside down on a cross in Rome, it was not therapy. It was a sacrifice of the self as joyful as it was painful, in the hope of Resurrection. Not a vain hope, for it was the confidence of the first man to have seen Christ's grave cloths lying neatly rolled up in the empty tomb. As Cardinal Newman wrote, "No one will die for his own calculations; he dies for realities."

A Year with Fr. Rutler (2017)

"Echoes from Home"

John Henry Newman (1801–1890), in addition to being one of the great theologians of Catholic history, was an accomplished violinist. Even at an advanced age, his most prized gift was a violin that he played until his fingers became too arthritic to go on. In one of his sermons, he said, in words that are a sacred song themselves:

> Is it possible that that inexhaustible evolution and disposition of notes so rich, yet so simple, so intimate and yet so regulated, so various, yet so majestic, should be a mere sound which is gone and perishes? It is not so. It cannot be. No, they have emerged from some higher sphere. They are the outpourings of eternal harmony in the medium of created sound. They are echoes from home. They are the voice of angels or the Magnificat of saints or the living law of divine governments or the divine attributes. Something are they beyond themselves which we cannot compass, which we cannot utter—though mortal man, and he perhaps not otherwise distinguished above his fellows, have the gift of eliciting them.[10]

Grace and Truth (2019)

---

[10] John Henry Newman, "The Theory of Developments in Religious Doctrine" (1843), in *Fifteen Sermons Preached before the University of Oxford*, ed. James David Earnest and Gerard Tracey (Oxford: Oxford University Press, 2006), 232–233.

Education

William James, a philosopher and brother of novelist Henry, said of liberal education that "our colleges ought to have lit up in us a lasting relish for the better kind of man [and] a loss of appetite for mediocrity." He understood what the golden mean was, and he understood what a sham mediocrity was. If he leveled this criticism of colleges in his day, can you imagine what he would say now, looking at our schools and other institutions? The enshrinement of mediocrity has virtually destroyed education in Western civilization, and it has dealt a mortal blow to our system of justice and politics.

Grace and Truth (2019)

While I am beguiled by the lure of learning, and never neglectful of the importance of the academy, experience has convinced me that the life of the mind can be exercised more vigorously and inventively in a parish than in a university. Since teaching is the *primum officium*, or primary responsibility, of a pastor, I might go so far as to say that teaching in a university is like fishing in an aquarium, while teaching in a parish is like fishing in an ocean. The demographics of the former are exclusive, whereas there are no admission requirements for entering the doors of a church.

A Year with Fr. Rutler (2017)

Many have supposed that sound education and good intentions can construct an ideal society, even if God is out of the picture and original sin is denied. The holocausts and pogroms of the modern age have exposed that deadly fallacy.

A Year with Fr. Rutler (2017)

Egg Hunts on Manicured Lawns

Thomas Merton recalled in *The Seven Storey Mountain* (1948) that before he became a Catholic, his Easter consisted of an abbreviated service of Morning Prayer followed by an egg hunt on a manicured lawn. Such Easters are like the festivals in the twilight of imperial Rome when, as Suetonius records, the great men spoke of the gods but secretly consulted the stars. Some have so lost confidence in the Resurrection of Christ that they keep little of Lent at all.

He Spoke to Us (2016)

The End of the World

All things are temporary, including the Temple in Jerusalem and the World Trade Center in New York. What matters is not when the world will end, or even when we will end, but rather the fact that we will end, and by God's grace be raised in glory. This is great good news from the viewpoint of all the saints, who with the angels join us at the altar at the Sanctus of the Mass.

A Year with Fr. Rutler (2017)

An Engine of Hysteria

In a recent talk to the Islamic Society of Baltimore—which the FBI warned him had radical allegiances—President Obama said that Thomas Jefferson and John Adams had copies of the Quran. He neglected to say that they were not seeking spiritual edification. They were trying to anatomize what was to them a fount of cruelty and an engine of hysteria. Our Lady knew that kind of mentality when she watched her Son dragged through the streets.

A Year with Fr. Rutler (2017)

The English Reformation *Redivivus*

We have heard many times, without careful definition, that the human race has entered an entirely new anthropological stage. Even speeches during Vatican II spoke of it. The very thought would be more thrilling if we knew what it meant. We do know that it does not mean that we have become a species different from our ancestors.... A case in point is the religious trauma of the English Reformation. It, too, claimed to its very bones that it was a thing more worthy than even a reformation: it was to be a restoration of an integrity hidden by the accretions of time and the allurements of superstition. The English reformers justified their work by claiming that they were, at once, going back to the oldest times and keeping up with the latest times. It still is hard to work our way through that ideological veneer, for it has become the idiom of our own ecclesiastical culture.

A Crisis of Saints (1995)

Enthusiasm

Benjamin Franklin (1706–1790) began his career as a printer in Boston, apprenticed to his brother James, and indicated by the epitaph he wrote for his remains, buried in the grounds of Christ Church, Philadelphia, that he never ceased being a printer; his desiccated frame was "the cover of an old book, its contents torn out, and stript of its lettering and gilding." As a high school student competing in an oratorical competition in the Franklin Club of Philadelphia, I saw a copy of those words but did not know then that they were probably Franklin's revision of a stanza of John Mason (d. 1694). Mason, the unbalanced son of a Dissenter, took Anglican orders to little effect and proceeded from the theological mire of Cambridge eventually to the rectorship of Water-Stratford in Buckinghamshire. There, later, the salubrious influence of his prodigious output of hymns on the Wesley brothers was ill matched by his suggestion that he was an immortal prophet. A large retinue flocked to his parish, where they sang in gibberish and danced and fainted. It is strange that Ronald Knox's *Enthusiasm* (1950) neglected this group of millenarians, for they anticipated the Jansenist convulsionaries of the eighteenth century whom he describes so vividly, gathering in the Parisian cemetery of Saint-Médard to speak in tongues and eat human waste. As with such vaulting neurotics, the clients of Mr. Mason continued in their ways for at least the next sixteen years, even though the new rector of Water-Stratford produced the decayed remains of his predecessor as evidence that he was dead.

The Stories of Hymns (2016)

Envy, Socialism, and Charity

Envy may be a lamentable attitude of the capitalist, but only as a moral accident; it is the socialist's essential motivation. Lingering behind each socialist panegyric to the poor is a ritual incantation against the rich. When a socialist reforms the world, he makes charity mean a soup kitchen; he will not let it mean anything like a banquet. But essential living is meant to be a banquet, and life eternal is an eternal banquet. This cannot be realized if one is obsessed with distribution while remaining naïve about production. The functional defect of socialism is that it is not social. It has not helped the poor man by eradicating the prince; it has only made the prince poor. If it has not put a chicken in every pot, it has removed the peacock from every lawn. It has made liberality a casualty of an artifact called liberalism. Such may satisfy the motive of envy; it is irrelevant to the motive of charity, and in the collectivist bosom it engenders the very greed it scorned.

The Curé d'Ars Today (1988)

Epiphany

In the Epiphany, the Second Person of the Holy Trinity was worshipped by foreigners who had been led to Bethlehem, but the Magi knew only that the Holy Child was the long-awaited Messiah. Fast-forward to the beginning of that Child's mature ministry, and there it is revealed that He is the Second Person of the Most Holy Trinity. Not until He was ascending to Heaven some three years later did He actually name the Trinity, but during the course of those years He gave hints of that triune economy.

A Year with Fr. Rutler (2017)

Errorland

The Constitution of Ireland begins: "In the name of the Most Holy Trinity, from Whom is all authority and to Whom, as our final end, all actions both of men and States must be referred, / We, the people of Éire, / Humbly acknowledging all our obligations to our Divine Lord, Jesus Christ . . ." The landslide vote in Eire for legalizing the fictitious form of marriage between persons of the same sex, in contradiction of all laws natural and divine, unearths the pulsating Druidism that St. Patrick and his fellow saints defied. The estimated $17 million from pressure groups in the United States is no excuse, for people will be pressured only if they are willing to be pressured. Another dismal fact is that more than 90 percent of the young people influenced to subscribe to this vote were formed in Catholic schools. . . . While most of Europe suffers from the deadly sin of indifference, or sloth, Ireland is in adolescent rebellion, virulent and irrational. This was exploited by political interests hostile to Christian civilization.

A Year with Fr. Rutler (2017)

Ersatz Charity

Timidity disguised as charity can do more harm than anger. The conceit that evil will melt away by ignoring it would be like Captain Smith on the Titanic saying, "Iceberg? What iceberg?" St. Augustine said, "God does not need my lie." St. John Fisher, speaking as the only one of his country's bishops who was a true shepherd, lamented: "The fort is betrayed even of them that should have defended it." Four hundred years later, Churchill would say, "An appeaser is one who feeds a crocodile, hoping it will eat him last."

A Year with Fr. Rutler (2017)

The Eternal *Logos*

It would be brainless to deny that irrationality is the very con-stitutive "reason" for terrorism. It would be doubly brainless to dismiss each terrorist as a "lone wolf," as though he were acting independently of a motive common to many. Lone wolves so numerous hardly seem lonely. When men are roaming about with meat cleavers and pressure-cooker bombs, it is not the moment to diagram the importance of logic. It is, however, the duty of those in civil authority to be logical, and they cannot do this without commitment to the eternal *Logos*.

Calm in Chaos (2018)

Eternity

Of the Four Last Things, Heaven is at once the most agreeable subject and the most perplexing. Hardened cynicism first asks if it is too good to be true, and then asks if it is all that desirable. A bliss beyond time and space confounds our existential idiom. Mortal man worries that eternity will be boring. But that is like a drowning man asking his rescuer if there will be anything to do on the beach.

A Year with Fr. Rutler (2017)

Euphemism

A common way to lie is to change words. Euphemisms are verbal gymnastics to avoid the truth. For instance, vice can be made to sound attractive by calling it "liberating." Or, as Stalin said, "One death is a tragedy; one million is a statistic." A recent headline on the front page of the *New York Post* told of a criminal horror: "Baby Ripped from Womb." The subtitle said: "Bronx Mom Slain for Fetus." Now, a baby is a fetus, and a fetus is a baby. Why not just call it a baby? It is hard to extricate oneself from euphemisms.

A Year with Fr. Rutler (2017)

Evangelization

Conversion of unbelievers starts with a daily conversion of believers themselves to more genuine and mature practice of the Faith. This Epiphany is a time to commit ourselves to that great project. Our parish church is dedicated to Our Saviour. It is a reminder that we have a special responsibility in the heart of this great metropolis to announce why Christ has come into the world: not just to edify or inspire or console, but to save souls. Christians must "comfort the afflicted and afflict the comfortable," and they do this by starting with themselves.

A Year with Fr. Rutler (2017)

Evidence for the Existence of God

While there are natural evidences for the existence of God, only God Himself can reveal to us the mystery of the Holy Trinity.

A Year with Fr. Rutler (2017)

Evil

The Jewish philosopher Hannah Arendt wrote a book about Adolf Eichmann, one of the chief architects of the Holocaust, called *Eichmann in Jerusalem* (1963). He was one of the most diabolical figures ever to have walked upon the human stage. Yet, Arendt remarked, what a surprise it was, when he finally was found and put on trial, to see what an ordinary man he was in appearance and speech. In him was nothing that looked or sounded like the devil. But that is what made his evil all the more palpable! Arendt used this example to coin the expression "the banality of evil." In other words, evil loves to work through mediocrity. Evil smiles. Evil will speak with a kind of humanitarianism, all the while holding virtue in contempt. It does not believe in the possibility of grace. It considers truth to be only a matter of opinion.

Grace and Truth (2019)

Evil and Its Material and Formal Agents

The question "Why do bad things happen to good people?" ... has occupied substantial writers through the ages. Theologians speak of "theodicy," which is the task of explaining the existence of evil in a world made by a good God. People who do not believe in a good God should logically have no problem with the existence of evil, but most of them do, because (1) they are not logical and (2) they are living off a remnant assumption of the rights of goodness over evil. Bad things often happen because they are allowed, and even made, to happen.... The evil of September 11 was the direct work of bad people. Perhaps it could have been prevented if in past years the world had taken the terrorists more seriously. Each day in the United States, the number of babies killed before birth is larger than the number of people who suffered and died on September 11. It is made to happen by "material agents" of evil who commit the act directly. It is allowed to happen by "formal agents" who pass evil laws, defend the evil as though it were good, and suppress the truth.

A Year with Fr. Rutler (2017)

An Examination of Conscience

If you go through the Passion narratives, you can identify every personality that has ever lived. All the foibles of the human race are on display in one character or another. We cannot look at these characters as though they are somehow distinct from us, for in every one of them is a part of our own soul. God has given us the Passion narratives, edited by the Holy Spirit, so that we can have the anecdotes and dialogues and characters He wants us to know. This heavenly script is an examination of conscience for us and our ego's intrigues against the divine design.

Grace and Truth (2019)

Excommunication

Jesus does not contradict Himself. He judges no one in the sense of an arbitrary assessment. But His blatant existence challenges any lies made against His law. Since He is the Incarnation of Truth, Christ's judgment is perfect. Ours is not. When the Church passes judgment by censure or excommunication, she is ensuring and communicating the judgment of Christ, and not a human opinion.

A Year with Fr. Rutler (2017)

The Expression of Ecstasy

At a formal dinner in a club frequented by Anglo-Saxons, I told a guest of different ancestry that the members might seem subdued and even somnolent, but such was their way of expressing ecstasy. That is a little like the way of the Church when she is faithful to herself: there are some celebrations too joyful for ordinary happiness. To be solemn is not necessarily to be sad; it can be expressive of a very high happiness.

The Stories of Hymns (2016)

Ex umbris et imaginibus in veritatem

One of the greatest minds that ever lived, John Henry Cardinal Newman, understood the meaning and mystery of truth. That is why for his memorial inscription he chose *Ex umbris et imaginibus in veritatem*, "Out of the shadows and imagining, into the truth." "Into the truth," not around the truth, or near the truth, or behind the truth. Our limited intellects are clever and learned enough to do that. But he wanted to go *into the truth*.

Grace and Truth (2019)

The Eye of a Mother

A while before my mother died, her mind began to grow tired. Often at the end of a day, she would seem to be imagining things that were not there. At sunset she would look at me and ask, "Where are the children?" She had been one of nine children and had cared for many. But she was not imagining what was not there. She could see that childhood itself is missing from the very life of our culture. This was the long memory of Rachel weeping for her children who were not. Our Lord had some officious followers who wanted to prevent children from seeing their Messiah. He said, "Let the children come to me, do not hinder them; for to such belongs the kingdom of heaven." Though very gentle, my mother would not tolerate anyone's criticism of four persons: the pope, because he is the pope; the queen, because she is the queen; the late Terence Cardinal Cooke of New York, because my parents were the last he received into the Church before he died in 1983; and Mother Teresa of Calcutta, because she was such a good mother.

He Spoke to Us (2016)

Faddists

By baptism, man is reborn into innocence. The traditional antiphon for the first Sunday after Easter quotes 1 Peter 2:2, "Like newborn infants ..." In Latin the first words are *Quasi modo*, and in Victor Hugo's 1831 novel about Notre Dame Cathedral, a crippled infant is abandoned at the cathedral on that day and is named from the antiphon, for he seems "almost like" a normal human. Hugo wrote the novel in part to publicize the danger to the great building that had suffered so much damage in the French Revolution. It actually was in danger of being torn down because of its decrepitude and also because its architecture was considered "old fashioned." Hugo helped inspire the Gothic Revival and saved that great building from the hands of faddists who in their nervous ways resembled those who in recent decades have done so much damage to our own fine churches.

A Year with Fr. Rutler (2017)

Faith, Catechesis, and Geometry

Pope Pius X's "Oath against Modernism" was neglected and even mocked in the adolescent rebellion following Vatican II, but it is a remarkable subject for meditation, as prophetic now as in 1910. At its core is this: "Faith is not a blind sentiment of religion welling up from the depths of the subconscious under the impulse of the heart and the motion of a will trained to morality; but faith is a genuine assent of the intellect to truth received by hearing from an external source." The first Bishop of Rome said that Christians must use their brains: "Always be prepared to make a defense to anyone who calls you to account for the hope that is in you" (1 Pet. 3:15). The Church suffers today in consequence of impoverished catechesis, and earnest young people are finding themselves on the front lines of spiritual combat without ammunition for their minds. Even in exalted corridors of the Church there is a remarkably casual neglect of systematic theology when discoursing about the reason for hope. Etienne Gilson wrote in *Christianity and Philosophy* in 1936: "We are told that it is faith which constructed the cathedrals of the Middle Ages. Without doubt, but faith would have constructed nothing at all if there had not also been architecture; and if it is true that the façade of Notre Dame of Paris is a yearning of the soul toward God, that does not prevent its being also a geometrical work. It is necessary to know geometry in order to construct a façade which may be an act of love."

Calm in Chaos (2018)

Faith and Reason

Faith is not a substitute for reason. It is an extension of reason that is dimensions beyond our limited human intelligence. "Eye has not seen, nor has ear heard, nor has it even entered the heart of man, the wonderful things God has prepared for those who love him" (1 Cor. 2:9). It takes faith to trust that those we love and mourn deeply are now alive in a more glorious state. This is a reasonable belief because Our Lord, who is Truth, says it is so.

A Year with Fr. Rutler (2017)

The Fall of Man

Christ fell three times beneath the Cross. He also got up three times. We fall all the time. The whole human race fell in its first generation. The Fall of Man is misery writ large. What matters for our eternal happiness is that we get up again. So a great saint said, oblivious to his own sanctity, "Not all the saints started well, but they finished well."[11]

A Year with Fr. Rutler (2017)

False Gods

The Latin historian Suetonius wrote of the emperor Tiberius and his theological quandary. Tiberius reigned at the start of Christianity, and in fact, the Sea of Galilee was sometimes referred to by his name. He concluded that the pantheon of the gods that he had been taught as a child was fiction. Suetonius tells us that

---

[11] This was one of the famous sayings of St. John Vianney.

Tiberius looked at the stars in the heavens and consulted them, and he looked into the pantheon and found it vacant. That really is an analogy for the human condition at the end of the modern age. The problem is the people have not only lost heart in the false gods, but they have also been told that the True God doesn't exist. It is not only the pantheon that seems empty to them; it is the Church of God, and indeed the entire universe that has been voided.

Grace and Truth (2019)

False History

People try to forget the truth when they want to lie. But since lies contradict the way things are, liars have to fabricate a false history. So it is that liars need a good memory. They have to remember what they have denied. This is the protocol of all moral confusion.

A Year with Fr. Rutler (2017)

False Religions

The way of perfection is the way of truth—not a sensual alternative to truth. The history of false religions is a catalogue of how they confuse truth with emotion and then fall into decay when sentimentality no longer sustains them.

A Year with Fr. Rutler (2017)

False Witness

The Church's teaching about human life, especially with regard to abortion and euthanasia and contraception, doesn't fit the modern theory of the way the world is supposed to work. It doesn't fit the temper of the times. And yet respect for life is one of the things that Our Lord was thinking about when He said that He had done His Father's work: He manifested to us the dignity of life from the moment of conception. If we deny these things, we are bearing false witness — false witness against our human dignity, as well as against our God.

Grace and Truth (2019)

Faithful Witness

In 1955, the bishop of Shanghai, Ignatius Kung, was arrested by the Chinese Communists and taken into an arena, where he was put on the platform and instructed before thousands of his fellow Christians to deny the pope and the Catholic Church. The bishop of Shanghai, who was little more than five feet tall, reached up to the microphone and shouted, "Long live Christ the King! Long live the pope!" He was dragged away, and false witnesses accused him of treason — but his only treason was his loyalty to God. He spent thirty years in prison in one of those slow-motion martyrdoms of which we hear little. In March 2000 at the age of ninety-eight, Cardinal Kung — for he had been given the red hat by John Paul II secretly in 1979, then publicly in 1991 — went to his eternal reward. And when we speak of such a man as Cardinal Kung, we are not using a pious convention when we say that "he went to his eternal reward." Christ is faithful to those who bear faithful witness to Him.

Grace and Truth (2019)

Fame

The pantheon of fame has its cracks. I recently spoke with a college student who had never heard of Bing Crosby. The only recognition that matters is how we are known to the Lord. Should we be blessed to meet Him in glory, He will not say, "How do you do?" He will not even say, "I think I remember you." He will say, "Before I formed you in the womb, I knew you" (Jer. 1:5).

A Year with Fr. Rutler (2017)

The Family

Some politicians promote the destruction of the family and the legalization of counterfeit forms of marriage. Either by ignorance or demagoguery, some will try to lump the issues of abortion and marriage with issues of social polity. They will say we shouldn't be "selective" in giving preeminence to the right to life and authentic marriage over other matters, such as ecology, the death penalty, welfare reform, health care, and so on. Usually, they prefer to remain anonymous and shrink from debate. Such illogic would never have persuaded a more civilized age. It is a transparent way that the prince of lies would confuse people. Policies on air pollution, tax structures, seal hunting, and psoriasis do not have the moral weight of natural law as it pertains to the right to life of the unborn and the integrity of the family. Abortion is

intrinsically evil—*malum in se*—and it is not a prudential matter like capital punishment or other issues. Excommunication
from God's sacraments is automatic (*latae sententiae*) when one
participates in an intrinsic evil.

A Year with Fr. Rutler (2017)

The Family versus Social Engineers

It may take a long time to repair the damage done to society by
misguided social engineers who scorned the traditional family,
but the Church lives by the vision expressed by Pope Pius XI at a
time when a fascist government tried to usurp the role of parents:
"The family is more sacred than the state, and men are begotten
not for the earth and for time, but for heaven and eternity."[12]

A Year with Fr. Rutler (2017)

Fanaticism

Indifference is the fanaticism of the faint of heart.

He Spoke to Us (2016)

Fantasy

The denial of God and His grace—and therefore the denial of
the reality of the saints—is at the root of all fantasy.

Grace and Truth (2019)

---

[12] Pope Pius XI, *Casti Connubi* (31 December 1930), no. 69.

Fasting

We have all had the experience of meeting or knowing people who make a fetish of fasting, even to the length of weighing themselves in the process. With a deluded spirituality, they claim to fast but only diet. The scales of justice are not in the bathroom. Fasting is meant to teach humility: If I cannot do without a few sandwiches, I should speak with reserve about being a soldier of Christ.

He Spoke to Us (2016)

Fatherhood

The dignity of fatherhood is known by knowing God. There are those who would suggest that the Fatherhood of God is a psychological self-projection of a patriarchal society. This nonsense is an old heresy known as Gnosticism. The opposite is true. The social order fully knows the meaning of fatherhood only as an emanation of the Fatherhood of God. Christianity is virtually unique in its understanding of this. Even the Jews, chosen of God, usually referred to God as Father only symbolically, or metaphorically. The overwhelming science of the Fatherhood of God comes to us through Christ.

A Year with Fr. Rutler (2017)

Fatherhood and Civilization

As a priest and consecrated religious, St. Pio was "Padre." Civilization has been built by good fathers, and the Liturgy invokes "Abraham our Father in Faith" and all the patriarchs as witnesses.

Washington is the father of our country, and Lincoln was Father Abraham to an afflicted people. Father's Day is a civil tribute to the fatherhood that begins with God our Father, from whom all earthly fathers take their name. Bad fathers betray their families and their civilization. That is true of fathers of children and of our spiritual fathers who are bishops and priests.

A Year with Fr. Rutler (2017)

Faust and the Maternal Scream

When I was a college student, I remember going to the opera with my parents to see *Faust*. In the climactic scene, a woman in prison takes her baby and dashes it to the ground. We were close enough to see that the baby was, of course, a doll, but when that diva smashed the doll to the stage, my mother let out a scream! I was young and immature and naïve enough about life to be embarrassed by that maternal scream. Now I realize that in that maternal scream was the sense of truth that allowed me to be born and that has allowed, from all ages, every life to be born. That holy scream was also heard in Bethlehem soon after Our Lord was born. An insecure willful king massacred the innocents because wanted to live a lie: He wanted to be the only king. But the lie did not last (no lie does), and he ended up dying a miserable death. In the meantime, many infants paid the price for his lie. Notice this characteristic of King Herod, which is typical of people like him: He was sentimental, and he played on sentimentality in others. When the three mysterious figures from the East told him that the Great One had been born, he responded, "Go and search diligently for the child, and when you have found him bring me word, that I too may come and worship him" (Matt. 2:8). We can almost see the saccharine look on his face, the pretense to devotion, while his mind was sneering and plotting. Flannery O'Connor, the great Catholic writer, pointed out many times that the cruelest people are the most sentimental.[13] They don't live by truth, but by a lie. And when you live by a lie, you are governed, not by fact, but by feeling. Indeed, the worst crimes against life are always cloaked in sentimentality.

Grace and Truth (2019)

Feasts and the Cross

There is not a festival of the Church that is not a veneration of the Cross, through which all feasts come.

The Stories of Hymns (2016)

Feast Days

Since the Holy Trinity is the source and center of the Gospel, the Church did not think it necessary to have a special feast to celebrate this fact for about a thousand years. Special veneration of the mystery spread in France, and Thomas Becket brought it to England in the twelfth century. Pope John XXII, one of the

---

[13] "We lost our innocence in the Fall and our return to it is through the Redemption, which was brought about by Christ's death and by our slow participation in it. Sentimentality is a skipping of this process." Flannery O'Connor, "The Church and the Fiction Writer" (1957), in *Collected Works* (New York: Library of America, 1988), 809.

Avignon popes living in France, made it a universal feast in 1334, and in 1911 Pope St. Pius X made it a solemnity, which is the highest kind of feast. This is to be remembered when people think that the liturgical calendar is fixed and unchangeable.

A Year with Fr. Rutler (2017)

Fire Worship

God has endowed the human reason with the ability to harness light. This Creator is not like the mythic powers that punished Prometheus for stealing fire from heaven. The true God sent His Holy Spirit as fire for His Church. Every act of true worship is thanksgiving for this brightness. Fire worship among the pagans was an untutored prophecy of Pentecost.

The Stories of Hymns (2016)

First and Last a Parish Priest

With close to a hundred thousand pilgrims filling Ars in [St. John Vianney's] last year, missionaries had to be delegated to help with the confessions. The old shepherd's speech was becoming less intelligible; he had frequent coughing fits now, and sometimes passed out. "My head gets confused." Finally, he was obliged to give up kneeling during the Divine Office and allowed himself an afternoon nap. The sermons of these last days had become almost entirely public conversation with the Blessed Sacrament; a soul estranged from the saga of Ars would have been bewildered at the rapt silence of the packed church as the wrinkled and toothless Curé kept shaking his bony finger toward the gilded tabernacle, calling out words that sounded like "Love" and "God," and little more. One noon he sat down in his housekeeper's home: "Ah! my poor Catherine, I can do no more!" He returned to the presbytery for his nap but chose instead to head back to the church, surrounded as always by the indeterminable number of staring folk. Nothing was unusual about this, though he had taken an extra cup of milk from Catherine, and it seemed to her he needed it to live. On Easter Day, April 24, 1858, he noted that a half dozen parishioners had not made their Communion. In his customary way, Vianney did not count the swarms of visitors around the altar. He was first and last a parish priest and would have to answer for the souls of his "own people." Rod and staff both were instruments of the shepherd, and so long as he could move he prodded and pulled. The priesthood is the sacrament of spiritual fatherhood.

The Curé d'Ars Today (2018)

Forensic Testing and the Evidence for Easter

Accustomed to forensic testing, Sir Edward Clarke (1841–1931) wrote: "As a lawyer I have made a prolonged study of the evidence for the first Easter. To me the evidence is conclusive, and over and over again in the High Court I have secured the verdict on evidence not nearly so compelling. As a lawyer I accept it unreservedly as the testimony of men to facts that they were able to substantiate." St. Luke was a pioneer historian at a time when historical analysis barely existed. He writes that Jesus "presented Himself alive, after His suffering, by many convincing proofs, appearing to them over a period of forty days, and speaking of the things concerning the kingdom of God" (Acts 1:3).

A Year with Fr. Rutler (2017)

Formal Cooperation in Grave Sin

The archbishop of Saint Louis, the Most Reverend Raymond L. Burke, is both a bishop and a lawyer and has a legal competence that charitably shreds emotional equivocation about abortion. In an article in the journal *America* (June 21–28, 2004) he recalls that the bishops of the United States six years ago recognized the difficulties in legislating moral good, but also said that "no appeal to policy, procedure, majority will, or pluralism ever excuses a public official from defending life to the greatest extent possible." A correctly formed conscience cannot be "set in opposition to the moral law or the magisterium of the church" (CCC 2039). A politician's failure to protect the life of the unborn betrays the public trust. Canon 915 of the *Code of Canon Law* stipulates that those who "obstinately" persevere "in manifest grave sin are not to be admitted to Holy Communion." This is not a sanction of excommunication arbitrarily imposed by a bishop, as some people describe it. The exclusion is inherent in the nature of the sacrament itself. In other words, culpable individuals have, by their own public defiance of the moral good, excommunicated themselves. A bishop only declares the fact, and that is done when the contempt for the truth has become a public scandal. Unlike other moral matters that may involve prudential interpretation, abortion is a definitive moral evil, and supporting legislation that protects it constitutes formal cooperation in a gravely sinful act. This blatantly obtains in the case of Catholic politicians who support organizations such as Planned Parenthood and the National Abortion Rights Action League.

A Year with Fr. Rutler (2017)

The Four Last Things

If Christians let the Advent season pass without contemplating the four mysteries of Death, Judgment, Heaven, and Hell, they have shortchanged themselves and have quite missed the point of living in God's grace. Many writers have said in different ways what even so skeptical a man as George Bernard Shaw said cogently: "Hell is the place where you have nothing to do but amuse yourself." We were made to adore God and to give Him delight. Everything else follows, and without adoration, every attempt to delight the self becomes unsatisfactory and even self-destructive.

A Year with Fr. Rutler (2017)

The French Revolution and Secular Humanism

France in the last generations before the Revolution had hardly been a verdant grove of mystical vision. In some ways the mental furnishing of the Church had been as elegantly angular as a Louis Seize chair. Said Chateaubriand, "Priests in their pulpits avoided naming Jesus Christ and talked instead of the Legislator of Christians." The revolutionaries thought they were bringing in a newer and more reliable stability after the Church had succumbed to a confusing revulsion within itself. The anticlerical elite only made an anthem of the rationalism that had already been whispered by clerics. If the priests of the times had not worshipped isosceles triangles, neither had they said much about the Holy Trinity; if they knew Christ was more than Plato, they had not explained why. But they had greased the slide from theism through deism to the shriveled surrender of the will called atheism.

Neglect of doctrine had become a means of ascending the bureaucratic pole of peer respectability. Hilaire Belloc has remarked in his book on the French Revolution that the Church was "not concerned to defend itself but only its method of existence." And consequently, a kind of gentleman's agreement was established whereby the Church's ministers were honored by the court and the encyclopedists, or by the media and the intelligentsia, as we might say, so long as they did not insist too hard on matters of faith and morals. The pattern is no less blatant today, for but one example, in the temptation of Catholic universities to dilute their religious identity for the sake of government subsidies. And because the hierarchy over the years of social absorption had come to be drawn from that part of society that held the prevailing rationalist views, it was hard for them to detect any temporizing or betrayal in their conformity. As Belloc writes in his limpid way:

> It did not shock the hierarchy that one of its apostolic members should be a witty atheist; that another should go hunting upon Corpus Christi, nearly upset the Blessed Sacrament in his gallop, and forget what day it was when the accident occurred. The bishops found nothing remarkable in seeing a large proportion of their body to be loose livers.... Unquestioned also by the bishops were the poverty, the neglect, and the uninstruction of the parish clergy; nay ... the abandonment of religion by all but a very few of the French millions was a thing simply taken for granted.

Taking all that in, I cannot but think Belloc was wrong in saying the Revolution's quarrel with the Church was against this negligent form of the Church and not against the Christian life genuinely lived. It is true that there is nothing in Catholicism that is hostile to democratic life and republican order; it is even truer that the Catholic systematics of natural law, human dignity, and social order are the most amiable constituents of solid democratic polity. But to make this point, Belloc may have exaggerated the moral neutrality of republican theory in the Enlightenment. He does say that only the course of years will show whether or not this particular theory and Catholicism were irreconcilable tangents. But we may say that the years since he wrote are enough to show how they were indeed irreconcilable, and that while democracy and Christianity are compatible, the materialist underpinnings of the eighteenth-century republicanism sowed the seeds of modern secular humanism.... The heaps of corpses in the twentieth century are the consequence of the rationalists' false confidence.

The Curé d'Ars Today (1988)

The Gentleness of Christ

One would risk glibness if not irreverence to say that Christ was a gentleman, but in His human nature He habitually put those around Him at ease.... When Our Lord had "opened their minds to understand the scriptures," He told those in the Upper Room to "stay in the city until you are clothed with power from on high" (Luke 24:45, 49). We know that Peter listened very carefully, for when he was clothed in that elegant spiritual haberdashery that is sanctifying grace, he delicately told the crowd in Jerusalem that they had acted out of ignorance, but if they repented, the Lord would grant them "times of refreshment" (Acts 3:19). For the Lord—unbending to evil and fierce in the face of the Evil One—is also gentle in all His ways.

A Year with Fr. Rutler (2017)

The Gates to Eternal Life

The liturgical reliving of the Passion is different from nostalgia. A wit said that nostalgia is history after a few drinks. The solemn liturgies walk us through the events that open the gates to eternal life, and this aperture into eternity is as real as the Golden Gate that opened on the first Palm Sunday and the tombstone that rolled away on the first Easter.

A Year with Fr. Rutler (2017)

Gaudete Sunday

Some mistakenly have thought that Paul exchanged letters with Seneca and was something of a Stoic himself. He does say: "We rejoice in our sufferings, knowing that suffering produces endurance" (Rom 5:3), but, unlike the Stoics, he believed that hardships and spiritual disciplines shouldered uncomplainingly prepare the soul for the joys of Heaven. So, on Gaudete Sunday in penitential Advent, a little unearthly light seeps into earthly darkness, and the Church chants: "Rejoice in the Lord always; again, I will say, Rejoice. Let all men know your forbearance. The Lord is at hand. Have no anxiety about anything, but in everything by prayer and supplication with thanksgiving let your requests be made known to God" (Phil 4:4–6).

He Spoke to Us (2016)

Ghosts

In 1899 the American poet William Hughes Mearns (1875–1965) wrote about a ghost:

> Yesterday, upon the stair,
> I met a man who wasn't there.
> He wasn't there again today
> I wish, I wish he'd go away.

Terrorists are not ghosts, and they will not go away, even if reasonably intelligent people misuse their brains to pretend they are not there.

Calm in Chaos (2018)

Edward Gibbon, Margaret Thatcher, and Public Virtue

As a typical eighteenth-century rationalist, Edward Gibbon was cynical about Christianity, but as an historian he saw the staying power of civilizations in terms of natural virtue: "That public virtue, which among the ancients was denominated patriotism, is derived from a strong sense of our own interest in the preservation and prosperity of the free government of which we are members. Such a sentiment, which had rendered the legions of the Republic almost invincible, could make but a very feeble impression on the mercenary servants of a despotic prince."[14] And as England's prime minister Margaret Thatcher pointed

---

[14] Edward Gibbon, *The History of the Decline and Fall of the Roman Empire*, ed. J. B. Bury (London: Methuen and Co., 1909), I, 10–11.

out, when the people's deepest desire becomes security, rather than freedom, wanting "not to give to society, but for society to give to them," they lose both their security and their freedom.[15] I expect that Gibbon would have understood modern saints no better than he did the early martyrs and confessors, but he would have seen in them a selfless energy that builds noble societies, and that neglect of such energy pulls them down. Our own nation is facing these realities as it decides what it wants to be. The present crisis in culture cannot be resolved if it is addressed only in terms of economics and international relations. The real leaders are not those who hypnotize naïve people into thinking that they are the source of hope but those who can rescue nations from servility to selfishness.

A Year with Fr. Rutler (2017)

The Gift of Awe

It is not falsely optimistic to think that ordinary people of common sense can grasp the truths of holy religion, once they are given the facts, and it is not falsely pessimistic to assume that the educated despisers of religion will reject the facts in order to sustain their personal theories. But true wisdom can guide both, and that requires the gift of awe, which is the "holy fear" of which the psalmist speaks: "The fear of the Lord is the beginning of wisdom" (Ps. 111:10; see Sir. 1:16).

A Year with Fr. Rutler (2017)

---

[15] Lady Margaret Thatcher, "The Moral Foundations of Society," lecture at the Hillsdale Center for Constructive Alternatives seminar "God and Man: Perspectives on Christianity in the 20th Century" (1994).

The Gift of Faith

The gift of faith, which comes to us from God, is a sublime grace. But we are not intended to keep it to ourselves — in effect, to bury it in the ground. The apostolic fishermen were ordained to be fishers of souls and not custodians of an aquarium.

Hints of Heaven (2014)

The Gift of Motherhood

I remember looking at a painting of the Crucifixion with my mother. I played the part of the art historian by explaining the artist, the biography of the artist, why he is considered a master painter, what techniques he used, and so on. That's how I explained the Crucifixion scene, with Our Lord on the Cross and His Mother weeping. But when I finished, my mother simply said, "How difficult it must have been for her." I got the painting right; she got the Mother right. That intuitive gift of the mother is passed down to each generation through the Church, Our Holy Mother. The gift of motherhood must never be taken for granted.

Grace and Truth (2019)

Gilbert Keith Chesterton

For thirty-one years, beginning in 1905, Chesterton wrote weekly columns of about two thousand words that were read widely in the English-speaking world. Against the background of nearly a hundred books and plays and collections of poetry, he continued this outpouring of 1,535 columns for the *Illustrated London News*, whose editors required that he declare early on (April 7,

1906) the constraints of his contract: "I am not allowed in these columns to discuss politics or religion, which is inconvenient as they are the only two subjects which seem to me to have the slightest element of interest for a sane man." He remained sane ... by writing about the great euphemism for politics and religion: that is, he wrote about the world. The columns constituted, in fact, some of the century's most astute political and theological discourse. His subject, addressed in a thousand ways under a thousand titles, was the soul and body; every declaration he could muster doomed the idealist dogma of man as mind and mind alone.... His wife, Frances, chose lines from Walter de la Mare for his memorial card:

> Knight of the Holy Ghost, he goes his way
> Wisdom his motley, Truth his loving jest;
> The mills of Satan keep his lance in play,
> Pity and innocence his heart at rest.[16]

A Crisis of Saints (1995)

God's Largesse

In all portents, in the daily commerce of life, in the economy of the virtues, in matters touching on talent and imagination, in the sacraments and in the desire for the welfare of those we love, God gives freely, but He does not give for free.

A Crisis of Saints (1995)

[16] See Maisie Ward, *Gilbert Keith Chesterton* (London: Sheed and Ward, 1944), 552. De La Mare wrote the lines to support Chesterton's candidacy for the rectorship of Edinburgh University.

Good News

The gospel is good news because it is traumatic news, and it is shocking by having happened in an unshockable world.

The Curé d'Ars Today (1988)

Gnosticism

Devotees of Gilbert and Sullivan's *Iolanthe* know the lament of Strephon, who was half man and half woodland sprite: "My body can creep through a keyhole, but what's the good of that when my legs are left kicking behind?" This came to mind when a picture of Bruce Jenner dressed as a woman appeared on a magazine cover. He received ESPN's Arthur Ashe Courage Award for having "shown the courage to embrace a truth that had been hidden for years." Sixty-five years, that is. Anyone listening to the conversations of sedentary former athletes on ESPN is perhaps not seeking the deeper significance of things, but the declaration that a man is a woman must astonish alert minds — including the Olympic judges who awarded Mr. Jenner a medal under the impression that he was a man. The longest-simmering heresy in Christian history is Gnosticism, which opposes things spiritual to things material, with the consequence that one's authentic identity is "trapped" in the body. The Christian knows that the body is a temple and not a prison. Philosophers like Immanuel Kant gave Gnosticism a sophisticated veneer, but the invariable result is a creature like Strephon — in mind one thing and in body something else. John Milton wrote, "The mind is its own place, and in itself can make a heaven of hell, a hell of heaven." Modernity paid the price for opting in favor of Gnosticism when the myth of Superman replacing God led to a world war. In 1941, Cardinal Gerlier preached in Lyons: "The world of the future will be Christian or it will be hell." Our culture is succumbing to a predilection for a mental construct that seems not far from hellish.

A Year with Fr. Rutler (2017)

God's Greatest Gift

The greatest gift of God to us is Himself in the Holy Eucharist. Pentecost Sunday celebrated the coming of the Holy Spirit into the Church, and Trinity Sunday celebrated the central mystery of the Faith, the dogma of the Holy Trinity. Today, in a feast formally decreed by Pope Urban IV in 1264, the celebration of the Body of Christ, Corpus Christi, becomes a celebration of a celebration, for it rejoices in the Eucharistic action during which the Church prays to God the Father, invoking God the Holy Spirit to change the bread and wine into the Body and Blood of God the Son. All this is a unified action, indeed a sacred dance, ritualizing the unity and harmony of the Three Persons of the Holy Trinity.

A Year with Fr. Rutler (2017)

Goethe's Window Shades

Light and life go together, and there are countless "last words" that have to do with light as life ends. As he was dying, the poet Goethe cried out, "*Mehr Licht!*" (More light!) — but in his case, it most likely had no spiritual meaning. He had also been a scientist, one who considered that his best book was

The Theory of Colours, and he probably was just asking that the window shades be raised.

A Year with Fr. Rutler (2017)

Grace

There is nothing inherently wrong with finding a treasure without working for it. Were it otherwise, no heir could be canonized, and many have been. I summon as a fresh and modern witness St. Katherine Drexel. Crudely put, the entire history of salvation is an account of how the bumbling and stumbling human race won the Great Lottery. Grace is gratuitous. As the Catholic knows, from the age of the apostle James to the moral tonic of Trent, faith without works is vain; but faith is faith, and as such, it is a gift. Should we make the mature examination of our souls in the second before the Particular Judgment, we may be astonished at how many times holy grace dropped into our laps without our recognizing it.

Hints of Heaven (2014)

The Great Treasure

Heaven is not for the religious but for the heavenly, and Heaven breaks through the bounds of earth when the clumsy soul chances upon the great treasure and takes it to himself with an exuberance that publishes the news in spite of all the proprieties of limited reason and habitual custom.

Hints of Heaven (2014)

The Greatest Drama of All

The actor Alec Guinness, a convert to the Faith, said in his book *Blessings in Disguise* (1986) that the thing he regretted most in life was not having become a Catholic sooner. You might say that an actor makes a profession of lying, but that's really not what acting is about. Real acting is playing out the truths of life on the stage in symbolic form, in appropriated language, but all the while serving the truth. And I think a great actor like Guinness realized that the greatest drama of all is on no other stage but the stage of human history, and that there is no theme more compelling to an audience than the Passion and Resurrection of Christ. Certainly, the good thief knew that. God in His infinite mercy reminds us of that with great delicacy time and time again.

Grace and Truth (2019)

Greeting Cards

The kingdom of heaven is like treasure hidden in a field.... There was a householder who planted a vineyard.... The land of a rich man brought forth plentifully.... There was a rich man who had a steward, and charges were brought to him that this man was wasting his goods.... A man was going down from Jerusalem to Jericho.... These familiar lines open the most exquisitely austere and natural of all stories, the parables told by the Word who uttered the world into existence. The only proof I have of their literary superiority is that no one has ever been able to match them. Those who try are like a man standing before a masterpiece of painting who says, "I can do that," takes up a palette, and produces a greeting card.

Hints of Heaven (2014)

Hagiography

Hagiography may flatter saints but, when it does, it insults them.

The Curé d'Ars Today (1988)

Happiness

Many have ridiculed the nineteenth-century professor of logic Richard Whately, who said, "Happiness is no laughing matter." I think he has had the last laugh. The happiness of which he spoke is beyond jocularity, although the outward smile is a serene tribute to it. St. Teresa of Avila prayed to be spared from gloomy saints. God came to us in Christ to show us our purpose, and to lead us to it. "Take up your cross" is not a pathology of suffering for its own sake, but a movement of the self beyond the self, to reach our ultimate purpose with God, a happiness that has no end.

A Year with Fr. Rutler (2017)

A Happy Day for Goodly Fat People

Was it not a special favor from God to watch the joint beatification of Pope Pius IX; Abbot Columba Marmion, O.S.B., third abbot of Maredsous Abbey in Belgium; and Pope John XXIII? It was a happy day for goodly fat people … and a day of abasement for aesthetical ascetics … who want only gaunt saints on their prayer cards. Enthusiasts who cut down on food principally to improve their tennis game would be less eager to fast if it added weight. In a perversely affluent culture where thinness is an outward sign of wealth, getting fat is not necessarily a way to humility, but it does guarantee humiliation. To paraphrase Chesterton on the angels, the key to heroic virtue may not be in being light but in taking oneself lightly.

He Spoke to Us (2016)

Harbor Lights

In our day, stormy controversies attend questions of biotechnology on the micro level and world politics on the macro level. The answers are not easy, but they are simple: Everything will be fine so long as human rights respect the rights of God. The deepest question is, "Why did God make you?" The simplest answer that calms every storm is this: "God made me to know Him, to love Him, and to serve Him in this world, and to be happy with Him forever in Heaven."

He Spoke to Us (2016)

Heaven

God came to earth in Christ to show us how to get to Heaven. It was the most "worldly" thing that ever happened, because He reconciled the world to Himself. Nothing is more "unworldly" in an impractical sense than to reject all that Christ told the world about Heaven.

A Year with Fr. Rutler (2017)

Dennis Clinton Graham Heiner

Dennis Clinton Graham Heiner (1927–2008) crossed 38th Street daily for Mass at Church of Our Saviour, where I was pastor for many years. Outwardly, Dennis had a coddled childhood in New York City, and his parents sought the best for him, sending him to St. Bernard's School, whose establishment aura was complemented by his parent's devotion to the progressive principles of John Dewey. Robert Graham Heiner and Frances Eliot Cassidy were friends of Margaret Sanger and promoters of her eugenic theory. Their home resonated with the peaceful intercourse of curious savants from Planned Parenthood who met to discuss the annihilation of unfit people, blithe in their assumption that their sort was not threatened.

Dennis may have misrepresented himself to enlist in the Navy as a teenager, and so he served in World War II, if only at the tag end. From there it was Harvard and then Yale Law School. Mental exhaustion from the war, and growing interior conflict with his parent's view of creation, or the lack thereof kept him from ever practicing law. Instead, he pursued medicine at the University of Paris, but never practiced that either.

He had become a Catholic in contradiction of everything his parents understood to be rightly ordered, though he never broke with them in bonds of affection. That only increased his tense nature, and then he met a psychiatrist in the form of a stately Cuban woman, Helena Reina, who left all behind in the Marxist revolution of Castro. They were married for more than fifty years, and all the while I knew them he was her nurse, for she had become blind and nearly comatose. Even toward her end, whenever I brought her the Blessed Sacrament, he sat her under an oil portrait of herself in youth. Not once did I ever hear him speak of her as anything but a blessing, or of her infirmity as anything but a benison, and he seemed never so joyful as when he tried to make her drink through a straw.

I envied his quiet library of the Greek classics and modern apologists up to Ronald Knox, and so I was astonished when bookish Dennis was arrested on December 16, 1999, at the age of seventy-two. The Brooklyn Museum had staged a postmodern exhibition called "Sensation" whose centerpiece was a painting of the Virgin Mary covered with elephant dung and pornographic symbols. Dennis had stepped over a barrier and smeared a tube of white paint over it. The incident won international attention and got the mayor involved, and all Heaven broke loose. At his trial, he was his own defense and recited a list of the holy images of the Blessed Mother around the world, concluding by saying that he was answering speech with speech.

The prosecutor demanded probation, community service, and one day of sensitivity training, besides an order of protection forbidding him from entering the Brooklyn Museum. Brooklyn Supreme Court Judge Thomas Farber, a Jew, said that he had expected to hear nothing but hate from the defendant but only heard love. He rejected the prosecutor's request and encouraged Dennis to visit any museum he wanted, albeit without a tube of paint.

He never came to weekly confession or daily Communion without a pro-life pin in his lapel, and every Saturday he led the Rosary outside an abortion clinic. He was crossing the street to early Mass when a vehicle struck him and, though he told me he was steady, he died two days later. Months before, he had arranged Masses to be said for Helena, who had died the previous April, and his mother, who had never abjured her eugenics. Helena's Mass was the day before he was buried, and his mother's Mass was one hour after his funeral. A couple of years before his death, I informed him that the notorious painting had been destroyed in a London fire. He expressed no satisfaction, but in his silence one sensed that God's judgments are severe.

Cloud of Witnesses (2009)

Hell

Nothing could be more hellish than the possibility that there is no Hell, for it would mean that there is no moral judgment.

A Year with Fr. Rutler (2017)

Hell and Heaven

It seems odd that as Christmas draws closer, the Church makes a point of reminding us of Hell. We have little need of reminding, if we are awake to the manifestations of sadness and suffering along our city streets. The whole world is a hodgepodge of things we instinctively call "hellish" or "heavenly." ... Christ warns and consoles us, with His loving admonitions and promises, that He would have none lost and all saved.

A Year with Fr. Rutler (2017)

Once, when a reporter shouted to the thirty-third president: "Give 'em Hell, Harry!" Truman replied, "I don't give them Hell. I just tell the truth about them and they think it's Hell." Our Lord gave people Heaven, and if that frightened them it was because their duplicity made Heaven hellish.

A Year with Fr. Rutler (2017)

Heresy

The Church suffers in many ways, most conspicuously (even if neglected by much of the secular media) by physical persecution in many countries. Indeed, this oppression is on the increase.... A subtler form of suffering is by heresy. The word means choosing a wrong understanding of the truth, and this can be more dangerous than physical wounds, as it damages souls and not just bodies. Martyrdom glorifies and enriches the Church, while the spread of error weakens the Body of Christ on earth.

A Year with Fr. Rutler (2017)

Heretics

Heretics usually start out with a sincere desire to make obscure things clearer.

A Year with Fr. Rutler (2017)

Heroes and History

In recent days, as eyes look warily and perplexed on the spreading threat of Islam, I have thought of the genuine heroes who confronted that challenge in their various generations. If we are shocked at the genocide of Christians, the beheading of children, the torture and crucifixion of fathers and their young sons, we should remember the real heroes who were familiar with such slaughter in their own day. In Tours in 732, the Frankish king Charles Martel defeated the Islamic army using clever weaponry against great odds. Then there were Richard the Lionheart, St. Louis IX, János Hunyadi, St. John of Capistrano, Don Juan of

Austria, Andrea Doria, St. Pius V, and Jan Sobieski, all of whom lived lives that could constitute an entire college course in history, psychology, politics, and religion. If some of these names are now obscure, that is the fault of those who do not appreciate how, if any one of them had failed, our world would be far more miserable today and its institutions unrecognizable, and it is entirely possible that none of us would be alive.

A Year with Fr. Rutler (2017)

No Heroism for Average Christians?

Pope Benedict XVI, who lived during the hard days in Germany, said in 2002: "Heroic virtue properly speaking does not mean that one has done great things by oneself, but rather that in one's life there appear realities which the person has not done himself, because he has been transparent and ready for the work of God." This is the universal call to holiness about which St. Francis de Sales preached so solidly.[17] Recently, the German cardinal Walter Kasper described a "Revolution of Tenderness and Love" that would seem paler than the bold summons of Pope Benedict and St. Francis de Sales. In 2014, Cardinal Kasper

---

[17] "The proud man, who trusts in himself, has just reason not to attempt anything; but the humble is so much the more courageous by how much the more he recognises his own inability; and the more wretched he esteems himself the more confident he becomes; because he places all his trust in God, who delights to display His omnipotence in our weakness." *Introduction to the Devout Life from the French of St. Francis de Sales* (London: Longmans Green, 1891), 102.

said: "Heroism is not for the average Christian."[18] Many seem to have accepted that, for the German Church is in demographic meltdown: priestly ordinations have dropped by half in the last decade, and Mass attendance has plummeted to 10.4 percent. This contrasts with the amazing growth of the Church in Africa—but Cardinal Kasper has said: "They should not tell us too much what we have to do."

A Year with Fr. Rutler (2017)

Hillary and Hildegard

Addressing the 2015 Women in the World Summit, Hillary Clinton declared that "deep-seated cultural codes, religious beliefs and structural biases have to be changed." Not present at that summit was Saint Hildegard of Bingen, who could have enlivened the proceedings by her description of the wiles and ways of Alinsky's Lucifer:

> Religion he will endeavor to make convenient. He will say that you need not fast and embitter your life by renunciation.... It will suffice to love God. He will preach free love and tear asunder family ties. He will scorn everything holy, and he will ridicule all graces of the Church with devilish mockery. He will condemn humility and foster proud and gruesome dogmas. He will tear down that

---

18 "Cardinal Kasper: 'Heroism Is Not for the Average Christian,'" *Catholic News Agency*, May 9, 2014, https://www.catholicnewsagency.com/news/cardinal-kasper-heroism-is-not-for-the-average-christian.

which God has taught in the Old and New Testaments and maintain that sin and vice are not sin and vice.[19]

Calm in Chaos (2018)

History

Refusing to believe that Jesus was the Messiah, and to thwart any Messiah's entrance in the future, the Ottoman Sultan Suleiman I blocked up the Golden Gate in 1541 and placed a cemetery outside it. But he had closed the barn door too late. Christ cannot be kept out of history. He can be kept out of individual lives, though, and He can be repudiated by the civilization He shaped. Many who despise the Christian civilization of which they are part refuse to acknowledge that without the Holy Spirit, those attributes of civilization they enjoy, and even exploit, cannot be sustained.

A Year with Fr. Rutler (2017)

Holy Awe

Empty confessionals empty churches, and empty churches empty the soul of holy awe.

The Seven Wonders of the World (1993)

---

[19] Hildegard of Bingen, *Scivias*, trans. Columba Hart and Jane Bishop, quoted in Joseph Pronechen, "14 Saints Reveal Details about the Antichrist," *National Catholic Register*, October 11, 2016.

The Holy Eucharist

Each of us has the grace of contacting Heaven every day when the Light of the World casts out moral darkness and comes to the altar in the Holy Eucharist. In the Rosary, we have the privilege to add the Fatima prayer: "O my Jesus, forgive us our sins, save us from the fires of hell, lead all souls to Heaven, especially those most in need of Thy mercy. Amen."

A Year with Fr. Rutler (2017)

In the "darkest days" of the year, the Light of the World begins to be seen, in order to "cast off the works of darkness" (Rom. 13:12). Contemplation of Death, Judgment, Heaven, and Hell in the season of Advent dignifies the human intellect by showing us how to know the Christmas joy of the "Word Made Flesh," not as amiable nostalgia, like Civil War battle reenactments or dressing up like Washington crossing the Delaware, but actually realizing Heaven in that daily Christmas, Good Friday, Easter, and Pentecost which is the Holy Eucharist.

A Year with Fr. Rutler (2017)

The Holy Name

When we receive our names in baptism, they radiate the Holy Name, for every Christian is a spark of the Savior. We should say the Holy Name with reverence and make reparation when we hear thoughtless people use it as a curse. They do not know its power, but Satan does, and that is why he wants us to twist it if he cannot blot it out.

A Year with Fr. Rutler (2017)

The Holy Spirit

Every misunderstanding about God, in one way or another, comes from denying what the Holy Spirit has taught the Church. To think of God only as Creator is a rather passive kind of inert deism, and to think of Him only as the Incarnate Son easily becomes humanism, and to focus only on the Holy Spirit becomes an emotional kind of spiritualism.

A Year with Fr. Rutler (2017)

The power the Holy Spirit gives the Church is the truth. Truth is the ultimate power because it is reality. "Men may all lie, but God is always true" (Rom. 3:4). Truth always wins in the long run. In the short run, it may seem that lies win. But truth sustains life, while falsehood destroys it. Jesus said that Satan "was a murderer from the beginning, and does not stand in the truth, because there is no truth in him. Whenever he speaks a lie, he speaks from his own nature; for he is a liar, and the father of lies" (John 8:44). Lies do have power, but it is a fatal power and eventually self-destructs. In our society there are lies that an unborn baby is not human, and that marriage is not naturally the union of male and female, and that truth is only opinion. When a society accepts these lies, it eventually clashes with inescapable reality and crumbles. Even Satan is forced to tell the truth in the presence of Christ: "I know who you are, the Holy One of God" (Mark 1:24).

A Year with Fr. Rutler (2017)

Today a bishop, as a successor of the apostles, will give a number of our children their first Communion and will confirm some with the sevenfold gifts of the Holy Spirit. It is hoped that when they are older, the Holy Spirit will have made them more able to explain the Eucharist. But they will never be more open to God's grace than in this time of innocence. The three little children in Fatima encountered the Eucharist more profoundly than any doctor of divinity. In 1916, the year before Our Lady appeared to them, they saw the "Angel of Portugal" suspended in the air and prostrate before a Host from which drops of blood poured into a chalice. The angel then gave the children Communion: "Take and drink the Body and Blood of Jesus Christ." On May 13, 1917, the Mother of God appeared to the children with light pouring onto them from her hands. By a common inspiration, the untutored children knelt and repeated: "O most Holy Trinity, I adore You! My God, my God, I love You in the most Blessed Sacrament!" The daughter of the Father and mother of the Son and spouse of the Holy Spirit was joining them in Eucharistic praise of the Most Holy Trinity.

A Year with Fr. Rutler (2017)

The Holy Spirit as the Comforter

I am fond of the Latin line embroidered into one panel of the Bayeux Tapestry, depicting the Battle of Hastings. Under a depiction of Bishop Odo, brother of William the Conqueror, who is striking at reluctant troops with a war club, we read, "*Hic Odo episcopus baculum tenens confortat pueros,*" "Here Odo the bishop holding a club comforts the boys." It is not the sort of comfort the young soldiers may have appreciated, but it is precisely what "to comfort" really means: to strengthen, to fortify, to prod. Thus,

Scene from the Bayeux Tapestry depicting Odo, Bishop of Bayeux, rallying Duke William's troops during the Battle of Hastings in 1066 (image courtesy of Wikimedia Commons, public domain).

Jesus refers to the Holy Spirit as the Comforter. In Advent, we hear the opening lines of Handel's *Messiah* from Isaiah 40: "Comfort ye my people, saith the Lord."

A Year with Fr. Rutler (2017)

Holy Week

It is tempting to embrace Holy Week as the greatest of all allegories — "the greatest story ever told" — for the tragedy and triumph of Christ do indeed surpass all other stories. The flaw, indeed, the danger is that such rhetoric might give the impression that it is only a story, loose with facts and too emotive to have actually happened. The apostles did not think so. They were so shocked by it that the Risen Christ had to coax them out of their moral stupor and show them that He was not a ghost, just as He berated the two men on the Emmaus road for not having understood that these events had to happen.... The life of Christ is not an allegory; our lives are an allegory of the life of Christ. "You have not chosen me: I have chosen you" (John 15:16).

A Year with Fr. Rutler (2017)

Holy Week and the Core of Reality

To approach Holy Week is to approach the core of reality. The Incarnation of Christ, by which the divine Second Person of the Holy Trinity also became a real man, contradicts the mood of oriental religions that seek to escape the body. In a problematic world, the limited human intellect prefers excarnation to incarnation. Incarnation makes solemn and magnificent moral demands on the realist. The tragedy of the human condition is its failure to be really real. Holiness is the realization of what we are supposed to be. It does not happen by overcoming the body; it happens by overcoming the ego. This is the "oneness with God" intended by Christ in His agony in the garden: "And now I am no more in the world, but these are in the world, and I come to thee. Holy Father, keep through thine own name those whom thou hast given me, that they may be one, as we are one" (John 17:11).

A Year with Fr. Rutler (2017)

Hope and Change

When people want change without knowing what kind of change, they take a risk. As all good change protects and advances the supreme gift of life, the moral integrity of a government is measured by how it does this. The *Catechism* warns against a secular messianism that roots hope in things other than God: "Before Christ's second coming the Church must pass through a final trial that will shake the faith of many believers. The persecution that accompanies her pilgrimage on earth will unveil the 'mystery of iniquity' in the form of a religious deception offering men an apparent solution to their problems at the price of apostasy from the truth" (675). We shall know whether a change in government is good or evil when it protects innocent life or legalizes its destruction.

A Year with Fr. Rutler (2017)

Hot Cross Buns and Ashes and All

We live many Lents during our lives, and we should not make a big burden of them. We should come to know them well and even cherish them, hot cross buns and ashes and all. But when Lent is done, souls attain to the stature of Heaven by having measured their own smallness, and they become strong enough to bask in the blaze of glory by sensing their own fragility and turning it into the transparency of grace.

He Spoke to Us (2016)

How Not to Become a Saint

It has become something of a trend in pious corners for well-intentioned entrepreneurs to declare that they want to die poor so that they might become saints. Dying poor guarantees nothing but a modest funeral. Spoken carelessly, this avowal carries the subtle scent of the calculator; it is a little like the remark I once heard from a cleric who said he had become a priest to save his soul. No one becomes a saint by wanting to be one; it happens by loving God. No priest will save his own soul unless his first and selfless desire is to save other souls. Otherwise, the profession of faith becomes a demeaning little question whispered behind the gauzy curtain of unction: "What's in it for me?"

Hints of Heaven (2014)

How to Be a Good Catholic at the Polling Booth

While one may vote for a flawed candidate, one may not vote for anyone who advocates and enables immitigably evil acts, and that includes abortion.

A Year with Fr. Rutler (2017)

How to Revere the Beloved Dead

One way we revere the beloved dead is to apply indulgences for them, just as can be done for the living. "An indulgence is the remission before God of the temporal punishment due to sins whose guilt has already been forgiven, which the faithful Christian who is duly disposed gains under certain prescribed conditions through the action of the Church which, as the minister of redemption, dispenses and applies with authority the treasury of the satisfactions of Christ and the saints" (*Indulgentiarum Doctrina*, I). Indulgences respond to the reality that there are two consequences of sin:

> Grave sin deprives us of communion with God and therefore makes us incapable of eternal life, the privation of which is called the "eternal punishment" of sin. On the other hand, every sin, even venial, entails an unhealthy attachment to creatures, which must be purified either here on earth or after death in the state called Purgatory. This purification frees one from what is called the "temporal punishment" of sin. These two punishments must not be conceived of as a kind of vengeance inflicted by God from without, but as following from the very nature of sin. A conversion which proceeds from a fervent charity can attain the complete purification of the sinner in such a way that no punishment would remain. (CCC 1472)

Showing one's respect for the beloved dead also requires devotion to one's country, for which one should especially pray at election times. The nearly fifty million babies destroyed by abortion since *Roe v. Wade* do not need prayers for the dead because the Lord has already received them according to His merciful will. But our nation is accountable for allowing this deepest outrage against innocent life to continue and expand. Holy Church has widely published the fact that no one is morally justified in preferring any political candidate who promotes abortion over one who does not. Only the invincibly ignorant can hope to escape severe penalties, eternal as well as temporal, if they reject this counsel.

A Year with Fr. Rutler (2017)

Humanae Vitae

Many Christians do not understand the moral implications of artificial birth prevention as explained in Pope Paul VI's encyclical *Humanae Vitae*. In 1968, his prophetic warnings were widely ridiculed as nonsense: moral breakdown, increased infidelity and illegitimacy, and pornographic exploitation of women by men. Then he asked: "Who will prevent public authorities from favoring what they believe to be the most effective contraceptive methods and from mandating that everyone must use them, whenever they consider it necessary?" Who, indeed? Within a decade of *Humanae Vitae*, the Chinese government began a program of forcing sterilization and abortion on women having "unauthorized" children. The program enjoyed the financial support of the United Nations and of the administrations of U.S. presidents Bill Clinton and Barack Obama.

A Year with Fr. Rutler (2017)

As a maelstrom of dissent swirled around the publication of *Humanae Vitae*, the Catholic philosopher Elizabeth Anscombe and her husband toasted it with champagne. I rather thought her brilliant essays on abortion academic exercises until she was dragged into court for demonstrating outside an abortion mill. A picture of her standing before the judge, with Professor John Finnis as her barrister, should be painted as an icon for the coming generation.

Cloud of Witnesses (2009)

Since 1968, many have mocked the Catholic Church's warnings, in the encyclical *Humanae Vitae*, about the consequences of contraception and abortion. They now have to deal with the fact that in Germany the most popular name for newborn boys is not Carl or Hans or Dietrich, but Mohammed. With respect to the author of *Humanae Vitae*, it may not be too late for reasonable people in a self-indulgent society to admit that Pope Paul VI was—if they do not want to say infallible—accurate.

A Year with Fr. Rutler (2017)

Humility

Without Christ, the plastic and musical arts would not have attained their highest achievements, nor would there even be humor in its most benign and self-satirical forms—for that is based on humility, which is not a developed virtue outside the Judeo-Christian tradition. The noblest pagans had no concept of humility.

A Year with Fr. Rutler (2017)

Humpty Dumpty's Imperium

When the state tries to establish an imperium over nature itself, it vandalizes all sane instinct and abdicates its duty to promote the tranquility of order by tranquilizing it. The carnage both physical and moral issuing from the disastrous legalization of the destruction of unborn children proves that. Now its dismal postlude sounds in shrill attempts to "redefine" marriage. So far, eleven countries have done it, along with nine of our own states and our nation's capital. In Paris, close to a million public demonstrators have opposed the attempt of France's Socialist president to play Master of the Universe, or at least Master of its Universal Laws. George Orwell said, in a review of Bertrand Russell's book *Power: A New Social Analysis*, "We have now sunk to a depth at which the restatement of the obvious is the first duty of intelligent men." It should be obvious to all except the dense and the willfully ignorant that the next step will be to attack the Church through civil penalties and fiscal appropriations for refusing to accept the authority of the state to invert the natural order of which the state is only a steward. There was a veiled intimation of this in our national discourse as early as a letter to Madison from Jefferson, whose latitudinarian attitude toward religious bodies still had about it something of the cynicism of the French revolutionaries: "This principle, that the earth belongs to the living and not to the dead, is of very extensive application and consequences. It enters into the resolution of the questions, whether the nation may change the descent of lands holden in tail; whether they may change the appropriation of lands given anciently to the church, to hospitals, colleges, orders of chivalry, and otherwise in perpetuity."

Pope Benedict XVI gave all this priority in his address to the Roman Curia on December 21, 2012, widely ignored by the major American media, which seem jealous of their cohabitation with the present government. He established some sort of precedent by quoting a rabbinical voice not from first-century Galilee, but that of the Chief Rabbi of France, Gilles Bernheim, formerly rabbi of the synagogue de la Victoire in Paris and husband of a psychoanalyst.

> If there is no pre-ordained duality of man and woman in creation, then neither is the family any longer a reality established by creation. Likewise, the child has lost the place he had occupied hitherto and the dignity pertaining

to him. [Rabbi] Bernheim shows that now, perforce, from being a subject of right, the child has become an object to which people have a right and which they have a right to obtain. When the freedom to be creative becomes the freedom to create oneself, then necessarily the Maker himself is denied and ultimately man too is stripped of his dignity as a creature of God, as the image of God at the core of his being.

As the state did not invent marriage, neither did the Church. But Christ transformed marriage, as He did baptism, building upon its nature by investing it with supernatural graces to represent the indissoluble love of the Bridegroom for His Bride, the Church. Thus, the Council of Trent condemned polygamy as divinely forbidden since it is contrary to the nuptial meaning of the Church, but the council's theologians hesitated to denounce multiple marriages explicitly as contrary to natural law, for such marriages at least obliged normal conjugal union. The natural fecundity of the marriage bond is mocked by substituting for it a disorder intrinsically infecund. Our Lord's miracle at a wedding, the first of the seven Johannine miracles, brings to a potency in the spiritual order the seven acts of creation in the physical order. Trying to redefine marriage by human fiat is to pretend that man is creator and not procreator. This old and regressive conceit began with the first lie in Eden: "You will be like God." At the wedding in Cana, Christ's mother said, "Whatever my Son says to do, do it." We are free not to do what He says, but we are not free to undo what He did. We are free even to play Humpty Dumpty with nature, only asking which is to be master of words instead of acknowledging the Word as Master. But when the social order has a great fall in consequence, all the politicians will not be able to put it back together again.

He Spoke to Us (2016)

Hymns and C. S. Lewis

Hymns, as individual compositions distinct from the Church's official collective prayer, have always been susceptible to aesthetic lapses, like any other form of art. More than a generation ago, C. S. Lewis complained that most hymns are "fifth-rate poetry set to fourth-rate music." The situation is worse now for two reasons: the degraded state of our culture and the banality of our liturgical life.

The Stories of Hymns (2016)

Hymns and the Mass

Hymns, when they are worthy and worthily understood, should enhance the classical Liturgy which, by God's grace, will soon rise from its aesthetic stupor. A right understanding of the hymn form means a right understanding of prayer, the psychology of collective song, and the integrity of the Eucharistic action. Properly sung, the Mass has its own liturgical hymns. Sacred hymns were primitively held to be sacrosanct indeed: until the seventh century in the Roman Rite, only the priest sang the Our Father, and it stayed that way in the Mozarabic Rite; the Gloria was generally reserved for bishops until the eleventh century. The Creed was understood as a hymn from the fifth century; Pope

Symmachus introduced the Gloria deliberately as a hymn in the early sixth century; and Pope Sergius made the Agnus Dei a hymn intrinsic to the Liturgy in the late seventh century. And all because a hymn was sung in the Upper Room.

The Stories of Hymns (2016)

An Ignatian Antidote to Futility

Instead of surrendering to indignation and dying with a sense of futility, it is far better to follow the example of the saints. In particular, we could take as our model that saint whose very name means "fire": Ignatius Loyola. He prayed in his *Spiritual Exercises*, and the Church has taken up his prayer ever since:

> Take, O Lord, and receive my entire liberty, my memory, my understanding, and my will. All that I am and have, You have given to me. And I give all back to You to be disposed of according to Your good pleasure. Give me only the comfort of Your presence and the joy of Your love, and with these, I shall be more than rich and shall desire nothing more.

Grace and Truth (2019)

Ignorance

Only the ignorant think that ignorance is bliss.

A Year with Fr. Rutler (2017)

The Imperial Church

As a seed is nourished by the soil, so the Church thrives in indigenous cultures, transfiguring what is worthy, shucking off what is not, giving new vitality to old customs. The Druid's fire becomes the Yule log, Saturnalia shines brighter as Christmas, and the classical diocese and presbyter, vestal and pontiff are grafted onto an imperium that will never end. Here is a consolation, too: in the mustard bush all manner of birds will gather. Canaries are there, but there will be crows cackling along with them; vultures may share a perch with doves; common sparrows may feel a little intimidated next to peacocks; and for every wise owl you may expect a few cuckoos.

Hints of Heaven (2014)

Incense

A church-supply catalogue recently delivered to our rectory advertises a special blend of incense "like that used by St. Paul when he was in Rome." We can credit that to an overactive imagination, or good salesmanship, or both, but it worked: I could not resist ordering some.

A Year with Fr. Rutler (2017)

Information

No king in his silken bed at Versailles knew the luxury of instant information that we have.

A Year with Fr. Rutler (2017)

The Inheritance of Salvation

An ephemeral perception of things makes it hard to understand public significance apart from celebrity-based "popularity" and "approval ratings." I mention this because of the continuing celebrations of the Diamond Jubilee of Queen Elizabeth II. It is the nature of her office, and confounding to anyone who does not understand the institution, that she did nothing to earn her position other than being born. But that notion is reassuring to all of us who are made heirs of salvation by the gratuitous mercy of Christ the King.

A Year with Fr. Rutler (2017)

Innocence

Innocence is the love of Heaven, and thus the gateway to the glory of Heaven.

Grace and Truth (2019)

Insanity

People who say, "Don't be judgmental" are usually guilty of something. The inability to make a right judgment is a symptom of madness. Nietzsche expressed the cynicism of his age when he said that man as Superman would replace God, who had died. Yet in the confusion of his own illusory judgment, Nietzsche spent the last eleven years of his life in an insane asylum.

A Year with Fr. Rutler (2017)

Intellect and Sin

Each enslavement to sin calls itself a new form of liberation as it tightens its chains. Rare is the tyrant who does not cloak his extravagant selfishness in the titles of altruism and affected goodwill. Pope Pius XII addressed this in *Humani Generis*: "Now the human intellect, in gaining the knowledge of such truths, is hampered both by the activity of the senses and the imagination, and by evil passions arising from original sin. Hence men easily persuade themselves in such matters that what they do not want to believe is false or at least doubtful."

The Curé d'Ars Today (1988)

An Interior Light

Read St. Paul's hymn of love (1 Cor. 13:4–7), and you'll find described what he had not been before the Resurrection and what he became after his conversion. As a persecutor of the first Christians, he certainly had not been patient, kind, humble, gracious, selfless, calm, virtuous, or honest. Pope Benedict XVI preached:

On that Easter morning something extraordinary happened, something new, and at the same time very concrete, distinguished by very precise signs and recorded by numerous witnesses. For Paul, as for the other authors of the New Testament, the Resurrection is closely bound to the *testimony* of those who had direct experience of the Risen One. This means seeing and hearing, not only with the eyes or with the senses, but also with an interior light that assists the recognition of what the external senses attest as objective fact.

A Year with Fr. Rutler (2017)

Intrigue

The word "intrigue" can refer to two different phenomena. The first is simple fascination. Certainly no one who ever lived was more intriguing than Jesus of Nazareth. He intrigued those who saw and heard Him in His own day, and He continues to intrigue.... But there is a second kind of intrigue. And that, says the book of Proverbs, is an abomination to God (6:18). This fascination is not harmless or morally neutral, and it certainly is not the first level of an approach to God. It is really rejection of God and His goodness. This kind of intrigue, condemned by the rabbis and then by the prophets and the Fathers of the Church, is the devising of wicked imaginings, the distortion of the imaginative faculty to plot against God. The whole Passion narrative of Christ is a drama of that kind of intrigue. When He was preaching, people began to plot how they could capture Him. When He proclaimed His Messiahship in His native synagogue in Nazareth, the crowd tried to grab Him and throw Him off the brow of a hill. It was not yet His time, and He escaped from their midst. The human intellect is a gift from God, and it must be used as He intended—to glorify Him. The imaginative component of the intellect can remember the past and can anticipate the future. And so the imagination can civilize us by collecting and organizing the inheritance left by those who have gone before—their stories and wisdom and experience. And it can encourage us through contemplation of what we can build, what we can design, what we can hope for. But that same imagination can turn in on itself. We can be haunted by the past. We can be threatened by the future. And we can use its power for destructive purposes.

Grace and Truth (2019)

"It's All Good"

A young businessman told me that on a recent trip to California he was struck by how insipid the art of conversation had become among those he met there, and that the stock reply to almost every observation or critical comment on any subject was: "It's all good." Although New Yorkers might breezily pass this off as typical of the insipidity in what they call "La-La Land," this insouciance has infected all parts of our society. To say of everything, "It's all good" is to imply that nothing is bad, and that, in turn, means that nothing is either really good or really bad. Judgment is the act of distinguishing bad from good — and consequently, wrong from right. The inability to make a right moral judgment is a form of insanity.

A Year with Fr. Rutler (2017)

Stanley Jaki

Father Jaki (1924–2009) was the bane of editors, writing brilliantly in English but with thoughts within thoughts and rambling asides that he refused, with the ferocity of a Hungarian hussar, to have retooled. In one book on which we collaborated, he asked permission to add a "small footnote" to one of my paragraphs.

Upon publication of the book, I found myself calling Kant a rank amateur in science and recommending Father Jaki's translation of Kant's "shockingly incompetent" cosmogony. It was by far my most erudite footnote, though I had not written it.

Cloud of Witnesses (2009)

Jansenism

No doubt, in Vianney's time, the spirit of Jansenism was still much a part of French Catholic piety. This form of rigorism, a truncated view of human nature and creation, or what is known as deontological spirituality, is endemic in many modern spiritual movements; like the modern movements, its imprudence was born of a worthy reaction against aridity, formalism, and the vices of the times. Although named for the seventeenthcentury bishop of Ypres, it was associated primarily with the convent of Port-Royal, whose nuns were "pure as angels and proud as devils," and had a pronounced influence even on rural France, an influence lasting long beyond its condemnation by the bull *Unigenitus* in 1713. Heresies tend to exaggerate a basic truth that has lain fallow in regular practice. For instance, distortions of the doctrine of the Blessed Trinity give rise to three fundamental errors: distorted attention to the Fatherhood of God leads to deism, as the Sonship of God as an autonomous doctrine tends to immanentism, and an exclusive cult of the Holy Spirit foments spiritualism. In reparation for years of cynicism, probabilism, and moral laxity, Jansenism tried to recast and restore St. Augustine's doctrine of grace. Bishop Jansen had read Augustine's anti-Pelagian books at least thirty times; but in a way, he overread them, knowing all the pieces but not seeing the finished puzzle. His *Augustinus*, published two years after his death, has been called a delayed-action time bomb; if it shed light on the great Augustinian architecture, it did so as an atom bomb does. The battlements of the City of God were smashed beyond recognition.

During discourses in public audiences, John Paul II has reminded the Church of the similarity between Jansenism and Lutheranism in their misperceptions of original sin. They understood the Fall of Man to be the burial of an important part of man; consequently, they called into question the integrity of the free will. The Council of Trent told the truth of these things in the sixteenth century, as the Council of Orange had done in the sixth: as man is corrupt, but not irredeemably so, his will and reason can still lead him toward the font of redemption. In the *Credo of the People of God*, Paul VI repeated this: to be "fallen" is to be deprived of sanctifying grace, but we speak of a relative, and not absolute, deterioration. The human race is fallen, but the human race is also redeemed. The persistence of Catholic teaching on this central truth is an ornate example of the Church's unremitting stand for penance and reason against pessimism and secularism. Emotional rigorism is most agreeable to the impatient rationalist who likes to have details spelled in artificial detail, and to the impulsive pietist who suspects that anything of importance is a kind of uncontrollable spell. Jansenism has been, more than anything else, a superstition of science and a science of superstition.

In the modern experience, individuals who think they are liberated from Jansenism may be the most subtle victims of it. For Jansenism is not so much a wrong body of doctrine as it is a wrong doctrine of the body, and as long as we have bodies we will be tempted to deny the bodiliness of them. There is an example of it in the young modern agnostic who mocks any discipline of the soul while making a positively military onslaught against his flesh: I mean the young upwardly mobile professional who has not learned which end is up, who would laugh at the rigors of Port-Royal as he stands on his head in a health club. It is just as odd to think the body can be healthy by becoming superior to other bodies, as it is unhealthy to think souls can become holy by becoming superior to other souls. The notion is an obsequious form of hysteria that cannot tell the difference between a collapse and a lapse. The human race, body and soul, has been thrown into confusion by the Fall, but it has not been crushed.

The Curé d'Ars Today (1988)

Jargon

Theological terms such as "ontology" and "eschatology" are useful shorthand expressions for "the meaning of existence" and "the end of time," but they are mere jargon if they are not explained. St. John does not say that Jesus is the ontological essence: he says, "In Him was life" (John 1:4). St. Paul does not speak of realized eschatology: He says, "This present world is passing away" (1 Cor. 7:31).

A Year with Fr. Rutler (2017)

Jerusalem the Golden

Fondly do I hope that we may sometime, not too far off, be able to purchase hymnals that have a wider range of congregational singing, including more of the great hymns of the Church. Any such collection has to include St. Bernard's magnificent verses on Heaven. My most beloved relatives and friends have been buried to strains of Bernard's lines:

> Jerusalem the Golden, with milk and honey blest,
> Beneath thy contemplation, sink heart and mind
>   oppressed.
> I know not, oh, I know not what joys await us there.
> What radiancy of glory, what bliss beyond compare.

On the third Sunday of Advent, the Church preaches about Heaven. The liturgical antiphon of the day, "*Laetare, Ierusalem*" (Rejoice, Jerusalem), refers to the Heavenly Kingdom, of which earthly Jerusalem is the type. Every Christian doctrine is a way of speaking about Heaven.

A Year with Fr. Rutler (2017)

Jeunesse Dorée

It is a chilling thought that the spoiled youth on campuses today, rather like what Shakespeare's Brabantio called "the wealthy curled darlings of our nation," may be our nation's leaders not long from now.

A Year with Fr. Rutler (2017)

The Jeweled City

The virtue of faith enables us not to lose balance when perceiving the immensity of things. God does not measure by size or strength. The whimper of a baby is to Him as mighty as that pulsar's energy with its magnetic field 15 trillion times stronger than the earth's. A lost sheep is as important as an X-ray nebula spanning 150 light years. St. Peter fell to the ground after he saw light emanate from the transfigured Christ and then heard a voice coming from "bright cloud" overhead, saying: "This is my beloved Son, with whom I am well pleased; listen to him" (Matt. 17:5). Heaven is eternal, while the created universe in all its beauty is not. Only by worshipping God can we gradually adjust to St. John's strange images of the jeweled city and the sea of glass.

A Year with Fr. Rutler (2017)

Dr. Johnson and the Eulogizing of Celebrities

According to our friend Dr. Johnson, who was more intuitively Catholic than many putative Catholics: "No man is a hypocrite in his pleasures." If churchmen insist on eulogizing, they might get right to the point by describing what sort of pleasures occupied the dead in their lifetimes. The thought could restrain them from jumping into celebrity graves. It certainly would temper any propensity for Shakespeare's "Sweet words, low-crooked curtsies, and base spaniel fawning."

He Spoke to Us (2016)

Joy

Joy is more than happiness, if you take happiness to mean feeling good. Joy is a fact beyond feeling, and the fact is the actual possession of what is good. As only God is good, true joy is being with God. Because "God was in Christ, reconciling the world to himself," only Christ can make our joy "full" (see 2 Cor. 5:19; John 15:11). Gaudete, or "Rejoice," Sunday is, like Laetare Sunday in Lent, a glimpse of joy along the way to joy.

A Year with Fr. Rutler (2017)

Judgment and Taste

Tastes can vary, it is true, but it is only the barbarian who says that all taste is subjective. There is a hierarchy of standards for the good, the true, and the beautiful. If we do not conform ourselves to God as the source of these things, then we lose that triad. The good becomes mere sentimentality. The truth becomes mere pedantry. The beautiful becomes mere aestheticism.

Grace and Truth (2019)

Judgment Day and the Catholic Politician

If a politician promotes or defends a political party's platform that violates essential moral norms while boasting that he is a Catholic, and that he once was an altar boy, or some such fatuity, he brings a grave judgment on himself.[20]

A Year with Fr. Rutler (2017)

---

[20] Regarding the passing of the Reproductive Health Act, *National Review* reported: "The Act codifies *Roe v. Wade* in New York law and removes abortion from the state criminal code, legalizing the procedure up to the moment of birth in cases where the mother's life or health are endangered or where the baby is non-viable. It also allows individuals other than doctors to perform abortions. Previously, doctors in New York were only allowed to perform

The Judgment of God

During the 1976 Eucharistic Congress in Philadelphia, a relatively unknown figure, the Archbishop of Krakow, said: "We are now standing in the face of the greatest historical confrontation humanity has gone through. I do not think that wide circles of the American society or wide circles of the Christian community realize this fully. We are now facing the final confrontation between the Church and the anti-Church, of the Gospel versus the anti-Gospel. This confrontation lies within the plans of divine Providence; it is trial which the whole Church, must take up. It is a trial of not only our nation and the Church, but, in a sense, a test of 2,000 years of culture and Christian civilization with all of its consequences for human dignity, individual rights, human rights and the rights of nations."[21] The speaker was the future

---

an abortion after 24 weeks of pregnancy if the mother's life was in danger. 'Today we are taking a giant step forward in the hard-fought battle to ensure a woman's right to make her own decisions about her own personal health, including the ability to access an abortion,' Andrew Cuomo said. The governor, a Catholic who recalled his days as an altar boy in his State of the State address earlier this month, publicly celebrated the bill's signing by ordering One World Trade Center and other landmarks to be lit up in pink." Mairead Mcardle, "Catholic Leaders Call for Cuomo to Be Excommunicated over Abortion Bill," *National Review*, 28 January 2019.

[21] Regarding this reference to the "final confrontation," Paul Kengor, professor of political science at Grove City College, notes that it did not refer merely to the confrontation between the Western democracies and Soviet communism, which, of course, ended with the end of the Cold War. "Since then," Kengor writes, "the problems faced by and within the Church—and arguably posed by an anti-Church—seem to have only gotten worse. They stem from controversies over sex abuse, over

Pope John Paul II. His words in Philadelphia certainly were as prophetic as the voices in Judea thousands of years ago. In the subsequent generation, crammed with breathtaking events of universal and historic significance, heroic and tragic, we can count the manifold ways in which John Paul II seemed to see the judgment of God at work.

A Year with Fr. Rutler (2017)

In the moral order, people have to make judgments for the sake of sanity, but those judgments must be based on standards outside one's sentiments — rather the way we measure objects according to the standards set by the Bureau of Weights and Measures. Jesus submitted to the judgment of Pontius Pilate, and by so doing, He

---

corrupted priests and bishops and cardinals, over Church doctrine, over the current Holy Father himself, and, worldwide (especially in the West), over matters once seemingly settled since the dawn of humanity but now openly contested: sexuality, gender, family, marriage and the very nature of humanity. One of those who stood firmly against this dictatorship of relativism (as Pope Benedict XVI called it) was Cardinal Carlo Caffarra, who helped found the Pontifical John Paul II Institute for Studies on Marriage and Family in 1981. Cardinal Caffarra reminded us of the words of Fatima seer Sister Lucia and of what he called an "anti-creation." He shared a letter written by Sister Lucia, where she warned that "there will come a time when the decisive confrontation between the Kingdom of God and Satan will take place over marriage and the family." We are in quite a confrontation right now. The sheer fullness and explosive breadth of that confrontation today would seem more in keeping with the sweeping, apocalyptic warnings of Cardinal Karol Wojtyla back in 1976." "John Paul II's Warning on 'Final Confrontation' with the 'Anti-Church,'" *National Catholic Register*, 5 October 2018. Father George Rutler has also been a stalwart critic of "the dictatorship of relativism," as this anthology shows.

took on the suffering of those who are wrongly judged. Jesus did not deny Pilate's right to pass judgment, yet He reminded Pilate that he was answerable to a higher authority: "You would have no power over me were it not given to you from above" (John 19:11). The Christian command not to judge others is about defining justice without accountability to God. "He who rejects me and does not receive my sayings has a judge; the word that I have spoken will be his judge on the last day" (John 12:48).

A Year with Fr. Rutler (2017)

The Justice of God and Man

Without respect for God as the author of justice, justice itself suffers. G. K. Chesterton said, "When you break the big laws, you do not get freedom; you do not even get anarchy. You get the small laws." There are those in our society who have come to think that all laws are little and that the courts can change the big laws by human will. So we have activist courts even attempting to abolish the basic natural laws of life as ordained by God. Christ reminded Pontius Pilate that governors are responsible to Heaven. A characteristic of tyrants is that they subvert the law. During the terrible years of National Socialism, Cardinal Faulhaber of Munich risked his own life when he preached: "The State, as an institution built by God, can establish its laws, and its subjects are under the obligation to obey them, for the sake of their conscience. The State has the right to levy taxes and to demand sacrifices of property and life in the defense of the Fatherland. The State, however, has no right to make laws which are incompatible with Divine Law and the Natural Law." St. Augustine said, "Love God and do whatever you please." But that does not mean lawlessness.

God "never commanded anyone to be godless. He has given no one permission to sin" (Sir. 15:20). Many who quote Augustine omit the rest of his sentence: "for the soul trained in love to God will do nothing to offend the One who is Beloved."

A Year with Fr. Rutler (2017)

Just-War Criteria for the Battle of Life

St. Augustine said that there are seven standards by which we can justify going into battle, known as *jus ad bellum*:

- *Just cause*: War must be in response to a direct and unjust attack upon the just order of life and freedom.
- *Proper authority*: War must be declared and prosecuted by a legitimate government, entrusted by the people to decide whether or not the cause is just.
- *Right intention*: The intention in going to war cannot be revenge, but must involve correcting a wrong, preventing a miscarriage of justice, protecting life, and so on.
- *Proportionality*: The just war must be fought in such a way that no more evil results than the good that results. That's a very hard thing to guarantee, but at least there must be an intention to promote the good and not to compound evil.
- *Reasonable chance of success*: A just war cannot be a suicidal adventure, a manifestation of mere bravado. Remember the story of the charge of the Light Brigade, when British troops in the Crimean War went on a suicidal charge against an overwhelming enemy. A French officer who watched the scene said, "It is magnificent, but it is not war."

- *Last resort*: All other attempts at peace must have been explored; all discussion must be exhausted.
- *Peace*: The just war must end in peace. That, again, is hard to guarantee, but the intention of establishing peace must prevail over the desire simply to create a situation in which another war is inevitable.

Our civilization is engaged in a deep, spiritual war for the dignity of life itself that manifests itself outwardly in political and legal confrontation. We can take those standards of warfare that St. Augustine gave us and apply them to the crusade to protect life in the womb. This is the most just of wars. What could be a more just cause than the protection of the most innocent life at its very beginning? And who has a better authority to protect life than the mother, the father, and the government, which is ordained to protect the right to life and liberty and the pursuit of happiness? In all these ways, God is testing the courage of our society, because we have not only the privilege but the duty to defend life.

Grace and Truth (2019)

President Kennedy and Justice Brennan

Descent to the phosphorescent obsequiousness of Mr. Justice Brennan's funeral was greased by the efficient compact John F. Kennedy made in his run for the presidency, telling the Protestant clergymen in Houston that he would never be under the thumb of a pope.[22] He should have stuck to the advice of Pius

---

[22] "In a traditional Catholic ceremony at Washington's majestic St. Matthew's Cathedral, the late Justice William J. Brennan Jr. was

VII on the lengths of accommodation: "We are prepared to go to the gates of Hell, but no further." After Kennedy nudged public Catholicism from the snows of Canossa to the sands of Palm Beach, eulogists claimed that his gnostic kind of religiosity was Catholicism come of age, but it was Catholicism ashamed of its age: God's good servant, but the King's first.

He Spoke to Us (2016)

The Killing of Unwanted People

On the day of the Medal of Honor ceremony in the White House, the abortionist Kermit Gosnell was on trial in Philadelphia, charged on eight counts of murder, including one adult and seven newborn infants who had survived their abortions. One of his "medical" assistants had already testified to having "snipped the spines" of more than a hundred babies. The silence of most media outlets concerning this astonishing criminal case was eloquently portrayed by a photograph of the press box at the courthouse — which was nearly vacant. Clearly, many people were made uncomfortable by the way that this case represents the logical denouement of the perverse logic of the Supreme Court's *Roe v. Wade* decision, the foundation of our Culture of Death. What happened in Gosnell's house of horrors has, in fact, been defended theoretically by some "ethicists" who hold

---

remembered in eulogies yesterday that captured his vast liberal legacy, trademark compassion and enduring good humor." Joan Biskupic and Saundra Torry, "Rites Celebrate Justice Brennan's Enduring Legacy," *Washington Post*, July 30, 1997. Central to that "vast liberal legacy" was his pro-abortion record, which did not say much for his "trademark compassion."

positions in our universities. And many of our nation's highest officials have defended "partial-birth abortion." The misuse of reason can rationalize contempt for life, just as happened in the Weimar Republic when the jurist Karl Binding and the psychiatrist Alfred Hoche published their defense of killing unwanted people: *Die Freigabe der Vernichtung lebensunwerten Lebens* (*Permission to Destroy Life Unworthy of Living*). Binding died in 1920, when the book was published, but Hoche lived until 1943 after privately objecting to the "euthanizing" of one of his own relatives by Nazis who had read his book and followed its principles.

A Year with Fr. Rutler (2017)

A Kind of Historical Duty

I would hope, not in a spirit of recrimination but as a kind of historical duty, that future generations will label the various ruins of our age with the names of the movements and movers who wrecked them: that each denuded church sanctuary resembling a cocktail lounge would bear the name of the renovator who whitewashed the florid faces of the saints, that each ugly commercial building would advertise the architect who relocated human life to fester in it, that the epitaph of each victim of vice might name the sirens who sang a sexual revolution, that each asylum be named for each psychoanalyst who said there is no sin. I propose it only as a guide away from the intolerable cruelty of unreality. Chesterton proposed something like it himself in an encounter with the lady who announced that the craving to do a thing shows you ought to do it. As the train in which they were traveling rolled on and the insanity flitted away, he saw the moral carnage of such flippancy on the passing fields of England and the world:

> Madam, you will not, I am sure be anything but delighted to learn that you have convinced me. A man should always do a thing as long as he has a genuine craving to do it. How true that is! How illuminating! And yet how simple! My present genuine craving, which is to strike you suddenly and sharply on the bridge of the nose, is one which as it is far less destructive than meat-eating, will certainly command your theoretical acquiescence, and which also has this advantage, that it will give some sort of glimmering notion of what sort of world you are living in. As you say, I may survive the craving. After beating you on the nose for a day or two the desire itself may leave me. Then, no doubt, I shall pass to a higher plane.[23]

It remains to be seen whether natural virtue and its respect for natural law can withstand the general onslaught against them.

A Crisis of Saints (1995)

The Kingdom of Heaven

"The kingdom of heaven is like treasure hidden in a field, which a man found and covered up; then in his joy he goes and sells all that he has and buys that field" (Matt. 13:44). Salvation requires a

---

[23] *Illustrated London News*, April 28, 1906 in *G. K. Chesterton: Collected Works*, vol. 27, *Illustrated London News, 1905–1907*, ed. Lawrence J. Clipper (San Francisco: Ignatius Press, 1980), 177–178.

response of the will, and in this parable, the response is deliberate recognition of the worth of grace. The man who chanced upon a hidden treasure acknowledged that it was a treasure. Not always does the believer appreciate the richness of the gospel. What is granted can easily be taken for granted, without the faintest amen. Otherwise our hymns in church would be louder, and the breast-beating at the Agnus Dei would bruise.

Hints of Heaven (2014)

True Kings

The ass was the royal beast and a signal that Messiahship was being claimed. True kings see no contradiction between the beast of burden and royalty and no incongruity between humility and majesty.

The Stories of Hymns (2016)

Krasinski Square

Orlando is not Warsaw, and Orlando's Disney World is not Krasinski Square, which was a buffer between the Warsaw Ghetto and the rest of the city during the Nazi occupation. Sleeping Beauty's castle is safe in Orlando, but the Nazis demolished the Badeni Palace facing Krasinski Square. If Catholics in the United States would learn about zeal for the Faith, they might consider a trip to Krasinski Square, where in place of Mickey Mouse is a monument to the Warsaw Uprising. It is a silent instruction about "the dignity of the human person."

Calm in Chaos (2018)

Labels

This was a time, in the nineteenth century, when liberals and ultramontanists in the Church were closing their ranks, but the abstruse concerns of both signified little to Vianney.... In retrospect, it might be tempting to pin a party label on him, but such would have been implausible: his one party was Catholicism.

The Curé d'Ars Today (1988)

Lambs among Lambs

At a vigil service before the burial of a friend who was a Knight of Malta, a comfortable attorney who was a self-styled progressivist took umbrage at a phrase I had read from the daily prayer of that order: "Be it mine to practice and defend the Catholic, the Apostolic, the Roman faith against the enemies of religion." He told me that there are no enemies of religion anymore. Yet when Our Lord sent His disciples out, He disabused them of such dangerous naïveté. They would be lambs among wolves, not lambs among lambs.

A Year with Fr. Rutler (2017)

The "Land O' Lakes" Statement and John Henry Newman

The "Land O' Lakes Statement"[24] was hardly innovative, save in its destructive influence on Catholic education, being

---

[24] "In a recent address, Bishop James Conley of Lincoln recalled the 50th anniversary of the Land O' Lakes Statement describing

a reactionary return to the early-nineteenthcentury materialist pedagogy in Prussia that developed after the shock of its defeat in the Battle of Jena-Auerstedt (October 4, 1806), and to the utilitarian syllabus of Jeremy Bentham in England. In many ways, John Henry Newman faced crises parallel with those of 1967 when he delivered his "Lectures on the Idea of a University" in 1854. He was founding the Catholic University of Ireland in Dublin when most of the Catholic bishops themselves were conflicted about what constitutes university education. Newman's vision extended beyond their parochial borders, and his genius was a perplexity to prelatical mediocrity. Newman saw even more clearly than those at Land O' Lakes that there is a distinction between natural knowledge and revealed knowledge and that indoctrination is malignant only when it does not see the difference. Orthodoxies should be thought out, lest they become independent of reason. The ambiguous Catholicism of Land O' Lakes invoked a phantasm guised as freedom for truth which was nothing more than liberty to reject truth.

Calm in Chaos (2018)

---

it as the '*non serviam* moment of many of America's Catholic universities'—a reference to Lucifer's words ("I shall not serve") in the Old Testament. The statement 'rejected the authority of the Church, and of her doctrinal teaching,' said Bishop Conley. 'It rejected the idea that faith and reason work best in communion with one another. It prioritized the standards and culture of secular universities over the authentic mission of Catholic education. It was a statement of self-importance, and self-assertion.'" "Bishop: Land O'Lakes Statement Was *Non Serviam* Moment for Many Catholic Universities," Catholic Culture, July 25, 2017, https://www.catholicculture.org/news/headlines/index.cfm?storyid=32191.

The "Land O' Lakes Statement" Distilled

The Land O' Lakes Conference was to higher Catholic education what the Yalta Conference was to Eastern Europe.

Calm in Chaos (2018)

A Lantern on the Stern

A solid sense of the Christ in history cannot be learned or taught by anyone who speaks of things preconciliar and postconciliar the way we speak of things B.C. and A.D. Coleridge wrote: "If men could learn from history, what lessons it might teach us! But passion and party blind our eyes, and the light that experience gives us is a lantern on the stern, which shines only on the waves behind us!"[25]

The Seven Wonders of the World (1993)

Latin Doctors of the Church All Songbirds

St. Ambrose joins St. Jerome, St. Augustine, and St. Gregory the Great in the quartet of Latin Doctors of the Church. Poetry and song were essential to the intellectual economy of these men, even for the blunt Jerome. Thought that does not begin and end in acts of praise is sterile speculation. Thus Ronald Knox explained why the Modernists do not compose hymns: "Birds of prey have no song." St. Ambrose, by his life of daylong praise, was granted his petition: *Te nostra supplex gloria/ Per cuncta laudet saecula.* Or, in the masterful translation of John Mason Neale,

---

[25] Samuel Taylor Coleridge, *Table Talk* (1835), December 18, 1833.

who in his lifetime of forty-eight years became the greatest hymn translator of the nineteenth century: "To thee our morning song of praise/ To thee our evening prayer we raise."

The Stories of Hymns (2016)

Laughing with Caesar

We are not a Christian nation now. In 1783, Washington spoke of "our blessed Religion," and on D-Day Roosevelt prayed for "our nation, our religion, and our civilization." This would not be allowed in our secularized culture. Shepherds of the faithful cannot charm into reason the forces that now preside over our nation. We can dance to Caesar's intolerable music, but he will call the tune. We can feast with Caesar, but he will soon feast on us. We can laugh with Caesar, but he will soon laugh at us. *Risus abundat in ore stultorum.* There is abundant laughter in the mouth of the foolish.

He Spoke to Us (2016)

Laughter and Humility

G. K. Chesterton said, "Almost without exception the greatest philanthropists in the world lack two things: laughter and humility." He was very suspicious of millionaires. The philanthropist, with all his good works, is not pleasing to God (or really to man) unless he can also spread God's grace and God's truth. Andrew Carnegie, the most famous magnate in the world in Chesterton's time, drove the writer almost to distraction. He said, "Andrew Carnegie is a good man, but he could be so much more if only someone were to roll him in a barrel down the street."[26] Laughter and humility are the two things lacking in secular humanism. Laughter is a gift and manifestation of grace. Humility is a gift and manifestation of truth.

Grace and Truth (2019)

Lee, Orwell, and the Scourge of Vandalism

After the Civil War, Robert E. Lee, son of one of Washington's generals, urged that no monuments be erected to figures however noble, so as to smooth the way to peace. It was only on the fiftieth anniversary of that war that monuments appeared on a big scale. When a freed black slave stunned the congregation in Saint Paul's Episcopal Church in Richmond by kneeling at the Communion rail, General Lee caused more of a stir when he knelt beside him. Descriptions vary, but there seems solid substance to the story, and its image in words is better than any in bronze. Lee did not even want a statue of himself at his Washington College, where he spent his last years promoting the liberal arts and classical virtues. In one letter, he wrote: "All I think that can now be done, is to aid our noble & generous women in their efforts to protect the graves & mark the last resting places of those who have fallen, & wait for better times." These days the latest hysteria is the toppling of statues by immoderate and ignorant people. Someone as bereft of a knowledge of history as some media pundits and politicians has even vandalized a statue of St. Joan of Arc in the city of Saint Louis, apparently under the impression that she was either a transgendered Confederate

---

[26] *Illustrated London News*, December 29, 1906.

general or a symbol of that ultimate scourge of the vandals of culture: the Catholic Church.... George Orwell, in his novel *Nineteen Eighty-Four*, described the sterile world of the New Man shorn of the dignity conferred by God and natural law: "Every record has been destroyed or falsified, every book rewritten, every picture has been repainted, every statue and street building has been renamed, every date has been altered. And the process is continuing day by day and minute by minute. History has stopped. Nothing exists except an endless present in which the Party is always right."

Calm in Chaos (2018)

Lent

Lent is not for the fey.

He Spoke to Us (2016)

Lent and the Public Executioner

For a long while, when there was a compact and coherent Christendom, Lent as the "truce of God" was a palpable social fact: charity was flaunted, wars were suspended, and executions were postponed. This last was not because anyone thought capital punishment intrinsically evil. It was because the law courts closed for Lent. To meet the Lenten deadline (yes, I said deadline), executions in the Papal States were speeded up to get them over with by Ash Wednesday. The salutary moral effects of the papal executions often brought about a celebratory spirit inconsistent with Lenten sobriety. With a flair alien to the morbidly edifying public posture of contemporary social engineers, the papal executioner sometimes wore a carnival costume. Blessed Pius IX's octogenarian executioner killed five hundred criminals during several papal reigns, including Pius's, but Lent was time off for him.

He Spoke to Us (2016)

The Campaign of Lent

Lent is a campaign against the aboriginal evil one, who seeks the ruin of souls. Even soldiers in a victorious army can be killed. Christ has defeated the foe, and He protects us with "the shield of faith with which you can extinguish all the flaming arrows of the evil one" (Eph. 6:16).

A Year with Fr. Rutler (2017)

The Gift of Lent

It would be rash to run a marathon without training. And it would not be wise to plunge into Lent without getting ready for it. The old liturgical calendar had three weeks to get ready for Lent: Septuagesima, Sexagesima, and Quinquagesima, meaning "seventieth," "sixtieth," and "fiftieth." These were not exact configurations: Quinquagesima Sunday marks the fiftieth day before Easter, if you include both of those Sundays, and Septuagesima and Sexagesima Sundays are really sixty-four and fifty-seven days before Easter. But the point is that these are signals to get ready for the gift of the Lenten season, which itself is a serene anticipation of Easter joy and therefore has a joy of its own. St.

Benedict said back in the sixth century, "In these days, therefore, let us add something beyond the wonted measure of our service, such as private prayers and abstinence in food and drink. Let each one, over and above the measure prescribed for him, offer God something of his own free will in the joy of the Holy Spirit."

A Year with Fr. Rutler (2017)

Lent and St. John Chrysostom

Lent is an occasion of sin, for it is a time when the flesh is made weak. It is the only occasion of sin that one can seek out legitimately. St. John Chrysostom preached: "God does not impede temptations, first, so that you may be convinced of your strength; secondly, that you may be humble, not proud; thirdly, that the devil, who may doubt whether you have really abandoned him, will be certain of that fact; fourthly, so that you may become as strong as iron, understanding the value of the treasures which have been granted to you."

He Spoke to Us (2016)

The Small Disciplines of Lent

The small disciplines and penances of Lent help to move us from moral slumber to a deeper consciousness of God. Earthly dreams are fantasies, but what God shows us when He detaches us from earthly distractions awakens the soul.

A Year with Fr. Rutler (2017)

A Lesson in Splendor

It is a little parable, this one about the mustard seed—deliberately so, I think. Its size teaches a sullen world a lesson in splendor. The Church learns as much from little verses as from long discourses; some of Christ's most pointed revelations are to be encountered in His asides. There is a lot of ecclesiology—not to mention botany and biology—to be garnered from the elliptical bits of God's Word that seem like breathing spaces between the grand panegyrics and pericopes. But the breath breathed is the breath that made the world.

Hints of Heaven (2014)

Lessons Learned from Studying World War II for *Powers and Principalities*

World War II, the world's most worldwide war, begun for mixed reasons and fought on many fronts, can only be understood in its essential dynamic as a spiritual combat between forces of great good and palpable evil. It had not only heroes and cowards, but saints and sinners, and as it unfolded, the Church's governing and prophetic and priestly duties were on full display. The French editor of a Protestant newspaper wrote: "The militant Catholics in our country have taken a place which is important and, we do not fear to say, preponderant at the head of the movement of resistance, in which very often they have taken the initiative and of which they remain the inspiration."

I would list a sampling of the things I learned in writing the book. For example, on the Vigil of the Assumption in 1942, the Salesians announced that 120 members of their order had been

An American soldier before a statue of the
Mother and Child during World War II (public domain)

executed by the Gestapo in Poland. It was the first anniversary
of the death of Father Maximilian Kolbe at Auschwitz, by an
injection of carbolic acid. A month later, Father Jan Piwowarczk
received a new class of seminarians in Krakow, including Karol
Wojtyla. As pope, he would canonize Kolbe and beatify the thirty-
one-year-old Salesian Father Josef Kowalski, who was killed for
refusing to trample on a rosary.

The eighty-one-year-old auxiliary bishop of Paris, Emanuel-Anatole-Raphael Chaptal de Chanteloup, wore a Star of David in protest against the deportation of Jews and soon was buried wearing it. The collaborationist Vichy radio mocked Cardinal Gerlier of Lyons for hiding Jews and resistance fighters: he was "an ex-lawyer who late in life became an Archbishop, thanks more to the omnipotent grace of the House of Rothschild than to the laws of Holy Mother Church." When German officials ordered the Jews of Beauvais to register at the municipal headquarters, Bishop Felix Roeder claimed a distant Jewish antecedent and was the first to register, processing through the street in full pontifical vestments and preceded by an acolyte carrying the Cross.

In the Pacific Islands, the Japanese killed the Vicar Apostolic of New Guinea and a group of his missionaries. Other Catholic missionaries, including an American, Father Arthur Duhamel, were bayoneted on Guadalcanal. Pope Pius XII's message on the Vatican radio on the feast of the Transfiguration, broadcast in German, said: "God's ship is destined to reach port safely. She will not sink, for Christ is the helmsman, and the gates of hell, the onslaught of the wildest waves and of the spiritual U-boat action ('Geistige U-boot Arbeit') of godless neopaganism, will not harm her. For while paganism cannot build up, still less can neopaganism, which lacks even that nobility of mind and true humanity which was found in the old pagans."

In Syria, the Nationalist Socialist Party hailed Hitler as "Abu Ali," and the Young Egypt Party called him "Muhammad Haidar." The Grand Mufti of Jerusalem, Haj Mohammed Effendi Amin el-Husseini, visited Hitler, secured the deportation of five thousand Jewish children to death camps, and obtained a promise from Hitler to liquidate the Jews of Palestine after a Nazi victory. In Belgium, the University of Louvain was purged of its Catholic faculty, and Mass was forbidden. The Italian Fascist propagandist Roberto Farinacci blamed Allied bombings in Italy on a conspiracy of Myron Taylor, Winston Churchill, British Catholics, the Church of England, and the Vatican. When Christmas came in 1942, the *New York Times* said that Pope Pius XII "is a lonely voice crying out of the silence of a continent."

Almost at the same time, the Bishop of Berlin, Johann Konrad von Preysing, persuaded that Germany had "fallen into the hand of criminals and fools," wrote in a pastoral letter that the world's present miseries were "the result of human contempt for natural and divine law." His secretary, Father Bernhard Lichtenberg, died en route to Dachau, which had an entire wing meant for priests. Among the inmates was Father Titus Brandsma, a scholar of Nijmegen, who gave his rosary to the Allgemeine SS doctor who administered his poison injection. Two months later, a twenty-seven-year-old priest, Father Alois Andritzki, of Dresden, spoke out against the eugenics policies in the Saxon sanatorium in Pima. By the end of the war, some sixteen thousand patients, disabled or mentally ill, were killed there as "life unworthy of life." In Dachau, Father Alois asked for Communion, and the guard injected him with acid. By decree of Benedict XVI, he was beatified as a martyr on June 13, 2011, in Dresden cathedral.

Typical of the "greatest generation" who defied all reason save virtue to fight the good fight was the RAF's Flying Officer Charles Robert Cecil Augustine Allberry, killed in action in the Netherlands at the age of thirty-two. The vice-master of his Cambridge college called him "daring and merry as well as kind" and noted that he had already attained, at the age of twenty-seven, front rank as a Coptic scholar by his edition of a Manichaean psalter. He was received into the Catholic Church a little more than a year before his death. No less dashing was the Crown Prince of Saxony, who relinquished all claims to the royal succession in order to become a Jesuit. This Father Georg was found drowned in Berlin under suspicious circumstances. Brendan Eamon Fergus "Paddy" Finucane died at twenty-one, the youngest Wing-Commander in the history of the RAF, having shot down thirty-two German flyers, twenty-six single-handedly. A friend remembered: "A casual onlooker might be pardoned for thinking him a dare-devil type: I shall like to think of him as I saw him the Sunday before he met his death — kneeling down at Mass, saying his beads with complete simplicity."

He Spoke to Us (2016)

Let There Be Light

Artificial light is so available now, at the flip of a switch, that we are losing a sense of wonder at the gift of light. The first creature was light itself: "Let there be light." It is hard to describe light without referring to its opposite. "The people who walked in darkness have seen a great light" (Isa. 9:2). The first thing one learns in painting, after tackling perspective, is that colors seem bright only by contrast, and that principle of chiaroscuro was known well before the likes of Caravaggio and de la Tour. You do not have to spend a winter in Lapland to know that: just spend a few dim days in February, or try selling an apartment without a view.

He Spoke to Us (2016)

Liberal Protestants

The liberal Protestant denominations are evaporating. One of their leaders has said that their numbers are dropping because their members are too well educated to have children. It is hardly intelligent to design one's own demise. Our social fabric will have to adjust to the disappearance of these groups, which for a long while defined the public face of society.

A Year with Fr. Rutler (2017)

The Life of the Holy Catholic Church

Socrates used to look at newborn babies and marvel at how old they looked, for really there is nothing that looks more like an old man than a little boy who has just come out of his mother's womb—hairless, toothless, fragile. Socrates surmised from this that each baby had a previous, long life, and the process of birth was the blocking of the memory of that life. Education, he proposed, would consist in recovering the memory, just as a midwife brings life out of the womb. His method of teaching was called the midwife method. Of course, Socrates was wrong about that preexisting intelligence. But, analogically, he was on to something: by the fact of our very existence, we have inherited a life larger than our own: the life of culture. Our Lord says that He must leave this world in order to send us the Holy Spirit who will lead us into all truth. The Holy Spirit opens our memory through the virtues of faith, hope, and love, and through those particular gifts of prudence, justice, temperance, and fortitude, by which we put the memory to work. We have to give thanks that in the midst of the culture of death there is life. And that life is found in the Holy

Catholic Church. "With His own blood He bought her," says the hymn. The Church is our Mother, and she confers upon us the dignity of sons and daughters of an ancient ancestral procession. If we forget that, we can recover the memory through the life of grace. There's nothing so dead as a grown man or woman who has forgotten the past. This is how civilization gets lost. The only way to find the way out of the woods is to remember how you got there. The Old Testament prophets did that, but they were only pointing to the Source of all memory, Christ Himself. He comes into the world and says, "Before Abraham was, I am" (John 8:58). That's not bad grammar. It would be for us, since we are not divine. For Jesus, though, it means that He started it all. And all those sages, seers, and prophets who have become part of the collective memory of the Church were sent by Him to waken us up to the fact that there is a life and that it is passed on through the Church, as a mother passes on life through her womb.

Grace and Truth (2019)

Lies

The twentieth century came to revere lies — not only to believe them, but to extol them, to admire them, and to celebrate them. Some of the most influential books of the twentieth century were anthologies of lies. In London, at beginning of that century, the naïve but prominent couple Beatrice and Sidney Webb set up in their house a little shrine to the man they thought was the prophet of the new age, Vladimir Lenin. Of course, they conveniently ignored the horrors he was perpetrating, the forced famines he was engineering, and the assassinations he was plotting. They were living a lie. Beatrice and Sidney Webb wrote one book after another claiming that Lenin's new order really was ushering in a workers' paradise. Margaret Mead wrote a book that made her the prophet of modern anthropology. She, like Rousseau two centuries earlier, denied, for all practical purposes, the fallen nature of man, Adam's inheritance in our blood. She wrote about Samoa and the idyllic life led by the indigenous peoples before civilization corrupted them. Her own peers have since had to admit that she cooked her statistics and misrepresented what she saw. And there was another Margaret, Margaret Sanger, who did far worse damage. She came to persuade a whole century that life is an enemy, that children are a threat to civilization, and that we alone are creators—not *pro*creators with God, but the engineers of the human race. She employed and popularized the eugenic theories of the Nazis. She wrote lie upon influential lie, and today she is still revered by many.

Grace and Truth (2019)

Light from Light

None of Our Lord's utterances was more startling than "I am the light of the world. Whoever follows me will never walk in darkness, but will have the light of life" (John 8:12). As the Light itself, He declares that He is not a creature, but the Divinity who creates, and He does so together with "the Father of lights, with whom there is no change, nor shadow of alteration" (James 1:17), and with Their Spirit, who will "enlighten the hearts of the faithful" with the fire of love. That is the essence of the words in the Creed: "Light from Light."

A Year with Fr. Rutler (2017)

The Light of Christ

The light of Christ pierces the soul's vision most vividly in the darkest times, just as a city's lights seem brightest at the winter solstice. As the late Yogi Berra said in his typical diction that makes great sense in spite of itself: "It's getting later earlier." In the same way, when "the days are waxing late" there is an intuition of something new coming into the world. That newness is the enfleshment of the Second Person of the Holy Trinity.

A Year with Fr. Rutler (2017)

The Billboard Lights of Times Square

The light of life that God gives us is to be kept burning brightly. We can make that light beautiful or garish. G. K. Chesterton, entranced by the billboard lights in Times Square advertising soaps and cigarettes and hair tonic, remarked: "How beautiful this would be, for someone who could not read."

A Year with Fr. Rutler (2017)

The Light of Truth

A recent survey by the Intercollegiate Studies Institute shows that 44 percent of our elected officials cannot identify quotations from the Declaration of Independence or the Gettysburg Address—and yet they are making judgments about the moral course of our nation. In the last election, the majority of voters were more concerned about finances than legalized infanticide or terrorism. Christ Himself surveys this scene, which soon will shatter in the sheer light of Truth. That is how civilizations collapse, and why Advent is a season of warnings.

A Year with Fr. Rutler (2017)

The Lord of Creation No Genetic Engineer

The Lord of Creation knew, and knows, more about the intricacies of His creation than any modern microbiologist or geneticist. His earthly contemporaries would have been confounded by the system that encodes in the first inkling of a life all that the organism will become. In modern bioethics, it is easy to lapse into a primitivism by claiming that a thing becomes alive only when it looks alive, but that contradicts genetic fact. A stem cell has as much claim on reverence for its life as a pope or a president or a Nobel laureate. A seed is alive, even if it looks like little more than lint, and the first cell of human life is alive, even if a clinician chooses to call it a blastocyst. The mustard bush is implanted with its mustardness and bushness even when it is a negligible seed, prey to rapacious birds, as the first cells of human life are prey to genetic engineers.

Hints of Heaven (2014)

Human Love

Human love opens to eternal joy when it is lived as a type of God's perfect and unfailing love. For instance, marriages lived as images of Christ's love for His Church will be faithful and sacrificing, but by being indissoluble they will also be eternal. To say "Catholics can't get divorced" is a stuttering way of saying that love is given and never withdrawn. Of course, it is possible to think that love is given by humans, when in fact it is only given to them. It is a deliberate act of God; if you deny that, you lapse into strange and vague language about "falling in love." And in the next breath those who fall in love speak of "falling out of love." It is a strange object, indeed, that we can both fall in and fall out of. It is in fact a fiction. And the Cross of Christ stands as the perpetual sign that love is nothing unless it is what you have to climb up to, through every obstacle that pride puts in the way.

The Seven Wonders of the World (1993)

Jean-Marie Lustiger

I said Mass with Cardinal Lustiger (1926–2007) in his residence in Paris shortly before the 1997 World Youth Day there, which would gather one million people. The French government had tried to block the whole event. The cardinal said his part of the Mass in English, which he was trying to perfect for the great event, and assigned to me the rest in French. Afterward in the sacristy, he asked, "Where did you learn to speak our language the way you do?" The pregnant ambiguity of the compliment, or its opposite, was a vintage way of the French being French.

Cloud of Witnesses (2009)

George Edward Lynch

George Edward Lynch (1917–2003), auxiliary bishop of Raleigh, saw in Thomas Lynch (no relation), one of the signers of the Declaration of Independence, a model of the men who would "mutually pledge to each other our lives, our fortunes, and our sacred honor." I have a copy of his personal transcript of those words, in handwriting as neat and precise as he was in figure and regimen, tall and white-haired with a gentle manner and soft speech more Carolina than Bronx. Over the years of his pro-life work, he was arrested twenty-one times around the United States and abroad, including Russia. The circumstances of his confinement often were harsh, and yet he enjoyed the chance to evangelize men who were imprisoned for less altruistic acts. During a demonstration outside an abortion center in West Hartford, Connecticut, he was severely beaten by policemen who had removed their nameplates and badges.

Gradually all this took a toll on his health, and once during Mass he fainted and returned after resting briefly on a vesting table in the sacristy. From behind the scenes, Cardinal O'Connor approved and encouraged his apostolate in the pro-life movement, and when Bishop Lynch died in his sixtieth year of priesthood and thirty-third as bishop, the cardinal privately remarked only half-jokingly when the funeral was over that it might not be too soon to start work on his canonization.

It was during his sabbatical in Rome a few years before his retirement that I got to know him, he celebrating Mass and I preaching in the church of our patron, San Giorgio in Velabro. At the time I was most conscious that it had been the titular church of Cardinal Newman, but now I also think of it for Bishop Lynch having offered the Holy Sacrifice there.

No one in that church of St. George had to persuade George Lynch that dragons are real. He dueled with them much of his life. In that letter of his that I have here on my desk, he says that "many who have been penalized by heavy fines, long prison terms, and in various other ways" for protesting against abortions could "say and mean" the pledge made by Thomas Lynch of South Carolina and his fifty-five fellow signers in 1776, "and I am willing, come what may, to be numbered among them."

Clouds of Witnesses (2009)

The Magi

In "The Journey of the Magi," T.S. Eliot portrays the Magi as utterly changed by what they saw and more than uncomfortable with their homeland—present-day Iran—when they went back:

> We returned to our places, these Kingdoms,
> But no longer at ease here, in the old dispensation,
> With an alien people clutching their gods.
> I should be glad of another death.

Like the Magi ... saints are never able to call their old home their true home, for they set their sights on their promised home in Heaven, and that hope makes them all the more useful in this world. "Hope does not disappoint, because the love of God has been poured out into our hearts through the Holy Spirit that has been given to us" (Rom. 5:5).

A Year with Fr. Rutler (2017)

Making All Things New

Religions contrived merely by humans tend to be exotic. But in the only actual instance of perfect divinity and perfect humanity united in an historical figure, Christ does not go about dressed as a wizard, and He tries to keep His miracles confidential: "Tell no one" (see, e.g., Matt. 8:4). He makes all things new (Rev. 21:5), but He does not make new things. Thus, Aquinas wrote: "Grace does not destroy nature, but perfects it."[27]

A Year with Fr. Rutler (2017)

The Man Himself

Vianney's voice sounded like a fiddle at a barn dance, and when he got excited, it got higher, as though he were running out of strings. At first he tried to memorize each sermon, a disaster; his memory was no better than his pitch. Then he would lose the train of thought and stumble over the words; the gaunt little figure would hang its powerful chin over the edge of the pulpit as if pleading for rescue, only to stare at helpless looks from below. His collected sermons have been edited, and none of this pathos is left in them; but even edited, they should not be used as models. He is the model, and the sermons are to be read with a mental image of the occasional panic of the man who preached them. He continued preaching long after most of his teeth were gone and many of his words had become incoherent. The crowds continued to grow and were largest when the old man gave up preaching sermons altogether.

The Curé d'Ars Today (1988)

March for Life

There was a theologian who, when discouraged, would keep repeating to himself, "I have been baptized." Since the prince of lies has discouragement as his chief strategy and purpose, the

---

[27] *Summa Theologica*, I, q. 1, art. 8.

Rite of Baptism includes an exorcism: an explicit renunciation of Satan, and all his works, and all his empty promises.... Ever since the legalization of abortion in our country, the Church has resisted the temptation to discouragement in defending innocent life. January 22 will mark the forty-first annual March for Life in Washington. The March has gone on in weather fair and foul, whether government administrations have been friend or foe. In those years, more than 56 million babies in our country alone have been destroyed in their mothers' wombs. We lament the loss of at least 110 million soldiers and civilians worldwide in the two World Wars and can barely imagine with what talent and invention so many of them might have endowed the arts and science. The same dirge can be intoned for all those babies.

Last year at this time, I cited a statistical abstract using the ratio of professions to population and the number of infants aborted. The resulting estimate showed that in the last thirty-five years, those lives destroyed could have included: two U.S. presidents; seven Supreme Court justices; 102 U.S. senators and 589 congressmen; 8,123 judges; 31 Nobel Prize laureates; 328 Olympic medalists; 6,092 professional athletes; 134,841 physicians and surgeons; 392,500 registered nurses; 70,669 clergy, including 6,852 Catholic priests and 11,010 nuns; 1,102,443 elementary and high school teachers; 553,821 truck drivers; 224,518 maids and housekeepers; 33,939 janitors; 134,028 farmers and ranchers; 109,984 police officers; and 39,477 firefighters.

None of those infants lived to be baptized, and they are entrusted to the mercy of God. Our nation now has the lowest birth rate in its history and may be approaching the demographic winter that is destroying many other countries. The good news is that contending for life year in and year out has roused consciences, and the rate of abortions is at an all-time low. So when facing Satan and all his works and all his empty promises, say with good courage: "I have been baptized."

A Year with Fr. Rutler (2017)

Marriage

The sacraments of Holy Orders and Marriage bestow a "grace of state" (grace suitable for one's state in life) by which God enables the receivers, according to their consecrated status, to promote His justice in the world. The ordained man does that by teaching and bringing Christ to the people. The husband and wife do that by showing the relationship between Christ and His Church.

A Year with Fr. Rutler (2017)

One often-overlooked offense against God's justice is cohabitation before marriage.... Cohabitation increases the chance of divorce by 50 percent because of its wrong understanding of love. It also increases the tendency to adultery after marriage. Marriage is a social fact, and not a private matter. As it affects all of society, its misuse is unjust to everyone by distorting what God made marriage to be. It is unjust to the couple because it deprives them of grace. Those desiring to "walk in the ways of justice" should not receive the Eucharist without a firm purpose of returning to God through confession.

A Year with Fr. Rutler (2017)

As God is a just judge, He requires the best of those He loves. "Let marriage be held in honor among all, and let the marriage bed be undefiled; for God will judge the immoral and adulterous"

(Heb. 13:4). With thanks for so good a judge, we await the coming of Christ with holy awe — instead of the servile fear that is the neurosis of people who underestimate their own potential for holiness.

A Year with Fr. Rutler (2017)

From a secular perspective, Johns Hopkins University sociologist Andrew Cherlin has written about the harm done to children by the "Marriage-Go-Round" in the United States. Marriage has become a status symbol rather than an essential core of society. Marriages in our country are even more ephemeral than in Europe. After just five years of marriage, 23 percent of Americans had separated or divorced, compared with 12 percent in West Germany, 8 percent in Great Britain, and 3 percent in Italy. Dr. Cherlin's approach is utilitarian and ultimately defeatist: "I think our best hope is to find better ways of coping with the culture we have." Christ does not call us to cope with the culture, but to transform it.

A Year with Fr. Rutler (2017)

Martin Luther and St. Thomas

Popular myth has Martin Luther burning the *Summa Theologica* of St. Thomas Aquinas in the marketplace of Wittenberg. Not so. The hapless heretic wanted to destroy one of the world's greatest works, but none of the townsfolk was willing to surrender a copy. We should cherish Aquinas like that today, for he prevents a lot of pseudo-philosophical humbug.

A Year with Fr. Rutler (2017)

A Martyr's Love

The slaying of Father Jacques Hamel at the altar of the Church of Saint-Étienne-de-Rouvray in Normandy should be the envy of every priest: to die at Mass, the holiest hour of the world.... The venerable Dominican scholar Father Réginald Garrigou-Lagrange, who supervised the doctoral dissertation of St. John Paul II in Rome at the Angelicum, said: "The Church is intolerant in principle because she believes; she is tolerant in practice because she loves. The enemies of the Church are tolerant in principle because they do not believe; they are intolerant in practice because they do not love." We do not know what Father Jacques Hamel thought about capitalism or climate change, but it is obvious that he loved, and loved intolerably, and because of that, his last words to his killer were: "Va-t'en, Satan!" — "Begone, Satan!"

Calm in Chaos (2018)

Massacre of the Innocents

The great twentieth-century theologian Hans Urs von Balthasar said that "everywhere outside of Christianity, the child is automatically sacrificed."[28] That is not hyperbole: history shows it to be true. Whenever the dignity of the human person, founded in the redemptive power of Christ, is ignored, the selfish pride of man will find some excuse to attack innocence. With an indescribable sorrow from the Cross, Our Lord saw innocent life being shattered from the beginning to the very end of time. All

---

[28] *Wenn ihr nicht werdet wie dieses Kind* (Ostfildern bei Stuttgart: Schwabenverl., 1988).

the body parts of the fifty million babies who have been killed in the United States—those were before His eyes. And at the very beginning of the human race, Cain slew Abel. God said to Cain, "The voice of your brother's blood is crying to me from the ground" (Gen. 4:10). When the population of the world was one household, it was clearer that each one of us is a brother or a sister to one another. As time has moved on, though, it has become easier to reduce people to statistics. But God never looks upon us as a statistic.

Grace and Truth (2019)

Father Mathew

In the nineteenth century there was a remarkable character named Father Theobald Mathew, an Irish Capuchin who dedicated his life to the temperance movement.[29] There are those today who speak patronizingly of such work, but he was not a puritanical teetotaler, and drunkenness truly was a social crisis

---

[29] "By 1844, the Cork Total Abstinence Society claimed that more than 4 million members—half the population of Ireland—had 'taken the pledge' to abstain from alcohol for life. Whiskey production in Ireland fell by more than 50 percent from the mid-1830s to the mid-1840s. Crime rates also plummeted. Fr. Mathew became known far and wide as the 'Great Apostle of Temperance.' Work of his mission reached across the Atlantic to the Irish in the U.S. The *Boston Pilot* wrote of him in 1839, 'The people flock to him in great multitudes, and the number of those whom he has induced to abandon the horrible vices of drunkenness is beyond calculation.'" Edward T. O'Donnell, "164 Years Ago: Father Matthew Begins His Crusade," *Irish Echo*, February 16, 2011.

at that time. He had a higher vision, a vision of the human soul as a reflection of the glory of God. And it was so wonderful to him that he wanted people to understand that they were losing sight of something far more splendid than what alcohol or any drug could give. He was a virtual miracle-worker, giving the temperance pledge to hundreds of thousands of Irish and, on one occasion, to a multitude of a hundred thousand Scotsmen. He came to the United States and visited at the White House, where he presented his work to the admiration of President Zachary Taylor. The vice president at the time, who later became President Millard Fillmore, received him at City Hall in New York, and it is said that he even took the pledge. What Fr. Mathew faced in his day was no different from the drug culture we face today. Any sociologist can come up with an explanation for why alcohol was such a problem in the nineteenth century. The breakdown of social institutions, economic oppression, the suppression of religion, political tyranny, or any number of other things drove people to seek some kind of escape. But this good priest told the people that God gives us not an escape but an "inscape"—a vision of the good that challenges every attempt to contradict that good by doing evil.

Grace and Truth (2019)

May and the Mother of Fair Love

The fair month of May belongs to the "Mother of Fair Love." The first day of May was an ancient celebration of the start of plant growth. Hard and cynical people replaced the maypole with coarse Communist parades, but that illusion of a worker's paradise without God has fallen on the ash heap of history. Ancient Romans dedicated May to the goddess of blossoms, Flora, and prepared for her feast with late April "floral games" (*ludi florales*). Christianity did not extrapolate a Marian month from these customs; these customs were an unconscious intuition that there would someday be a Blessed Mother.

A Year with Fr. Rutler (2017)

The Media

Our Lord knew and knows all things, so in some way, He anticipated television when He preached from a boat in Galilee to be better seen and heard. None of His followers have had a better opportunity to spread His gospel than we do in our generation. It is dreadful to think how much we squander that opportunity and use the media so inadequately.

Grace and Truth (2019)

Medicina Mundi

It is possible to deny the Cross through the pessimistic notion that there is no solution for a sinful world, or through the optimistic notion that there is no sin to resolve. Lent shows a third way: there is sin, and it can be conquered by the Cross. Instead of pessimism and optimism, the Christian has repentance and hope. Jesus was crucified, and by His Resurrection He made the wood of the Cross *medicina mundi*—"the medicine of the world."

A Year with Fr. Rutler (2017)

Memory and God's Grace

By God's grace, memory confers youth. One has to be old to have a long memory, but that memory changes the weakness of age into strength. This is why the saints seem to get younger as they get older: they grow older biologically, but they grow younger spiritually. A friend of mine had a mother in her nineties who was overheard by a nurse shortly before she died saying into a mirror, "Is it not wonderful how something so old can be so beautiful?" Remember the Song of Solomon, "Arise, my love, my fair one, and come away; for lo, the winter is past, the rain is over and gone" (Song of Sol. 2:10–11). This is the voice that Our Lord speaks to the oldest people as they are dying: "My love, my fair one, arise and come away."

Grace and Truth (2019)

Memory, Holy Mother Church, and the Mass

The Church is not an "it." The Church is our Mother. She is the guardian of culture, and where the Mother is loved, there is a culture of life. When the Mother is scorned, we inherit a culture of death. When Pope John Paul II said that we are living in the Culture of Death, he meant that we have lost our memory of the human drama, of the combat between good and evil, and of the promise of grace. At the heart of a culture of life is the memorial of the Mass — Holy Mother Church's Sacred Meal. The Church has a memory that is not nostalgic but efficacious. She passes on the fact of the Eucharistic Meal, not a passive recollection of a one-time past event. The Church animates the Passover so that it becomes the presence of Christ, who leads us from the bondage of sin into the Promised Land. "Do this in memory of me," we hear, but the original word really means something far more subtle than our translation can easily capture. *Anamnesia* means recovering one's memory, not merely in the sense of recollecting what had been lost in the mind, but of bringing back into reality that which did exist but which we had forgotten. The memorial of the Mass does not just rivet our minds on the Christ of two thousand years ago; it passes Him on to us. Mothers have a very long memory, and Holy Mother Church has the longest memory, for she knows that there was a Paradise. She knows that there was a first man and a first woman created by the gratuitous love of God. And she knows everything that happened along the way until this day.

Grace and Truth (2019)

Metaphysics and Vianney

What once were thought to be scientific challenges to God are now more clearly clues to the complex order of His creativity, and the supernatural intuition of Vianney remains part of that stunning network. A considerable theological significance lies in the words of the Berkeley physicist Henry Pierce Stapp: "Everything we know about nature is in accord with the idea that the fundamental processes of nature lie outside space-time but generate events that can be located in space-time." When Copernicus flung the gauntlet down before Ptolemy, he also flung a red carpet before the mystery of divine particularity. Einstein's chalk marks on his blackboard intimated something deep about time and space, in which "I AM" is a name, and Alpha is Omega. If earth is not the center of the universe, then God's moral regard for

His human creatures is more miraculous than the Ptolemaists and flatlanders thought. In the confluence of physical and moral reality, which modern skepticism has tried to divorce, sin and virtue are intrinsic to physical meaning. And the ability Vianney shared with some other saints to converse with figures long dead, to perceive thoughts and anticipate events, is a graceful conforming to the deep facts of life: facts that are obscured by limited intelligence in the physical degree and by limited virtue in the moral degree. Brilliant without benefit of academic rank, elegant without benefit of social rank, and worldly wise without benefit of political rank, the Curé was one of the rare mortals who could command nature to be more real. Natural physics has reached a frontier so wide that the physicists can hardly open their mouths without sounding metaphysical. When the frontier is crossed, we will find that there really are giants in the land, and the giants will be what they have always been, what for want of a better name we call saints. Long before the fruition of subatomic physics, the saints knew what they did not know, and this holy and mystical lacuna was the secret of their powers.

The Curé d'Ars Today (1988)

Miracles

The well-known Pentecostal preacher Benny Hinn surprisingly admitted that most miracles happen in the Catholic Church because "Catholic people revere the Eucharist." If more Catholics themselves understood that, there would be more miracles. Now, miracles do not contradict nature: they are God's will at work at high speed. Christ promised to be with us "until the end of the world" (Matt. 28:20). Eucharistic adoration is simply the recognition of His presence. St. Clare prayed, "My Lord, if it is Your wish, protect this city which is sustained by Your love." The Lord answered, "It will have to undergo trials, but it will be defended by my protection."

A Year with Fr. Rutler (2017)

Misrepresentatives

It is offensive to God and conscience to neglect moral principles in order to vote for a particular political party or candidate out of custom. Many politicians advertise themselves as Catholic, or as friendly to the Church, and then hold Catholic moral principles in contempt. It is only the ignorance or self-interest of Catholic voters that keeps these misrepresentative representatives in office.

A Year with Fr. Rutler (2017)

Mit Brennender Sorge (1937)

Pope Pius XI, just as the horror of the Second World War was about to cast its shadow upon the entire globe, issued an encyclical that he arranged to have smuggled into Germany: *Mit Brennender Sorge*, or "With burning zeal." What was he inflamed about? The denial of natural law; the deification of the state; and the myth of biological perfection, especially as the Nazis interpreted it in their pursuit of the "master race." In that encyclical, he did not mention Fascists or Nazis or Marxists by name. Some thought this was a deliberate oversight or neglect or worse. But Pius had a supernatural perception of the root of the problem of discord—and it applied well beyond the threats of that moment. Government systems come and go. He knew that the principal of discord, though, will always haunt civilization—and that is why what he wrote in 1937, words that were read from the pulpits of Germany, is so prophetic for our generation and for our nation.

Grace and Truth (2019)

Modernity

The story of Job is not as old as Adam's, but not by much. In the thirty-eighth chapter of Job, God says: "Where were you when I laid the foundation of the earth? Tell me if you have understanding.... Have the gates of death been revealed to you, or have you seen the gates of deep darkness? Have you comprehended the expanse of the earth? Declare, if you know all this" (Job 38:4, 17–18). He says the same to us at the end of what we vainly call "the modern age."

Grace and Truth (2019)

Monarchical Trouper

The distinguished Catholic peer Lord Alton of Liverpool has calculated that during Elizabeth's reign, there have been six popes, and her Catholic subjects have increased from 4.4 to 6.6 million in Britain, and from 25 million to 140 million throughout the Commonwealth. One-third of the primary schools in England are Catholic, and they comprise two-thirds of the most highly rated ones. During the queen's reign, the number of Catholic charities in the United Kingdom has grown to 1,000. In the

Commonwealth countries, the Catholic Church runs 5,246 hospitals, 17,530 dispensaries, 577 leprosy clinics, and 15,208 homes for the elderly. After long centuries of conflicts between state and Church, this is a remarkable record, but it should not distract from the growing threats to religion from secularists throughout the world, and increasingly so in our own nation. Through it all, Elizabeth II has displayed a constant sense of duty and responsibility, knowing that with the perquisites of her office comes an unrelenting publicity that will not cease until her last breath — far different from public figures who may hope to retire and play golf. The example of growing old gracefully and publicly is another gift of a monarch — in contrast to mere celebrities who use the limelight to create an illusion of agelessness. It is said that when a Hollywood starlet, about to be presented to the queen, worried that the colors of their dresses might clash, she was told that Her Majesty does not notice what others are wearing.

A Year with Fr. Rutler (2017)

Vive la Monomanie!

There are those who would stifle the pro-life cause by calling it a single-issue obsession. Few would say that about the abolition movement or the struggle against child labor, even though such worthy causes did attract a fair share of distempered monomaniacs. But slaves and children have to be born first, and so the protection of life from conception must rank first among all dedications of philanthropy.

A Year with Fr. Rutler (2017)

The Moral Manners of Heaven

The moral manners of heaven, whose homely tokens are a sense of humor and an appreciation of paradox, would seem to us ... perverse ... and even horrible, without sanctifying grace or purgatorial refinement.

Hints of Heaven (2014)

Moral Memory

Advent awakens the moral memory to the most important facts. They can be erased from memory by ignoring Advent altogether. But then we would cease to be Christians entrusted with the memory of the human race. "I have said these things to you, that when the hour comes, you may remember that I told them to you" (John 16:4).

A Year with Fr. Rutler (2017)

A Morning Offering

Certain personalities may find hymn singing at an early hour to be a test of virtue. Before any song, a Morning Offering prayer is a Catholic custom for the first moment of rising:

> O Jesus, through the Immaculate Heart of Mary, I offer
> You my prayers, works, joys, and sufferings of this day for
> all the intentions of Your Sacred Heart, in union with
> the Holy Sacrifice of the Mass throughout the world,
> in reparation for my sins, for the intentions of all my

relatives and friends, and in particular for the intentions
of the Holy Father. Amen.

The Stories of Hymns (2016)

The Most Beautiful of God's Creatures

The most beautiful of God's creatures are the saints, who let the
Holy Spirit dwell in them. "Your beauty should not come from
outward adornment such as braided hair or gold jewelry or fine
clothes, but from the inner disposition of your heart, the unfad-
ing beauty of a gentle and quiet spirit, which is precious in God's
sight" (1 Pet. 3:3–4).

A Year with Fr. Rutler (2017)

The Mother of God

The last word Our Lord spoke to the human race from the Cross
was "Mother." Mary shows the way to her Son. People who try
to find God without His Mother will get lost, and those who
call themselves Christian without calling on Mary are confused
children.

A Year with Fr. Rutler (2017)

Every Mother a Prophet of Life

Every mother is a prophet of life. When a civilization abandons
its children, it is the mother who reminds us of the desolation.

Grace and Truth (2019)

Mother Saints

Name the great ladies of America, and you will get Mother Elizabeth Ann Seton and Mother Frances Cabrini and Mother Marianne Cope and Mother Theodore Guerin. There is an instinct to call them "Mother" as a title even nobler than "Saint." It is a reverberation from the Cross, when the Son gave us nothing less than a Mother. It was His last word to the human race before He died.

Calm in Chaos (2018)

Saint Mother Teresa of Calcutta

On that hot and depressing August 9, 1974, when Richard Nixon made his final address to the hounds of the media, he said: "My mother was a saint." With all his flaws, which by comparison to those of others in our national pantheon seem adolescent, his chief anchor and steadiest ballast was his mother long gone. A munificent grace was the day I introduced my own mother to Mother Teresa. Hearing the two of them was like eavesdropping at Pentecost. She thanked Mother Teresa for all her good work. Mother ignored that and thanked my mother for being a mother of a priest. I could shrink whenever I think of that, but Mother always made a priest feel big, despite his shortcomings. After Mass, she would kiss the hands of the priest and thank him for having brought Jesus to her. She also would ask the priest to remember her each time he put the drop of water into the wine in preparing the chalice at the Offertory. I try to do that each day. I shall not be at the canonization, but I know she will be at every altar everywhere, watching with Mary the Mother of the Church.

Calm in Chaos (2018)

Francisco de Zurbarán, Virgin Mary as a Child
*(1658–1660), Hermitage Museum, Saint Petersburg
(image courtesy of Wikimedia Commons).*

The Mother with the Longest Memory

There is a lovely painting by the Spanish artist Francisco de Zurbarán (1598–1662) showing the Blessed Mother as a young girl
seated on a chair.[30] On her lap is some embroidery she's working

---

[30] *Virgin Mary as a Child* (1658–1660), Hermitage Museum, Saint
Petersburg. Zurbarán completed the painting a few years before
his death. It can be compared to another by Zurbarán of a similar
theme in the Metropolitan Museum of Art, *The Young Virgin*
(1632–1633).

on, but when you look carefully, you realize it's the shroud of her Son. This image prefigures the role of the Mother from the very moment of Christ's conception. We are born to live. He is born to die and to rise again that we might live forever. And the only reason we know that is because the Church is not an "it." She's our Mother, the Mother with the longest memory.

Grace and Truth (2019)

Mourning in Festivity

If bad things happen at a time of festival, the feast can become more powerful. Sometimes those who mourn the death of loved ones at this time of year hear more clearly than anyone the voice that says, "So you have sorrow now, but I will see you again and your hearts will rejoice, and no one will take your joy from you." Likewise, just as the glory of Christ became most vivid in contrast to His crucifiers, so is the splendor of His Body, the Church, brightest in contrast to those who deface it.

A Year with Fr. Rutler (2017)

On the Murmansk Run

The first letter I ever received was sent to me by my father during the Second World War. He was sailing on a Liberty ship of the Merchant Marines on the Murmansk Run. His letter was addressed to me care of my mother because I was still in her womb. He told me to be good. He said his ship had gone through some storms and U-boats kept circling around, but "everything is fine." That was the clarion voice of a great generation.

He Spoke to Us (2016)

The Music of Worship

The finest music of worship inspires, and in turn is inspired by, the vaults to which it soars. The self-consciously "modern" church building (usually an acoustical disaster) houses suburbanites who sing like Icarus about rising up on eagles' wings while dashing out to the parking lot. After a generation of synthetic and unrealized "renewal," there remains a reluctance to tell the truth about this situation, while dwindling congregations in their imposed aesthetic squalor sing painful metaphors about satisfying the hungry heart and breaking bread on their knees. Such was not the voice of John Damascene in the desert and Bernard of Clairvaux in the abbey. They knew that Christ makes the soul sing in the brightest and best way.

The Stories of Hymns (2016)

The Mustard Seed

The mustard seed is a parable of the Church, nascent and fragile, yet inscribed by the Divine Word with all the saints and sinners, confraternities and schisms, shrines and hovels, golden and dark ages that will be until the Lord comes again. Zechariah prophesied it—who "has despised the day of small things?" (Zech. 4:10)—as did Daniel when he saw a stone becoming a vast mountain (Dan. 2:35). Every cathedral and miracle and converted nation was in the breath of Christ when He said to the woman of Samaria, "If you knew the gift of God and who it is who speaks to you ..." (John 4:10).

Hints of Heaven (2014)

The Mystical Body of Christ

If there is no urgency to tell others about Christ, then His Body —the Church—is misunderstood as an institution kept alive by bureaucrats who act as embalmers, cynically sustaining a corporate identity with mendacity and mummery. That is a formula for spiritual burnout. Such burnout is the malady of people who never were on fire to begin with. But those who encounter Christ say daily: "Did not our hearts burn within us . . . ?" (Luke 24:32).

A Year with Fr. Rutler (2017)

Jesus of Nazareth was killed, and then He killed death. This is why the Church exists. Jesus planned the Church during three years of preaching, provided the Eucharist in the Upper Room, fought Satan on the Cross, reappeared on the third day, gave the apostles power to forgive sins, spent forty days teaching, and then mysteriously entered eternity. The Holy Spirit entered the apostles and got the Church going on Pentecost. I apologize for this crude reporting of the events, but they are breathtaking.

A Year with Fr. Rutler (2017)

Napoleon and Trimmers

For all his odd little ways with God, preternaturally cynical Napoleon held trimmers of the Gospel in contempt, even as he made use of them.

He Spoke to Us (2016)

Neo-Paganism

Ours has become a neo-pagan culture, and that can be even worse than a simple pagan culture. Pagans did not know about Christ. Neo-pagans do know about Him and reject Him.

A Year with Fr. Rutler (2017)

Richard John Neuhaus

Many years ago I had the first of many dinners with Richard John Neuhaus (1936–2009), when he was still a Lutheran. He objected to the term "converting" for a baptized Christian who became Catholic because, for him, one "embraced" Catholicism. I demurred, as I thought I had converted, albeit not from so intensely dogmatic a confession as Lutheranism but from the pleasant perch of Anglicanism. That same evening, he pointed out that the heating system in a nearby building was being converted to gas, to which I replied that he should have said it was embracing gas. Our friendship was not thwarted.

Cloud of Witnesses (2009)

The New Grief Therapy

Our college campuses have become breeding grounds for self-absorption.... Professors who never attained moral maturity themselves reacted to the election of Donald Trump by providing "safe spaces" for students traumatized by reality. In universities across the land, by a sodality of silliness in the academic establishment, these "safe spaces" were supplied with soft cushions, hot chocolate, coloring books, and attendant psychologists. At least one university provided friendly kittens and puppies for weeping students to cuddle. A college chaplaincy invited students to pray, the implication being that their petitions might persuade the Lord to rethink His political leanings.

The average age of a Continental soldier in the American Revolution was one year less than that of a college freshman today. Alexander Hamilton was a fighting lieutenant general at twenty-one, not to mention Joan of Arc, who led an army into battle and saved France when she was about as old as an American college sophomore. In our Civil War, eight Union generals and seven Confederate generals were under the age of twenty-five. The age of most U.S. and RAF fighter pilots in World War II was about that of those on college junior-varsity teams. Catholics who hoped in this election for another Lepanto miracle will remember that back in 1571, Don Juan of Austria saved Western civilization as commanding admiral when he was twenty-four. None of these figures, in the various struggles against the world and the flesh and evil, retreated to safe spaces, weeping in the arms of grief therapists.

What will the frightened half-adults do when they leave their safe spaces and enter a society where there is no one to offer them hot chocolate? Christ formed His disciples in a more practical way: "I am sending you out like sheep among wolves. Therefore, be as shrewd as snakes and as innocent as doves" (Matt. 10:16). We are here today because those disciples did as they were told and were not shrewd as doves and innocent as snakes.

Calm in Chaos (2018)

The New Man

Pope Gregory the Great wrote:

> For unless the new man, by being made in the likeness of sinful flesh, had taken on himself the nature of our first parents, unless he had stooped to be one in substance with his mother while sharing the Father's substance and, being alone free from sin, united our nature to his, the whole human race would still be held captive under the dominion of Satan.

The Conqueror's victory would have profited us nothing if the battle had been fought outside our human condition. But through this wonderful blending, the mystery of new birth shone upon us, so that through the same Spirit by whom Christ was conceived and brought forth, we too might be born again in a spiritual birth; and in consequence, the evangelist declares the faithful to have been born not of blood, nor of the desire of the flesh, nor the will of man, but of God.

A Year with Fr. Rutler (2017)

Newman No Hegelian

One was perplexed at hearing Cardinal Christoph Schönborn say, at the press conference presenting the apostolic exhortation *Amoris Laetitia*, that it was an example of John Henry Newman's *Development of Doctrine* (1845).[31] At the heart of Newman's

---

[31] "Several questions [at the press conference] focused on the relationship between *Amoris Laetitia* and *Familiaris Consortio*, St. John Paul II's own apostolic exhortation following a Synod on

developmental economy is the "preservation of type," and it is hard to see that preservation in some of the ambiguities in chapter 8 of *Amoris Laetitia*. Newman's exposition of *Development* was a justification of tradition and not a training manual for altering that tradition. Newman's *Development* is not Hegel's "dialectic."

Calm in Chaos (2018)

No Dead Saints

The expression "living saint" can be misleading.... There is no such thing as a dead saint.

A Year with Fr. Rutler (2017)

Nostalgia for the Old Rites

Archbishop Marini complains about "a certain nostalgia for the old rites." In doing so, he contradicts Pope Benedict's distinction between rites and uses. He also fails to explain why nostalgia for the 1560s is inferior to nostalgia for the 1960s, except for the dentistry.

Calm in Chaos (2018)

---

the Family, which was published in 1981. 'I don't see that there is a change,' Cardinal Schönborn said, 'but certainly there is a development, just as Pope John Paul developed doctrine.... John Henry Newman explained to us how the organic development of doctrine works. Pope Francis is developing things in this way.'" "Cardinal Schönborn Praises 'Amoris Laetitia' Stance on Gay Marriage," Catholic News Agency, April 8, 2016.

The Notes of Sycophancy

In 2014 Pope Francis himself received only tepid applause when he complained to his Curia about prelates: "typical of mediocre and progressive spiritual emptiness that no academic degree can fill." Among such mediocrities are those who replace prophecy with political correctness. You can tell who they are by what they say about *Amoris Laetitia*. Like those bishops whom Chrysostom disdained for trimming their sails to gain preferment, the careerist cleric knows what he must say and what he must not say. For years I have saved the *Punch* magazine cartoon of the sycophantic curate timorously telling his bishop that parts of his bad egg are excellent. That was in a comfortable Victorian culture on which the sun would never set, though it did anyway. It was a world removed from that of Gregory the Great, who eventually moved the world instead of being moved by it. As Pius X said of the achievement of his great predecessor: "The ferocity of the barbarians was thus transformed to gentleness, woman was freed from subjection, slavery was repressed, order was restored in the due and reciprocal independence upon one another of the various classes of society, justice was recognized, the true liberty of souls was proclaimed, and social and domestic peace assured."[32]

Calm in Chaos (2018)

Odium Fidei

Countless Christians are being persecuted in *odium fidei* — "hatred of the Faith." Their bravery should humble those of us who live in

---

[32] Pope Pius X, encyclical *Iucunda Sane* (March 12, 1904), no. 36.

more peaceful places; but it is also a warning that echoes Christ Himself: "Everyone will hate you because of me, but the one who stands firm to the end will be saved" (Mark 13:13).

A Year with Fr. Rutler (2017)

O. Henry's Ancient Intuition

O. Henry, abandoned by his wife, Sara, said with his last alcoholic breath in the dim gaslight of his rented room: "Turn up the lights—I don't want to go home in the dark." However oblique his spiritual intuition may have been, it seems laden with an ancient appeal to One "in [whom] is no darkness at all" (1 John 1:5).

He Spoke to Us (2016)

An Old Wizard

In the same sense that the miracles of Christ were signs pointing to what He was accomplishing in time for the reorientation of mankind toward the will of God, and were not displays for some lesser gain, so Vianney's signs were didactic. He called himself an old wizard and sometimes feigned idiocy to discourage sightseers who were tempted to believe in him when he only wanted them to believe him. He wanted them to believe in something basic, the City of God, as believable as Paris or Ars or the hat on one's head. He made the Eternal City so tangible to rustics who had not seen a city that cosmopolitans came by carriage and train to learn such civility. Vianney would have been less than Catholic if he had spoken a language only for farmers or, for that matter, a language only for the landlords of farmers; but he spoke to them all in a tongue so direct that the way from anyplace to Ars became the way entire from Genesis to Revelation.

The Curé d'Ars Today (1988)

One Statue Left for the Statists to Tear Down

The architects of our mindless and soulless dystopia have one statue left to tear down, and it must be toppled if statists are to smash the image of God in men, and it is Rodin's *Thinker*.

Calm in Chaos (2018)

On Stage

In Holy Week, the Liturgies are not a performance that we watch. We are on the stage, and the stage is not a theater but the world itself. This is the one drama among all dramas that is real, for it is the entire experience of the human race, all that was and will be, encapsulated in a few days. Christ "recapitulates" the encounter of man and God in Himself. As Pope Benedict says, Jesus is "the face of God," and in these days that face is broken and bleeding as proof that God, who made the drama, is also in the drama.

A Year with Fr. Rutler (2017)

Ordinary Time

The Church calls the time outside Advent, Christmas, Lent, and Easter "Ordinary" because its weeks are numbered in an ordered series, the Latin word for which is *ordinalis*. Next to the very existence of the world itself, a most spectacular fact about this world is that it is orderly.

A Year with Fr. Rutler (2017)

"O Saving Victim, Opening Wide"

St. Thomas Aquinas wrote ["O Saving Victim, Opening Wide"] for Lauds of Corpus Christi.... One of these verses' most ardent and unlikely admirers was the humbug romantic Jean-Jacques Rousseau (1712–1778), who published a *Dictionary of Music* in 1767 and said, in what is quite an amazing admission from him, that all his works combined were not worth these few lines of the Angelic Doctor.

The Stories of Hymns (2016)

Pagans, the Dead, Christ, and Hope

The noble pagans flattered their dead because they could not absolve them. *De mortuis nil nisi bonum* is not a Christian dictum; speaking nothing but good of the dead bespeaks the Spartan decency of Chilon, who lived six centuries before the Incarnation of the Redeemer. Chilon may have been a wise magistrate himself and as merciful as a Spartan could be, but his mercy was not that of Christ the Judge, for Chilon had no power to summon the dead: "Come forth!" The noble pagan tried to make the best of a bad thing by recommending a social convention born of pessimism. The mercy of God changes pessimism to hope, and hope is the engine of honesty.

He Spoke to Us (2016)

Parables

The parables really are what Jesus said they are: hints of Heaven. Because the glory of Heaven is too great for us to bear just now, Christ uses parables as delicate and veiled indications of our true homeland. Every culture has to some extent sensed that the glory of Heaven is too bright for our eyes. The ancient Egyptians kept a veiled image of Ma'at, the goddess of Truth, in their temple at Saïs, believing that the actual sight of it would blind or even kill the viewer. The entire audience on the mount would have fled if Christ had plainly stated in His sermon that His kingdom was of another world. He saved that declaration for Pontius Pilate, who only shook his cynical head.

Hints of Heaven (2014)

Paradise

All we have to do to get rid of the old Adam and to embrace the new Christ is to say the most honest thing that a thief ever said: "This Man has done nothing wrong." And when anyone criticizes Christ, when anyone blasphemes His Holy Church, when anyone snubs the saints, ask them, "What have they really done wrong? What did Christ do that was wrong? And what is He doing now that is wrong?" It is the world that lies against Christ, but when we say that He has done nothing wrong, then He will say to us what Adam longed to hear: "This day, you will be with me in Paradise" (Luke 23:43).

Grace and Truth (2019)

Parish Life

Yesterday was not atypical in our parish. Within about eight hours, I offered the Sacrifice of the Mass twice, heard confessions, baptized a baby, married a young couple, and buried a man. Each of these actions was done in the name of the Father and the Son and the Holy Spirit, in whom "we live and move and have our being" (Acts 17:28). Though some of the Greek poets had used similar words, the Word of God made them real. That is why St. Paul died in Rome, not for a syllogist, but for a Savior.

A Year with Fr. Rutler (2017)

A Parish Priest

All that I write is written as a parish priest, and I am happy that is all I have ever been, and so I have had the privilege of being edified by souls in the daily traffic of their lives. If various passages in my essays are pedestrian, my one defense is that the men on the Emmaus road were pedestrians and the Man who walked with them was kind enough to explain that He had planned each step they were taking.

He Spoke to Us (2016)

Passion and Pride

The crossroads of every biography is this challenge to the soul: How will we choose? The soul that is governed by what it thinks is freedom but is, in fact, the delusion of pride, falls into slavery. It is pride, the pretense that we can live without the Cross that splits the soul. The soul is made of the intellect and the will: passion enslaves the will; pride then co-opts the intellect. That great voice of the nineteenth century and of all ages, John Henry Newman, spoke to a group of university scholars about pride, knowing that pride is a besetting sin of the intellectual. He said famously, "Quarry the granite rock with razors. Moor the vessel with a thread of silk. And then you may hope with such keen and delicate instruments as human knowledge and human reason to contend against those giants, the passion and the pride of man."[33] Passion and pride: This is what Our Lord is speaking of in announcing the hour of darkness. He is describing the prince of lies, who wants us to think that passion — not the Lord's divine and salvific Passion, but our fallen human passion — is the way to freedom, and that pride is the source of our dignity. Our Lord knows that passion and pride can be defeated only by suffering and failure. That's what the Cross teaches us. The Cross has been called the medicine of the world: It is the cure for this deep affliction, this neurosis within the soul that would have us mistake slavery for freedom. When the soul is divided, civilization begins to fall apart. The consciousness of God is the beginning of accepting the Cross. Once we understand that there is a God, He, by His grace, will show us that He is one, that He is merciful, and that He has the power to draw us unto Him. "I, when I am lifted up from the earth, will draw all men to myself" (John 12:32). Remember the way Our Lord revealed Himself to Moses: "I AM WHO I AM" (Exod. 3:14). He is the source of all life, and indeed of *being* itself. But if our souls are divided, if our civilization is split apart, we begin to lose the vision of God and His life-giving goodness that had been given to us. God told us,

---

[33] John Henry Newman, *The Idea of a University*, ed. Ian T. Ker (Oxford: Oxford University Press, 1976), 111.

"I AM." And yet, amid the remnants of a broken and decaying civilization governed by passion and pride, instead of proclaiming that God is the great I AM, we are reduced to sniveling observations about truth and eventually gasping out, "I don't even know what 'is' is!" Well, as long as we refuse to confront the reality of the great I AM, we will never really know what "is" is. We will never understand the grammar of civilization.

Grace and Truth (2019)

Pastors Poor Theorists

A pastor is too busy leading people in worship to attend workshops on how to lead people in worship, and his duties in the confessional prevent him from attending seminars on how to hear confessions.

Calm in Chaos (2018)

Perfection

We live in a generation that seeks to be dazzled rather than enlightened, amused rather than inspired, entertained rather than challenged and converted. The golden mean, as distinct from mediocrity, chooses the good over the convenient, the true over the plausible. And therefore, heroic virtue is needed to live the golden mean well. Jesus Christ not only showed the world the golden mean; He was the golden mean. This is why He confused so many people: some thought He was too rigid about the law while others thought He was too lax; some thought He was too worldly while others thought He was too supernatural. This balance is the content of perfection.

Grace and Truth (2019)

Perfection and Pity

Christ cannot be psychoanalyzed because He is perfect. It would be like seeking flaws in pure crystal or long shadows at high noon. That is why He may seem from our fallen state in a singularly ill-contrived world as both severe and merciful, ethereal and common, rebellious and routine, rustic and royal, solitary and brotherly, young and ageless. His perfection is a stubborn enigma to the imperfect, but if there were one hint of the art that moves His mind, it would be in His pity. It would be in His pity for the whole world when He weeps over Jerusalem; but most wrenchingly it would be in His pity for each soul when He sees us scattered on the hills like sheep without a shepherd.

Calm in Chaos (2018)

Perfectionists

Perfectionists are easily scandalized by what is not good. Saints are only scandalized by what is not glorious.

He Spoke to Us (2016)

"Personally Opposed, But ..."

For many painful years, serious social harm has been done by some Catholics in politics who compromised moral truth in order to get elected and enjoy the spoils of office. Their mantra on matters of moral evil has been that they are "personally opposed, but ..." St. Thomas More, appointed Lord Chancellor of England by King Henry VIII in 1529, knew that such duplicity can damn a man's soul and ruin nations. With elegance, kindness, brilliance, and cheerful wit he defended himself before a kangaroo court on the great Christian principles of the indissolubility of marriage, the primacy of the pope, and the freedom of the Church in relations with the state. False friends deserted him, his family was reduced to poverty, and he was beheaded on July 6, 1535. Once, when I read that a Catholic politician had removed a picture of the great martyr from his office during his election campaign, because it disturbed some of his staff, it struck me: while the loss of a head signaled the end of More's political career, it signaled the beginning of the political career of this other man. He won election to a governorship, through the inattentive voting of Catholics. At the University of Notre Dame he delivered a speech defending his compromise on abortion, which was enthusiastically received by the press. History will compare it unfavorably with St. Thomas More's speech before his accusers, so well portrayed in the play *A Man for All Seasons*.

A Year with Fr. Rutler (2017)

Pews: The Case Against

Pews contradict worship. They suburbanize the City of God and put comfort before praise.... Paradoxically, James Renwick, who designed the Cathedral of Saint Patrick in New York, was an Episcopalian, but he tried to explain to Cardinal McCloskey that pews were Protestant and inappropriate for a Catholic cathedral.

He was overruled by the cardinal, who installed the pews and rented some of the best ones for up to $2,000. This amount would be about $60,000 today. An engraving of the interior before it was consecrated, when a bazaar was held to raise money, shows how magnificent the space is and how that perspective is lost in a forest of wooden seats. I confess that a few years ago I restored worn pews in my former church, knowing that there was little time to form minds on the subject. In the few months that the church was empty of the pews, people came to admire the uncluttered proportions.

Ascetically, pews stratify the people as passive participants. There actually are churches where ushers, like maître d's in a cabaret, move down the aisle pew by pew, indicating when the people can go to Communion. Ensconced and regimented in serried ranks, the people are denied the mobility of sacred assembly.

Calm in Chaos (2018)

Pope John Paul II and Yalta

In the mid-nineteenth century, the poet and playwright Adam Mickiewicz dramatized the theme of his suffering Poland as the "Christ of Nations," and after the country had been deprived of its national identity for two centuries, the agony worsened, when Poland was crucified between the two thieves of Soviet Russia and Nazi Germany. It was not the West's proudest moment when President Roosevelt complained to Stalin at the Yalta Conference that "Poland has been a source of trouble for over five hundred years." The same Roosevelt had found it convenient to accept the Soviet propaganda attempt to blame the Katyn Forest massacres on the Germans. Pope John Paul II lamented Yalta in the encyclical *Centesimus Annus*. That will resonate in the annals of papal teaching more than recent magisterial concerns about the responsible use of air conditioning and the like. For those who have been crucified by tyrants, acquiescence in evil on the part of allies is more consequential than what can or cannot be done about the ozone.

Calm in Chaos (2018)

Porta Caeli

When looking at her calm features in the glass coffin in Nevers, we have to remember that, to the very end, St. Bernadette was aware of the devil's attempts to block life's heavenly progress. Racked with pain, she often murmured: "Heaven, heaven …" But as death came closer, she also cried out: "Go from me, Satan, go!" Ronald Knox's magisterial erudition on the subject of religious neuroses and delusions makes especially appealing his confidence in the integrity of Bernadette. Her practicality was polished by supernatural events to a lustre that philosophical pragmatism has never attained. Above the singing at Lourdes, her words form a descant: "When you are done with a broom, you put it behind a door, and that is what the Virgin has done with me. While I was useful, she used me, and now she has put me behind the door." The man who was known by thousands of Oxford undergraduates as "Ronnie" would remind them, with studied nonchalance, that the "door," by the way, was the Gate of Heaven.

The Stories of Hymns (2016)

Power without Truth

The Elizabethan philosopher Sir Francis Bacon ... said, "Knowledge is power." But hard experience has taught that knowledge of the truth is the key to the right use of power—otherwise, there is just raw power, which does not distinguish between right and wrong. Church law courts often bear the motto "There is no love without justice," which reaffirms the fact that love without justice is not love at all, but sentimentality, and justice without love is not justice at all but legalism. Mix sentimentality with legalism, and you have a diabolical recipe for cruelty. In the twentieth century, totalitarian systems separated power from truth. Once power is autonomous, independent of truth, it is unjust by its self-justification. In those ten decades of the twentieth century, apart from the horrendous deaths in wars, state-sponsored terror destroyed an estimated 170 million lives.

He Spoke to Us (2016)

"Praise to the Living God"

There is an unlikely congruity between the thirteenth-century Pope Urban IV, promoter of the Corpus Christi devotions, and the reviser of the hymn "Praise to the Living God," Thomas Olivers (1725–1799) of Montgomeryshire, in that the pope was the son of a French shoemaker and the orphaned Olivers was a shoemaker's apprentice. Their mutual patrons, the third-century shoemaker brothers Crispin and Crispinian, of course, shine in the speech Shakespeare gave his Henry V at Agincourt. That is about all that this eclectic group had in common, save for their saving devotion to Jesus Christ. Olivers came about it a hard way, having been expelled from his town of Tregonan for delinquency and then converting, not on the Damascus Road, but in Bristol, upon hearing George Whitefield preach. He became a Methodist preacher himself and is buried with John Wesley in London.

The Stories of Hymns (2016)

Prayer

Prayer indicates a desire to enter into God's plan for the universe.

A Year with Fr. Rutler (2017)

Preachers

There are two kinds of preachers: those who have something to say, and those who have to say something. Ars had a preacher with a whole gospel to preach.

The Curé d'Ars Today (1988)

The Price of Holiness

In the extraordinary events in Ars, which began in 1824 and lasted until a year before the saint's death, the terror and wonder of the confrontation between good and evil were palpable. Abbe Sandreau, an authority on exorcism, wrote in his treatise *The Mystical State*: "The devil acts on all men by tempting them; no one can escape those attacks; these are his ordinary operations. In other very much rarer cases, the devils reveal their presence by troublesome vexations, which are more terrifying than painful; they cause a great noise, they move, transport, knock over and at times smash certain objects; this is what is called *infestation*." Spiritual directors also list *obsession*, by which the individual is affected physically, and *possession*, by which devils act in and through the individual's consciousness. The Saint of Ars was victim of both infestation and obsession and had to deal with souls possessed. He paid the price of holiness, evoking the agony of the spirit of evil who has been vanquished by the Holy One, enduring a procession of explosive confrontations between enormous evil and greater good over a period of years almost identical to the life of Christ on earth.

The Curé d'Ars Today (1988)

Pride

At the age of sixteen, George Washington had laboriously copied out a long list of "Rules of Civility and Decent Behaviour" compiled by French Jesuits in 1595. Rule 47 said, "Mock not nor Jest at anything of Importance ... and if you Deliver anything witty and Pleasant, abstain from Laughing thereat yourself." Similarly, Rule 64: "Break not a Jest where none takes pleasure in mirth. Laugh not aloud, nor at all without Occasion." None of this was a formula for pomposity. This simply was a protocol for avoiding behavior that masks pride as humility.

A Year with Fr. Rutler (2017)

The Priest and the Judge

We ask the blessing of the Holy Spirit upon those who administer justice as judges and promote justice as attorneys because Christ taught the identity of the Holy Spirit with truth. The truth is bigger than any of us. Of this we are reminded when the priest and the judge both put aside their own clothes and put on robes that smother individuality and fashion and, by so doing, link them with a truth older than themselves and a power that is not their own.

He Spoke to Us (2016)

Priesthood

Last month, Pope Benedict XVI spoke of the priesthood when he went to Fatima and was heard by a throng even larger than the crowds that welcomed Pope John Paul II in 2000. He told half a million people, "We must cultivate an interior watchfulness of the heart which, for most of the time, we do not possess on account of the powerful pressure exerted by outside realities and the images and concerns which fill our soul." This is the power of holy meekness, which inherits the earth. The end of the Year for Priests is the beginning of a renewed response to St. John Vianney's definition: "The priesthood is the love of the heart of Jesus."

A Year with Fr. Rutler (2017)

Private Religiosity

The temptation to treat grace as a static commodity is as old as the gift of grace itself. St. Paul regretted that none of the other workers in the field of the Lord could match Timothy's zeal for souls: "They all look after their own interests, not those of Jesus

Christ" (Phil. 2:21). The apostle scorns the private religiosity of those who think keeping the Faith is justified in itself apart from spreading the Faith. Fidelity is not a spiritual form of intestinal retention.

Hints of Heaven (2014)

A Privilege of Professing the Creed

Our Lord's utterances stunned, enthralled, and shocked the crowds, but none was more startling than this: "I am the light of the world; he who follows me will not walk in darkness, but will have the light of life" (John 8:12). As the light itself, His human decibels shouted to the sky that His essence was not a creature but the Divinity, who creates physical light with the agency of the Father of lights with whom there is no variation or shadow due to change" (James 1:17) and who, with their Spirit, will "enlighten the hearts of the faithful" with the fire of love. Frail human voices have the inestimable privilege of professing that mystery each Sunday in the Creed: Jesus of Nazareth is "Light from Light" from beyond Nazareth.

He Spoke to Us (2016)

Proclaiming Christ to Non-Christians

Just as Our Lord commissioned the apostles to proclaim His triumph, so we have an urgent summons to do that today, for never has there been so much evil alive in the world, and so much ignorance about the Resurrection. The *New York Times* outdid its reputation for illiteracy about the Faith by publishing a correction: "An earlier version of this article mischaracterized the Christian holiday of Easter. It is the celebration of Jesus's resurrection from the dead, not his resurrection into heaven."

A Year with Fr. Rutler (2017)

Proclaiming Christ the Savior Is the Priority of Mission

An advertisement for a World Youth Day spoke of "celebrating life," "promoting the dignity of the human person," and "building a civilization of love." All well and good. But Christ was not mentioned once, nor was His gospel—because, I was told, there was a fear of alienating nonbelievers. This may be prudential proto-evangelization. But caution is not always prudent. General Sir Henry Macleod Leslie Rundle, GCB, GCMG, GCVO, DSO (1856–1934) "never took a risk and was rewarded by never suffering a reverse." At some point, the Lord of Life must be invoked as the cause of celebrating life, and some account must be given of the Source of the dignity being promoted, and someone will have to name the Author of the love that civilizes. I have never known anyone converted by a mere implication.

Hints of Heaven (2014)

Prodigies and Prodigals

We are prodigies by grace and prodigals by abuse of grace.

Hints of Heaven (2014)

Prodigal Son

God is a "righteous judge" who will not be swayed by clever attorneys or malleable juries. But the merciful Christ also says, "This is the will of him who sent me, that I shall lose none of all that he has given me, but raise them up in the last day" (John 6:39). It would be the sin of presumption to suppose that God's mercy does not require that we act justly. The prodigal son had to take the first step in the order of justice to return to the father.

A Year with Fr. Rutler (2017)

Progress?

A progress that is not toward God is an infinite regress.

The Curé d'Ars Today (1988)

Prophecy

Abraham Lincoln's self-effacement resulted in a most memorable miscalculation in the Gettysburg Address when he said: "The world will little note nor long remember ..." The Mother of Our Lord made an opposite and very accurate prediction, stunning as it was: "Henceforth all generations shall call me blessed." In her case, perfect humility dispensed with natural modesty. John the Baptist was the last of the prophets, which is why any religion that proposes Christ as a prophet but not the Son of God misses the whole point of true prophecy itself.

A Year with Fr. Rutler (2017)

Protestantism

Mainline Protestantism has practically disappeared, and endowments are its embalming fluid.

A Crisis of Saints (1995)

Public Life

Our society has come to take lying for granted. In fact, many people who lie in the public forum are admired for their cleverness in doing so. On the other hand, when a public figure is caught telling an inconvenient truth, we say that he has made a gaffe.

Grace and Truth (2019)

Public Penance

Catholics in America might consider performing in the near future some public act of contrition for the recent plague of miscreant church renovators and the vulgarities visited on Catholic altars.

Hints of Heaven (2014)

Public Thinkers

At a recent conference, I was introduced as a "public thinker." It was meant as a compliment, but I demurred, replying that the term is vague and, from my own experience, the only "public thinkers" I know are those poor souls I frequently see on the New York City subway talking to themselves.

He Spoke to Us (2016)

Publish or Perish

I remember with special affection a certain professor of mine, who once said to a prolific rival: "I see you've written another book. What are you calling it this time?"

Hints of Heaven (2014)

Quoting from the Saints

Vianney did not mind quoting reams from the saints: the treasury of merit, he said, was meant to be plundered. And with the sonorous ridicule of his old professors still loud in his ears, it seemed the safer course.

The Curé d'Ars Today (1988)

Rationalist, How to Define

Nothing can be more satisfying to reason than to be reasonable about it, and the definition of a rationalist is exactly one who is not reasonable about it.

The Curé d'Ars Today (1988)

Reality

We are the children of Adam and Eve. If we do not know that they walked this earth and fell for a terrible lie, we will live their lie as well. The prince of lies told our first ancestors that they could be as gods, and in accepting this lie, they entered into an imitation of reality where we are the focal point, the hinge on which reality bends. And when we live an imitation, we can no longer be at home with reality. Heaven is the ultimate reality, and if we lie and live a lie, we cannot be citizens of the eternal kingdom. That's why our first ancestors lost paradise.

Grace and Truth (2019)

The Reality of the Saints

There is nothing wrong in enjoying legends for their own sake, but the facts about the saints are more wonderful than any fable could be. St. Dorothy's apples, St. George's dragon, St. Nicholas's bags of gold are charming so long as they only charm. But they are something like the tinting of old black-and-white motion pictures by a new computer process: when a producer saw one of his old films colored that way, he said it was like pouring syrup on roast beef. To make St. Thérèse of Lisieux prettier than she was would diminish her great beauty; to parade St. Maximilian Kolbe as stronger than he was would mock his courage. You might say that St. John Vianney would become less brilliant than he was by any story that made him brighter than he was. It is good to remember that images of the saints should be severe and serious things, tokens of hard reality. And medals of the saints are not like the charms worn by people who do not know about the saints; holy medals ward off charm.

The Curé d'Ars Today (1988)

The Real Presence

Last week all of us were happily moved by the first Communions of some of the children of the parish. Aesthetically and ascetically, in beauty and in truth, I think all of us prayed that we might be able to make our Communion with Our Lord as directly and purely as did our newest communicants. He is truly with us, Body and Blood, Soul and Divinity, in a mystery beyond all adequate description but which the saints of the Church have called transubstantiation and have fallen down and adored. This is the heart of Christian life. Some ardent Christians who seek the power of the Holy Spirit have grown impatient with the forms of worship that Jesus Himself ordained and have drifted off into various heretical sects. Others continue to call themselves Catholics while substituting their own minds for the Infinite Wisdom that comes to us under the outward appearances of bread and wine. It is sad to seek Christ and settle for a substitute, but this is what the sectarians do when they remove themselves from the Real Presence of Christ in the Eucharist.

A Year with Fr. Rutler (2017)

Rebuilding Civilization

I know practically nothing about the inner workings of a computer, but I know a lot more about the history of the Saxon kings than the computer engineer who is patient when I have a problem with the Internet. Just as he does not think I am stupid for not knowing how to design a website, I do not belittle him for never having heard of the kings Aethelwald and Aethelberht. Together, resolving each other's ignorance, we might rebuild civilization.

A Year with Fr. Rutler (2017)

"Recovering Catholics"

Dissent within the Church can be far more raucous than assaults from without. Those who have never discovered Catholicism are not as caustic in their disdain as are those who claim to be recovering from it. Georges Bernanos said, "We do not lose our faith. We simply stop shaping our lives by it." The life that has lost its shape can be more destructive than the life that was not shaped at all, and this accounts for the "recovering Catholics" who are more bitter about why the Church is wrong than those who never thought the Church was right to begin with. Those who knew not what they were doing were forgiven from the Cross, while the man who knew what he was doing hanged himself.

He Spoke to Us (2016)

Reforming the Church

The Church Militant, which in its weakest moments may seem like a scattered and tattered regiment of the Church Triumphant, has supernal guarantees that the gates of hell shall not prevail against it. Any reformation of the Church that is not a transfiguration by the light of that confidence becomes a deformation.

He Spoke to Us (2016)

Regret

If there is any regret at all in Heaven, it may be the realization that in our short span in this temporal world, we did not discern the magnificence of ordinary things and did not perceive our true home in the House of God.

A Year with Fr. Rutler (2017)

Religion and Science

Parameters are measurable factors that define a system — like the parts that make the whole. The parameters of religion and science complement and serve each other but are not to be confused. Thus, Cardinal Baronio told his friend Galileo that the Bible tells us how to go to Heaven, not how the heavens go.

A Year with Fr. Rutler (2017)

Jesus loved the lilies of the field, more beautiful than Solomon in all his glory, but He beautified this world incomparably by passing through it with a reminder of its impermanence: "Heaven and earth will pass away, but my words shall not pass away" (Matt. 24:35). The Church has dogmas, but her parameters do not include making a dogma of unsettled science, just as in religion, "private revelations" are not binding on the faithful. Science, by its nature, is always unsettled, in any case. Today's certitudes may be disproved tomorrow, as with geocentricism centuries ago. Given these parameters, the Church must not allow herself to be appropriated by political and business interests whose tendency is to exploit benevolent, if sometimes naïve, naturalists.

A Year with Fr. Rutler (2017)

Revealed Truth

In recent times, the Church's desire for peace and unity among all people of goodwill has been misunderstood by some as a form of indifferentism to revealed truth, as if "all religions are basically the same" and "it doesn't matter what you believe as long as you believe something." The violence and terror in our world show that terrible things can happen when people believe wrong things. After September 11, 2001, Cardinal Biffi of Bologna reminded his people that Jesus commanded us to spread the news of His salvation: "It is an exact order from the Lord, and it does not allow for any sort of exemption. He did not tell us: Preach the Gospel to every creature, except for the Muslims, the Jews, and the Dalai Lama."

A Year with Fr. Rutler (2017)

The Reverent Expectancy of Advent

If the reverent expectancy of Advent has become, in the public square, drowned out by early, mostly secularized observances of Christmas, it is at least partly because a superficial culture is uncomfortable with the mysteries of Death, Judgment, Heaven, and Hell. But those subjects are discordant with the "Christmas spirit" only if that particular "Christmas spirit" is discordant with the Holy Spirit. Our nation and our entire world are engaged in a grave political crisis whose solution is to be found in what Christ has shown us about the Four Last Things. Mature adults do not distract themselves from threats of terrorism, war, domestic discontents, and their own mortality by singing "Rudolph the Red-Nosed Reindeer."

A Year with Fr. Rutler (2017)

The Richest Inheritance

William F. Buckley knew that piety is a virtuous combination of reverence for God and one's ancestors, and by making man ageless it saves him from the conceit that thinks that his generation is the first in history to have come of age. Some of his finest writing was the special art forms of obituary, eulogy, and panegyric. This he did with a special skill for members of his own family, which is the most difficult craft. His "autobiography of faith" is dedicated to his mother. His richest inheritance from his father was his religion. It is highly significant that he always added "Jr." to his name, long after his fame eclipsed his father's, for it was from his father that he learned the Faith of his fathers. It is also important that in a society in which marriage has become a temporary convenience instead of a sacrament, he was a faithful husband for fifty-seven years in sickness and in health until death. Without that covenantal understanding of human obligations, the philosophy of conservation is doomed to dwindle into an aesthetic sentiment.

He Spoke to Us (2016)

Right Judgment

St. Anthony Claret (1807–1870) said that right judgment is compromised by greed, sensuality, ignorance, and selfishness. He disparaged "independence of mind and will" as the inclination to see things as you want them to be, instead of as they are. This is the madness that does not let facts intrude upon judgment.

A Year with Fr. Rutler (2017)

On the Road to Damascus

St. Paul endured many hellish burdens and sufferings, and yet he never forgot the voice of Christ calling to him on the Damascus road, and that same voice inspired him with an ineffable joy through all his travels and preaching. As he wrote to the Christian believers in Corinth — which was a pretty hellish place for anyone of moral sensibility and aesthetic delicacy — "Eye has not seen, nor ear heard, nor have entered into the heart of man, the things which God has prepared for those who love him" (1 Cor. 2:9).

A Year with Fr. Rutler (2017)

Romans

John Henry Newman was a classical scholar. He had a particular fondness for the Latin writers, especially Cicero. Cicero was not only able to marshal the magnificent Latin language to express his ideas with eloquence, but he was able to convert others to his way of thinking. That is, he was not only a master of prose but a master of rhetoric. In a famous passage, Newman wrote, "Neither Livy, nor Tacitus, nor Terence, nor Seneca, nor Pliny, nor Quintilian is an adequate spokesman for the Imperial City. They write Latin. Cicero writes Roman." Now, whether or not we are familiar with that cataract of Latin writers, we can understand immediately what he means: Cicero did not engage in a mere literary exercise when he conjugated and declined the words of the noble Latin language; he put his heart into it. He was able to speak heart to heart.

Grace and Truth (2019)

Reform

Reform now, as always, will come about by our addressing the meaning and purpose of the human being. The worst times in human history have been caused by neglect of these realities; the best times have been the work of people humble enough to be shocked into the truth by the ugliness of such neglect. It can never be said enough: any crisis in culture is a crisis of saints, and no reform is radical enough unless it is a redemption from sin.

A Crisis of Saints (1995)

Relativism

Relativism is the attempt to realize unreality.

A Crisis of Saints (1995)

Remembering Mother Teresa

Mother Teresa silenced even a Jesuit who joked that she seemed to be getting smaller: "Yes, and I must get smaller until I am small enough to fit into the heart of Jesus." I still have the radiant memory of listening to her talk with my own mother on a visit to New York some years later, and it was like listening to two neighbors chatting over the backyard fence. Just as picturesque was the time in Rome when she led me by the hand through a large field of poppies on the periphery of the city and then served tea on a rickety table in the garden. Afterward, because there was a public transportation strike, she and another sister and I tried hitchhiking. No one gave us a lift, but Mother barely shrugged her shoulders. I have a picture of her wearing an insulated coat such as meatpackers wear when she arrived in the Bronx one winter night. When that picture was taken she winced because of the cataracts that had swollen her eyes. "Jesus told me to let the people take pictures, so I told Him to please let a soul out of Purgatory each time the light flashes." Her eyes could look ineffably sad, as when she heard that during Holy Hour in our hospice, a patient had hanged himself upstairs. There was no humbug about her.

Cloud of Witnesses (2009)

Of Rome and Salvation

Of Rome it has been said that one knows it well after a year and not at all after a lifetime. This is even more true of the mysteries of salvation.

He Spoke to Us (2016)

Theodore Roosevelt

On January 8, 1919, Theodore Roosevelt was buried in Oyster Bay. He was Dutch Reformed but rather skittish about theological matters. Natural virtue was his occupation, and he had an eye for it in others. He called Cardinal Gibbons the greatest living American, and he showed his admiration for St. Thomas More and St. John Fisher by hanging their pictures in his study. At Roosevelt's funeral, held in his wife's local parish church, which held far fewer people than ours, there was no eulogy and no music, although a minister recited the hymn "How Firm a Foundation." His estranged friend, President Taft, praised him by his silent attendance. All that might be said of bravery was testified to mutely by the battle flags on his coffin. In place of fulsome cant, the last prayer read was one written by Cardinal Newman. It had been the favorite of the president's son Quentin, who had been killed in battle the previous summer in France:

> O Lord, support us all the day long of this troublous life, until the shadows lengthen, and the evening comes, and the busy world is hushed, the fever of life is over, and our work is done. Then in Your mercy, grant us a safe lodging, a holy rest, and peace at the last.

A Year with Fr. Rutler (2017)

Rulers

If Christ does not rule our minds and hearts, mere men will try to do it, and they will do it badly.

A Year with Fr. Rutler (2017)

The eleventh-century King Canute is often mistakenly used as a symbol of arrogance for setting up his throne on an English beach and ordering the tides to withdraw. His goal was just the opposite: to instruct his flattering courtiers in the limits of earthly power. "Let all men know how empty and worthless is the power of kings, for there is none worthy of the name, but He whom heaven, earth, and sea obey by eternal laws." Canute then hung his gold crown on a crucifix in Winchester and never wore it again. It was commentary on God's words to Job: 'This far you may come and no farther.... Do you know the laws of the heavens?" (Job 38:11, 33).

A Year with Fr. Rutler (2017)

A Russian Proverb

A Russian proverb holds that when the Lord builds a church, Satan pitches a tent across the street. The endless agony of Lucifer without the Light is that he cannot get far enough away from the eternal brightness, and yet he is helplessly drawn to it, like an ugly moth to a lovely flame. There is some of that tension in those who talk incessantly about why they will have nothing to do with the Church. A Christ who does not inspire will seem to haunt. But only ghosts haunt, and Christ is not a ghost, for a ghost does not have flesh and bones as He has. This strange obsession is from a darker source.

He Spoke to Us (2016)

Sacraments of the Sacraments

The atheist denies God, but he ignores the saints; he would not do that had he not been influenced by a need to ignore them. The need assumes a paradoxical and even compulsive quality, like the nihilist insisting it is true that there is no truth or like the atheist believing that there is nothing to believe. But the saints continue to live visible lives. As the sacraments are outward and visible signs of an inward and spiritual grace, the saints are living sacraments; they are sacraments of the sacraments. And no story about them, no display of their souls' architecture, can be so grand and schematic as living their story with them. The voice of Ars said it: "At the Holy Altar I had the most singular consolations. I was looking at the Good God."

The Curé d'Ars Today (1988)

Sacred Music

In the Counter-Reformation, one of the most exuberant periods of Catholic artistic life, Giovanni Palestrina (1525–1594) promoted a system of intricate harmonies and descants that we call polyphony. Pope Marcellus assented to this, but he insisted that there be a *cantos firmas*, a consistent melody, which the harmonies may decorate but which remains consistent, audible, and predominate. In so doing, he gave us a musical model of what Newman meant by the continuity of type.

All great music is harmonious. It does not promote discord or evil passions. It has symmetry. It has a goal. Our friend Chesterton said that "jazz was the song of the treadmill." That may have been something of an arbitrary expression of taste, but he was expressing the essential principle that great music must have a goal; it must attain a finale. Plato banned from his ideal republic "corybantic" music, which was music that, through the use of repetitious drumbeats and nonsensical words, deliberately dimmed the intellect and inflamed the lower passions. Who could deny that popular music today is defined by precisely those aims?

We need not commit ourselves to any expression of arbitrary taste to say that Catholics must be committed to the exhibition and manifestation of grace in truth through the forms of art accessible to us. Pope Benedict XVI, in his wonderful writing on music, said that we must begin with the Gloria of the angels at the Incarnation, that celestial laughter that cheered the cold, neglected stable. He points out that in the traditional Mass, the Canon (the Eucharistic Prayer) was said silently as the Sanctus (the "Holy, Holy, Holy") was sung. This was because this celestial music of the cherubim accompanies, on the part of the gathered Church, the voice of the priest offering, in the name of Christ, the perfect sacrifice of the Body and Blood. With the choir and the clergy and the congregation all doing their part, they form a greater harmony, a kind of collective liturgical polyphony.

We have to wash out of our minds a lot of the more recent liturgical nonsense we've been fed. We have been afflicted with some of the most banal, brutal, ugly, destructive, and vicious substitutes for sacred music in our generation. Nevertheless, there endures that essential vision that motivates all the saints, the vision of the celestial laughter of Heaven come into our midst.

Grace and Truth (2019)

Safety

Nothing great or noble has been achieved by seeking safety.

A Year with Fr. Rutler (2017)

St. Anthony

St. Anthony ... was an Augustinian canon in Portugal who joined the new Franciscan Order in 1220, having been moved by the martyrdom of five Franciscans who had been beheaded by Muslims in Morocco. The year before, during the Fifth Crusade, St. Francis of Assisi narrowly escaped execution when he preached the gospel to Egyptian Muslims who had killed about five thousand Christians a few days before in Damietta. Anthony went to Morocco but became gravely ill, worked his way home via Sicily, and spent the rest of his thirty-six years preaching a combination of loving patience and mercy with bold insistence on Christ's truth and stern reproof of lax clerics. This is to be remembered when many voices today equate doctrinal orthodoxy with "rigidity" and portray the moral demands of Christ as distant ideals, if not impractical encumbrances. St. Anthony preached against the fanatical Albigensian heretics in southern France, whose misunderstanding of creation denigrated marriage and family life while promoting abortion, sodomy, and assisted suicide. They considered themselves more "spiritual" than Catholic "doctors of the law" and took Pharisaic pride in boasting that they were not Pharisees.

A Year with Fr. Rutler (2017)

St. Louis IX

One of the greatest men who ever lived was St. Louis IX, king of France in the thirteenth century. Louis represents all that was great and good about the High Middle Ages, which have been so misrepresented in recent times. Louis's father died when his son was only twelve years old, and so the boy's mother, Blanche, became regent. She was the daughter of Alfonso of Castile and Eleanor of England, and she was an extraordinary woman in her own right. She once said she would rather have her son die than commit a single mortal sin. Louis was dearly devoted to his wife, Queen Margaret, though it was difficult for Margaret to get along with her exacting mother-in-law. He was the father of eleven children, who were utterly devoted to him, as he and his wife were to them. There was in the family and their court that debonair spirit. Every aspect of culture felt his golden touch. In architecture, he gave us one of the most beautiful buildings in the world, the Sainte-Chapelle, as a shrine for what was believed to be Our Lord's crown of thorns. He cultivated reforms in the religious life, setting up several famous religious houses. In the administration of justice, he often listened to court cases himself. He was the court of last appeal, and people wanted to go before him because they knew he would rule justly. On one occasion, a young man was to be executed for treason for having participated in a rebellion led by his father. Louis refused to sentence him to death, saying, "It cannot be treason for a son to obey his father." He supported the theologian Canon Robert de Sorbon in establishing a center of studies that we know as the University of Paris, or the Sorbonne. For his charity, he was celebrated throughout Europe. He regularly served a dozen beggars at his table, and he established what is believed to be the first hospital for the blind. He also took the cross; that is, he enlisted in the Crusades. And it was on crusade in North Africa that he died, alongside his son, of typhoid. On August 24, 1270, at the age of fifty-six, St. Louis received the last sacraments. As he was dying, one of his final acts was to summon the Greek ambassadors and plead with them for the healing of the schism that had divided the Byzantine and the Latin churches. The next day, he lost his speech until noon, when he began to pray from the Psalms: "Lord, I will enter thy house. I will give thanks to thee in thy temple. And I will give glory to thy name" (Ps. 138:2, KJV). For the next three hours, just as Our Lord hung on the Cross from noon till three, he endured his last agony and then he uttered his last words: "Into Thy hands, I commend my spirit." That was a king. That was a man.

Grace and Truth (2019)

St. Patrick

If St. Patrick, whom the archdiocese of New York is privileged to invoke as its patron, could witness what has become of his feast in the streets of our city, he might think that the Druids were having their revenge.

A Year with Fr. Rutler (2017)

St. Patrick and Lent

There are places where there are Ash Wednesday and Easter and in between an extended St. Patrick's Day. Great Patrick would be the first to cry out against this from the heights of Croagh Patrick, his fasting place for all forty days. One could go to the other extreme and think of Easter as merely an interruption of a yearlong Lent. That is the piety of the rigorist for whom every silver lining has a cloud. Worse, there are certain Catholic types with the mottled spiritual complexion of the Jansenist nuns of Port Royal, who were "pure as angels and proud as devils." Patrick lit a Paschal fire, not a Lenten fire. All his fasts were for the feast ahead, and he knew that fasting is not only for the self, since in the Christian community one also fasts for the dead. A parable of the Lenten-Easter economy appears in the chronicles of Nennius the Briton and Tirechan the Gael. They wrote separately of how Patrick fasted another forty days on Mount Aigli near the end of his life:

> And the birds were a trouble to him, and he could not see the face of the heavens, the earth or the sea on account of them; for God told all he saints of Erin, past, present and future, to come to the summit of that mountain which

overlooks all others, and is higher than all the mountains of the West to bless the tribes of Erin, so that Patrick might see [by anticipation] the fruit of his labours, for all the choir of the saints of Erin came to visit him there, who was the father of them all.[34]

First, fast to starve the devil, then feast with the saints.

He Spoke to Us (2016)

St. Paul Unbound

We have inherited the tendency to rebel against the Lord of life. St. Paul analyzes himself: "For I do not do the good I want, but the evil I do not want is what I do.... Wretched man that I am!" (Rom. 7:19, 24). But he doesn't leave it at that. With a spirit of great joy, hope, and faith, St. Paul realizes and declares that Christ can get him out of that bind: "Who will deliver me from this body of death? Thanks be to God through Jesus Christ our Lord!" (Rom. 7:24–25).

Grace and Truth (2019)

St. Philip Neri

The feast of St. Philip Neri (1515–1595) falls this Monday, on the same day that the civil calendar memorializes those who gave their lives in the service of our country. Philip was a soldier, too,

---

[34] Quoted in the entry for St. Patrick in Herbert J. Thurston, S.J., and Donald Attwater, eds., *Butler's Lives of the Saints*, 2nd ed. (Allen, TX: Christian Classics, 1996), 615–616.

albeit a soldier of Christ, wearing "the helmet of salvation and the sword of the Spirit, which is the word of God" (Eph. 6:17). He lived in a decadent time when many who called themselves Christians chose to be pacifists in the spiritual combat against the world, the flesh, and the devil. In the battle for souls, Philip's most effective weapons were gentleness and mercy, though he was also a master of "tough love" when it was necessary to correct those inclined to be spiritual deserters. Although he was reared in Florence, Philip's pastoral triumphs gained him the title "Apostle of Rome." It was said of the emperor Augustus that he found Rome brick and left it marble, and in a moral sense the same might be said of Philip. The Sacred City was not so sacred in the minds of many, and his chief weapon for reforming it was penance. After eighteen years in Rome, Philip was ordained at the age of thirty-five. He polished rough souls every day in the confessional, where he might be found at all hours of the day and night for forty-five years. In the words of Blessed John Henry Newman, who joined the saint's Oratory three centuries later, "He was the teacher and director of artisans, mechanics, cashiers in banks, merchants, workers in gold, artists, men of science. He was consulted by monks, canons, lawyers, physicians, courtiers; ladies of the highest rank, convicts going to execution, engaged in their turn his solicitude and prayers." The oratorio is an audible relic of St. Philip: he invented that musical form as a means of catechesis. His magnetic appeal to the most stubborn and cynical types of people seems hardly less miraculous than the way he sometimes levitated during Mass, requiring that he offer the Holy Sacrifice privately. The pope prudently, if understatedly, explained that the spectacle might distract the faithful.

A Year with Fr. Rutler (2017)

Saints

Every saint is different in personality and in ways of serving the Lord, and for that reason certain ones will strike a sympathetic chord more readily than others. Some would have been easy to live with, and others decidedly difficult. But failure to rejoice in their sanctity is a judgment against us rather than against them. There is a line no less perceptive for having been mistakenly attributed to Plato: "We can easily forgive the child who is afraid of the dark, but the real tragedy is the adult who is afraid of the light." Sanctifying grace enables the light of Christ to shine not on, but through souls.

A Year with Fr. Rutler (2017)

The Saints and Their Current Cultural Reception

God has bestowed unspeakably great privileges on His people, and that is truer of us than of any generation: "Many prophets and righteous people longed to see what you see, but did not see it, and to hear what you hear, but did not hear it." But notice how our culture rejects the palpable evidence of miracles. The existence of saints is surely more taxing to the cynical observer than any miracles they perform. Still, it is wonderful how the inquisitive media, even in news reports about a pope declaring a new saint, almost completely black out information about the miracles that paved the way for the saint's canonization. You would expect these to be mentioned in the secular press, if only out of morbid curiosity or the desire for increased sales—but they are not. Similarly, the lives of the saints, the most vivid personalities in human history, are conspicuous by their absence from the university curriculum. Thomas More is the only saint mentioned in a sociology textbook used in a major New York university, and all the book says about him is that he was the "Father of Euthanasia." The authors apparently did not get More's joke: his *Utopia* describes an "ideal" society that practices euthanasia—but *utopia* is Greek for "nowhere," and the book is satire.

Hints of Heaven (2014)

The Saints and God's Grace

If you have the misfortune of arguing about religion, you will find yourself discussing doctrines, Church history, and the ups and downs of religious experience. But the one subject artfully avoided by the enemies of reality is the saints. The saints are living proof of how grace does not destroy nature but perfects it. Without grace, you cannot explain a saint. They are not people who are simply motivated by an exceptional interest in doing good. They are not people who just happen to have an extraordinarily high IQ. They are not people who manage to be at the right place at the right time. And they are not people who are able to manipulate crowds only by attractive personalities. Those excuses will not suffice to explain the saints. When St. Paul was still known as Saul of Tarsus, he had a highly trained mind and a degree of political influence. It was only after his conversion on the Damascus road, though, when he could cry out, "It is no longer I who live, but Christ who lives in me" (Gal. 2:20), that he became ever more vividly Paul the saint. He did not become less of a man because of Christ; he became more of a man. The denial of God and His grace—and therefore the denial of the reality of the saints — is at the root of all fantasy. To deny grace is to deny God's access to the soul. It would be very foolish indeed to say that a window is a window only at night. A window becomes ever more a window when the light shines through it. Well, that's the principal of grace; that's realism. The saints are powerful evidence that Christ works in history.

Grace and Truth (2019)

Saints and Legends

If legends attach themselves to the lives of saints, we should not be surprised. It is a way of acknowledging that saints are more than just heroes. For the most part, notables are chronicled instead of hymned. I am unaware of any description of congressmen, however remarkably honest, flying through the air on their own; even the most eloquent university presidents have not been alleged to carry their heads through the streets. The greatest heroes are honored for having done what they did, and not for doing more. But saints are sometimes said to have done more than they did, and this is because they were more than they were.

The Curé d'Ars Today (1988)

Saints and Trimmers

We recently celebrated the joint feasts of St. Thomas More, who was chancellor of England, and St. John Fisher, bishop of Rochester. Their personalities were different in many ways, and it was almost a miracle that an Oxford man and a Cambridge man got on so well and eventually were canonized together. The Act of Succession and the Act of Supremacy were the challenges that King Henry VIII threw at them, and the saints returned the challenge. The issues were rooted in natural law: the meaning of marriage and the claims of government. These are the same issues that loom large today. Whatever our courts of law may decide about these matters, St. Thomas says: "I am not bound, my lord, to conform my conscience to the council of one realm against the General Council of Christendom." In 1919, in *A Turning Point in History*, G. K. Chesterton predicted with powerful precision that, great as More's witness was then, "he is not quite so important as he will be in a hundred years' time." For every courageous saint back then, there were many other Catholics who instead took the safe path of complacency.

A Year with Fr. Rutler (2017)

The Saint of Ars and Father John Kronstadt

There are striking parallels between the Saint of Ars and his Russian contemporary, Father John of Kronstadt, to whom the French freethinkers were "learned men, yet did they not vividly personify the furies of hell!" His lifetime lasted from 1829 to 1908, during which he lived a life of great austerity, preaching the Risen Christ over against the ... myopia of rationalism. He lived on little more than almond milk, loved red vestments, absolved upward of three hundred penitents daily, instituted schools for technical job training, and lived the divine liturgy as heaven on earth: "Oh, my Lord Jesus Christ! Thou art all present! We see, touch, perceive, and feel thee here! The highest recompense for a Christian, especially a priest, is the presence of God in his heart. He is our life, our glory."

The Curé d'Ars Today (1988)

Salvation History

When Newman became a cardinal, he took as his motto a phrase of St. Francis de Sales: *Cor ad cor loquitor*, or "Heart speaks to heart." These words were vivified in Newman's life. The grace and truth of Christ passed through the soul of that great man Newman to his hearers, who ceased being only an audience and became participants in the drama of salvation.

Grace and Truth (2019)

Sanctity

The culminating evidence of sanctity is a joy that is not of this world. Saints always suffer in various ways as a consequence of their heroic virtue, which pits them against the "wickedness and snares of the devil," but there is no such thing as a sad saint.

A Year with Fr. Rutler (2017)

Sanctus, Sanctus, Sanctus

I was at the deathbed of a friend who had spent time in a Nazi prisoner-of-war camp. For the rest of his life—nearly seventy years—he thanked the Holy Trinity by regularly attending Nocturnal Devotion. While only mortal, kneeling before the Blessed Sacrament, he had the inestimable privilege that all of us have, of singing with all the angels and saints: *Kadosh, Kadosh, Kadosh. Sanctus, Sanctus, Sanctus.* Holy, Holy, Holy.

A Year with Fr. Rutler (2017)

Savonarola's Defense

In the moral order, one may not pass final judgment on another. Savonarola called that to the attention of a bishop who was damning him to all eternity.

He Spoke to Us (2016)

Science and Grace

The great Thomist Etienne Gilson writes in *Christianity and Philosophy*:

> A person always has the right to disdain what he surpasses, especially if what he disdains is not so much the thing loved as the excessive attachment which enslaves us to it. Pascal despised neither science nor philosophy, but he never pardoned them for having once hidden from him the most profound mystery of charity. Let us be careful, therefore, we who are not Pascal, of despising what perhaps surpasses us, for science is one of the highest praises of God: the understanding of what God has made.

As a man of profound rational equipment, Pascal took an almost sensual pleasure in humbling his reason. Nothing can be more satisfying to reason than to be reasonable about it, and the definition of a rationalist is exactly one who is not reasonable about it. By chalking up an outline of reason's limits, Pascal defined its rightful patrimony. He agreed with the ethereal votaries of Port-Royal so far as to say that the defective human will is a slave of concupiscence, but the inventor of the early computer saw what the morally blinded Jansenists would not see, that the sum of slavery minus its chains is liberty. In this he had a fraternity with Montaigne: the cultivation of habits, devotional practices, and the like can raise the basest souls to grace, for grace in its prevenient form disposes the soul to cultivate these things in the first place.

The Curé d'Ars Today (1988)

Science without God

Science without God is magic, and when science is magic it is also savagery.

The Curé d'Ars Today (1988)

Scripture and the Human Adventure

In every passage of Scripture and in every Eucharistic Sacrifice there is summed up the entire human adventure. We call this "recapitulation": this summing up is seen in every miracle of Our Lord and in every recorded human contact with Him. Our Lord wants us to understand these scriptural accounts as the summary of the big questions we ask about our history, our lives, our very selves. Consider the scene in Jericho, where Our Lord was passing by near that short fellow Zacchaeus. As a tax collector, he was a kind of quisling, a cooperator with a corrupt Roman authority. He was not a friend of His own people, and so he was despised. But he wanted to see Jesus. He knew what others thought of him, but that did not deter him. He was not obsessed with his self-image; he was obsessed with Christ.... Christ has been passing by throughout human history. Christ was passing by when the Roman

Empire fell. Christ was passing by when the Renaissance brought a momentary and blazing golden light to our civilization. Christ was passing by when the explorers crossed the ocean to discover what they thought was a New World. Christ was passing by when our own nation came into being. Christ was passing by when we were conceived. Christ is passing by every day of our lives. He's passing by when we are asleep and when we are awake, when we are at work and when we are at play. He's always there. Christ was passing by in Jericho, and He saw the diminutive Zacchaeus up on the branch of a tree, legs dangling. Zacchaeus knew he would be mocked, but he climbed the tree anyway. There's a lesson here: By being forgetful of the self, the self sees Christ. And Our Lord saw this funny man out of the corner of His eye. You might say Our Lord was being coy, for He really knew what was in the heart of that man, just as He knew the hearts of everyone in that crowd. Our Lord glanced up, and Zacchaeus looked down at Him. "Make haste and come down," Jesus said, "for I must stay at your house today" (Luke 19:5). This scene recapitulates every human life. The Christ who passes by from our conception to our death is always looking for us, and when He sees us make an act of humility, abandoning the self to see Him, He offers to come into our souls. Some lives are much longer than others, but everyone has a chance to invite Christ into the soul. And we do that by making ourselves accessible to Him.

Grace and Truth (2019)

A Second Nightcap for Socrates

Self-denial can strengthen the self as no glib kind of self-affirmation can. In California, I saw an advertisement for a preparatory school in which the top student in the senior class said that the school had taught her who she was, to feel good about herself, and to be satisfied with her choices. This Valley Girl vacuousness would have driven Socrates to drink a second nightcap. For those three smug confidences run afoul of the classical triad of erudition: self-knowledge is delusional without perception of eternal beauty; self-contentment eradicates the civilized discontent born of a quest for eternal truth; and satisfaction with one's choices is barbaric if one does not choose eternal good.

He Spoke to Us (2016)

Secularism

"Secularism" is not just a cultural fashion. It is the world's worship of its worldliness, the most degrading kind of narcissism. By its self-hypnosis, it is more subtle and thus more lethal than other heresies and tyrannies. All this was foreseen by Christ when He fortified His disciples with joy—while warning them of obstacles and obscurantists to come. "Rejoice, and be exceeding glad: for great is your reward in heaven: for so persecuted they the prophets which were before you" (Matt. 5:12, KJV).

A Year with Fr. Rutler (2017)

Secular Humanism

A mediocre civilization, as part and parcel of its rejection of the goodness of God, loses a sense of evil and, specifically, how evil came into the world. That is, it rejects original sin—but once you reject the idea of original sin, all you do is open the gates to it and all its cultural manifestations. A bland, naïve, secular humanitarianism is not Christianity. Christianity certainly must manifest itself in humane acts. But a humanitarianism that is separated from the realities of the human condition — that rejects both heroic virtue and the reality of sin — becomes antisocial and self-destructive. This kind of secular humanism in the political form of liberalism has been called "Christianity without the Cross." The golden mean led the noble minds of the past to understand, to one degree or another, the exercise of virtue. But it ultimately leads to the Cross, for the Cross is the ultimate balance between good and evil, between light and dark. This is the message that Christ came into the world to give. It is the message He displayed on the Cross, and it is the message that He empowered us to spread throughout the world through His Resurrection and Ascension and the gift of the Holy Spirit at Pentecost.

Grace and Truth (2019)

Secularists and St. Paul

Essentially, the secularist is not without religion: rather, he has made a religion of politics and wealth and rejects any religion that worships anything else. Now, to be secular is unavoidable for anyone who resides on this planet, except for astronauts, and even they have to come back down to earth. But secularism distorts secularity, just as racism makes a cult of race. The secularist makes a religion of irreligion and is different from the saints, who are "in this world but not of it," because the secularist is of the world but not rationally in it. This explains why the secularist's solutions to the world's ills are so destructive. The secularist is isolated from what is unworldly and thus lacks the perspective that adequately measures things of this world. In contrast, St. Paul was a most worldly-wise man and not least of all because he knew of a "third heaven" where a man, possibly himself, "heard things that cannot be told, which man may not utter" (2 Cor. 12:4).

He Spoke to Us (2016)

Sentimentalists

The cruelest people in history have tended to be extravagant sentimentalists, accepting flowers from children while they destroy infants, and glorifying mankind while despising men. The prince of lies is the definitive sentimentalist because he would have us live in a state of feeling instead of fact. He rejects the divine logic of Hell as the contradiction of Heaven and says they are the same. But logic wins in the end, as it did at the end of the twentieth century, when the utopias of tyrants were exposed as earthly hells.

A Year with Fr. Rutler (2017)

Separation of Church and State

The separation of the Church from the state was intended to free religion from the civil power. This does not mean that the Christian is not to be involved in the life of the state, nor does it mean that the state is to be run without obedience to God. In the encyclical *Immortale Dei* (1885), Pope Leo XIII said that rulers must set God before them as "their exemplar and law in the administration of the State."

A Year with Fr. Rutler (2017)

September 11, 2001

The horrific shock treatment of September 11 rattled three modern assumptions. The first was the politicized dismissal of natural law. The primacy of natural law was vindicated when people at the World Trade Center struggled to rescue one another, often sacrificing their lives to do so. A man leaving his apartment to go to work in one of the towers heard his wife crying that she was going into labor. Instead of going to his office, he took her to the hospital and watched his baby enter the world as his building collapsed. The baby's first act was to save his father. In a world of carnage in Bethlehem, men once heard the cry of the baby who saves all those who call upon Him, through all ages, even as late as September 11, 2001. The thousands of lives crushed on that day will make it harder to say that life does not count.

Secondly, the holy priesthood has been a victim of modern assault. God's gift of priestly intercession has recently become an object of incomprehension and mockery. Books were written on how the priesthood might be reformed out of existence. A saint once said that a priest is a man who would die to be one. On September 11, a chaplain of the New York City Fire Department was crushed while giving the last rites to a dying fireman. Members of his company carried him to New York's oldest Catholic church a few blocks away and laid him on the marble pavement in front of the altar. Each knelt at the altar rail before going back to the flames. I stayed a while and saw the blood flow down the altar steps. Above the altar was a painting of Christ bleeding on the Cross — the gift of a Spanish king and old enough for St. Elizabeth Ann Seton to have prayed before it. More than local Catholic history was encompassed in that scene. For those who had forgotten, the Eucharist is a sacrifice of blood, and it is the priest who offers the sacrifice. September 11 gave an indulgent world, and even delicate catechists, an icon of the priesthood.

The fall of the towers also toppled modern man's third error: his contempt for objective truth. The whole world said that what happened on September 11 was hideously wrong, and suddenly we realized how rarely in recent times we have heard things that are hideous and wrong called hideous and wrong. So many firemen wanted to confess before entering the chaos that we priests gave general absolution. They would not have wanted to confess if they had not known the portent of the moment; nor would they have made the Sign of the Cross if they had thought existence was a jumbled quilt of inconsequential opinions. A rescue worker next to me boasted that his lucky penny and his little crucifix had saved him when he was tossed ten feet in the air by the reverberations of falling steel. He got up, brushed himself off, and went back into the bedlam. If he was superstitious, he was only half so. Pope John Paul II has often been patronized by savants who thought that his description of a "Culture of Death" was extravagantly romantic pessimism. They have not spoken like that since September 11.

He Spoke to Us (2016)

The Sermon on the Mount

To understand the joy of the Sermon on the Mount, one has to look to the other mounts: Tabor, where the Light of Christ shone; and Calvary, where that Light shone in the darkness and "the darkness has not overcome it" (John 1:5).

A Year with Fr. Rutler (2017)

Serpents

Everyone wants to go to Heaven, even those who consciously deny its existence, and certainly those who would lengthen their earthly years; for Heaven, as the state of perfection, is the soul's ultimate good, and, in the stubborn conundrum of the Scholastic theologians, it is impossible not to will one's good. Were a man so perverse as to want to kill himself, that would be his twisted notion of what is good for him in that moment; and were he to desire Hell, he would want to go there because his infernal imagination gave Hell the quality of Heaven. The prophet promises "woe unto them that call evil good" (Isa. 5:20), knowing that there are those who do precisely that, and they do it not only because evil is the opposite of the good but because that opposition postures as good itself. The Serpent in the Garden did not tell our first parents that they would be as serpents.

The Stories of Hymns (2016)

The Seven Gifts of the Holy Spirit

In the sacrament of confirmation, the Holy Spirit completes His work begun in baptism, which washes away original sin, by placing ("infusing" or "sealing") seven gifts in the soul. These help one live the Christian life by perfecting the virtues. God does everything for a purpose. Four of the gifts of the Holy Spirit perfect the intellectual virtues. The purpose of the gift of *understanding* is to give an intuitive and penetrating perception of truth. *Wisdom* perfects love, by enabling a right appreciation of how God's love works. *Knowledge*, by discerning the divine plan in events, perfects the virtue of hope. *Counsel* increases prudence. Those four gifts, then, perfect the virtues pertaining to the intellect. The intellect is one element of the soul. Three other gifts perfect the other part of the soul, which is the will. The gift of *piety* perfects the virtue of justice by ... refining our relations with others and most especially with God. *Fortitude* strengthens ordinary courage in the face of dangers. *Fear of the Lord* perfects the virtue of temperance by disciplining unruly desires and destructive appetites.... The gifts of the Holy Spirit move the soul from philanthropy to sanctity.... Many earnest people are like those disciples in Ephesus who believed in Jesus but did not know there was a Holy Spirit. Parishes can lapse back into that ignorance, which is worse than starting out ignorant. Frequent confession and Communion help keep the seven gifts alive. And when they are alive, they can change the whole neighborhood, city, and all of civilization.

A Year with Fr. Rutler (2017)

Simplicity

Hell is all that Heaven is not; Satan is all that God is not; the angels are all that evil spirits are not; the saints are all that sinners are not; and the Church is all that chaos is not. That is putting it negatively; you can say the same thing positively just by reversing the order, and it is equally true. And it is also equally simple. Complications indicate that we have yet to understand the whole economy of the universe. What is called the Universal Theory of the Universe, or the Theory of Everything, or a variant of String Theory, is the Holy Grail of physics: the explanation of how all matter is coordinated and behaves. The physicist John Wheeler of Johns Hopkins and Princeton said some years ago that he did not know if such a formula could be found, but he expected that, if it were discovered, the most surprising thing about it would be its simplicity.

A Year with Fr. Rutler (2017)

Skeptics and Cynics

There is a difference between skepticism and cynicism. The skeptic questions the truth, while the cynic questions the existence of truth itself. A skeptic is cautious about being disappointed by a lie. A cynic has been disappointed. There is a saying: If you hug a skeptic, he'll ask if you really mean it; if you hug a cynic, he'll check to see if you took his wallet.

He Spoke to Us (2016)

Slavery

The mysterious and — for the lukewarm — unpleasant reality is that if we allow ourselves to be enslaved to mortal sin by the prince of lies, we are excommunicated for all eternity, and the word for that is damnation. In the first Eucharistic Prayer, we pray to be saved from this damnation. Christ saves us from that.

A Year with Fr. Rutler (2017)

A Slavic Aphorism

A Slavic aphorism, attributed to St. John Climacus, has it that "a man can be damned alone, but he can only be saved with others." Certainly, from about the time of the Enlightenment, this idea began to seem remote and exotic; the failure to understand it has led to middle-class cults of self-affirmation and hostility to apostolic institutions. By these mistaken routes, people isolated from their creation hold their own maturity ransom. They accuse saints like Vianney of neurotic sublimation, and then they proceed to socialize neurosis through a sublimation of private guilt which they do not understand and will not confess.

The Curé d'Ars Today (1988)

Soldiers and the Sick on Christmas

While many of our own parishioners travel away from the city on Christmas, many visitors come to us, some for the first time. As we gather, we remember those of the parish who are unable to leave home, who are in the hospital, and those of our parish serving as soldiers in Iraq and elsewhere. We are united around the altar of the Eucharist with all the saints and angels and the faithful departed, worshipping Our Savior in the angelic song of the Thrice Holy. If we have kept a good Advent, we can rejoice that Christmas does not fade wearily on Christmas Day. Christmas lasts twelve days—and for those who worship the Incarnate God, it lasts a lifetime.

A Year with Fr. Rutler (2017)

Solemnity

We celebrate the joy of eternal life with special solemnity in Eastertide, knowing that "solemnity" really means not dourness but elegant serenity.... In this spirit, we have to give thanks to all those who selflessly have helped with the joyful solemnities of Easter. St. Paul thanked his helpers in Rome and Galatia and Corinth, and we should thank our own helpers, hoping that our parish matches the good spirit of those churches without all of their concomitant enormities.

A Year with Fr. Rutler (2017)

The Soul in Harmony

When the soul is full of grace and truth, it sings. This is an instinct of the human condition: when we are happy, we sing; and when we are sad, we sing. One kind of song praises order, and the other mourns the collapse of an order. Harmonious music is heavenly laughter come to earth. When Our Lord was born, the heavens opened, and a great joy was heard as the angels sang, "Peace among men with whom he is pleased!" (Luke 2:14). In other words, it is only the soul in harmony with God that can understand the song of Heaven.

Grace and Truth (2019)

Spin

In an age that has abandoned most refinements of manners, lying has become a governing etiquette. This may be a result of the general philosophical confusion about truth, but a mental breakdown of culture is rooted in a deeper and more universal heartbreak, for the twentieth century has not ended as people at its start expected. Those who promised a golden age and those who feared an apocalypse have been disabused. We have a society of some who lost faith in faith and others who more wildly lost faith in faithlessness, and in the general whirlwind, "spin doctors" replace the venerable doctors of souls.

Calm in Chaos (2018)

The Spirit of the Age

Satan's chief enemy is the Church, for this is Christ alive in the world. From hard experience the Church knows the temptations of secularism (reducing Christianity to philanthropic humanism), clericalism (bartering supernatural grace for social power), and subjectivism (living in a parallel universe contemptuous of moral reality). To succumb to these temptations is to die, both personally and institutionally. The latest figures show that those denominations that surrendered to "the spirit of the age" are vanishing.

A Year with Fr. Rutler (2017)

Spiritual Discipline

Spiritual discipline, through acts of penance, also inoculates us against the sentimental attitude that measures reality according to our "feelings." What we feel about anything has nothing to do with what is right or wrong, and "feeling good" about ourselves is no guarantee that we are doing God's will. So prayer should be "constant in season and out of season" (2 Tim. 4:2), and not just when we feel like it. Our greatest dignity consists in the fact that God has made us able to think about Him, to serve Him, and to love Him. These approaching Lenten weeks of the Church year are His way of reminding us of that.

A Year with Fr. Rutler (2017)

Spiritual Warfare

As we are in the world, we are stewards of creation and fight daily in human struggles, but as we are promised eternal life, we also are engaged in a supernatural struggle against Satan himself. Human solutions to social problems are bound to fail if they do not acknowledge the reality of evil. King David was hounded by a madman, Shimei, who pelted him with stones. David was patient with him because, just as a broken clock is right twice a day, Shimei was shouting out some things that were at least partially true (2 Sam. 16:5ff.). But that was a strictly human confrontation, involving the natural virtues of prudence, justice, temperance, and fortitude. When Jesus was frequently challenged by Satan and his legion of evil spirits, the struggles were other-worldly, involving the theological virtues of faith, hope, and love. Unlike Shimei, who only suffered some sort of mental illness, the raver in the land of Gerasenes was possessed by demons. The townspeople were not only amazed at the power of Jesus; they also were eager for Him to get out of town, because they had grown comfortable with the brooding presence of evil and were unsettled by the presence of someone who was good beyond what they thought was possible. In short, practical solutions for daily problems are impractical if they do not invite Christ into the soul, guiding the intellect and the will.

A Year with Fr. Rutler (2017)

The State of Education in America

I don't think I'm telling tales out of school when I say that our schools are not what they should be. And that's putting it mildly. I think the state of education in the United States, on the whole, is in meltdown.

Grace and Truth (2019)

Syllabus of Errors

The disillusionment of Pius IX, expressed in the *Syllabus of Errors* five years after the death of the Curé d'Ars, was stamped with the same realism of Newman, and for that reason it was a specimen of hope. I say that because disillusion employs reality to subvert those illusions that, when mistaken for the way things really are, sow the seeds of a thousand pessimisms. The courage to be objectively disillusioned requires hope in objective truth, and hopeful the pope was. Indeed, he was so animated by the virtue that he braved wide ridicule in order to deny "that the Roman Pontiff can and ought to reconcile himself and reach agreement with progress, liberalism, and modern civilization." The phrase was laughed to scorn; but the laughter is now being drowned out by the disappointed howls of those who trusted progress, liberalism, and modern civilization. The pope did not deny the vernacular facts and goods of cultural advancement, or equality of social initiatives, or the scientific future; but he refused to impute to those things the naturalistic definitions of atheism. He dignified his opponents by using their terms exactly as they meant them, and his categories sound arcane only if they are not understood in that sense. So he was not Canute holding back the sea; but he was the fisherman who knows much about the sea, who knows that the sea rolls back and forth and that Christ has walked steadily upon it. Canute was the progressivist, the liberal, the modernist, who thought he could command the sea of time and events by reciting the molecular formula for water.

The Curé d'Ars Today (1988)

Tears

If all the tears shed in a parish church could be bottled, I think the oceans would look small. All tears. Not only of grief. Some are shed raucously at weddings and more softly when a baby is held over the baptismal font. But the greatest tears are in confession.

Hints of Heaven (2014)

Temptation and Holy Mother Church

A human mother knows the temptations that will beset her child, and if she lives long enough, she can observe and nurture that child, physically and morally, as he grows into maturity. But the Church, in her supernatural maternal character, knows the temptations of all stages of life, from infancy to the grave. And so she warns us that in youth we'll be tempted especially by lust, in middle age especially by the thirst for power and control, and in old age by that most insulting affliction of all—Satan's last chance to grab us — and that is greed. For greed is the weak and feeble human attempt to fabricate eternal life. The maternal memory of the Church knows how illusory all of these deceits are.

Grace and Truth (2019)

Terrorism

There are some today in public positions who underestimate terrorism, in some instances calling it "workplace violence." They are like Ambassador Joseph E. Davies (1876–1958) who said in 1938: "Communism holds no serious threat to the United States." Those who see good and evil as abstractions do not expect hatred of the holy to take any serious toll. The Quran says of Jesus, "They killed him not" (Sura 4). St. Paul says, "For many walk, of whom I have told you often (and now tell you weeping), that they are enemies of the cross of Christ" (Phil. 3:18). To deny this is to deny reality.

A Year with Fr. Rutler (2017)

Terrorist Reality Explicated

The chorus of shock after the terrorist attacks in Paris in 2015 became a cliché: the scenes were "unreal and inexplicable." Yet they were not without precedent. When the Nazis tramped along the leafy boulevards in 1940, there was shock, but there was also an air of inevitability about it. After all, there had been warnings and threats, and the defenses had not been what they should have been. True, Hitler was a madman, but — and I can attest after many years as a chaplain in a mental institution — one can be both insane and intelligent. Thus, the Chestertonian line about madness being the loss of everything except reason. So the madmen who attacked Paris this year were not wild but rather agents of a careful calculus scripted in the arabesques of the Quran nearly fourteen hundred years ago, when the jihadists rode throughout the Middle East from Palestine to Pakistan.... Only those hiding under their beds would call the latest slaughters in Paris "unreal and inexplicable."

Calm in Chaos (2018)

Thanksgiving

It is ironic that the Puritan settlers in the Plymouth Colony are so much associated with a thanksgiving feast, because they were dogmatically opposed to ritual feasts, and they had rejected the Holy Eucharist, which supernatural grace makes into the highest possible act of thanksgiving. We have been told often enough that "eucharist" is "thanksgiving" in Greek. Thanksgiving is almost a definition of civility, Puritan or Catholic. Parents begin to civilize their little ones when they get a gift: "What do you say?" And the answer, "thank you," starts the child on the paths of all good things. This is more than a lesson in etiquette. It is training in the art of an eternal grace: saying thanks to the giver changes a passive receiver into an active associate of some sort. That is not putting it well, but it does help to explain how gracious thanksgiving can make people into good citizens, earthly and heavenly, by making them patriots and saints. The categories are not inseparable, but neither are they contradictory.

A Year with Fr. Rutler (2017)

Things

If Catholics behaved as Catholics, our culture would not be satisfied with getting little things from elected officials in exchange for our moral dignity. If we only want things, we shall only be things.

A Year with Fr. Rutler (2017)

To Tempt God

Unsought mortifications are more difficult than self-prescribed ones. Patience with long lines at the supermarket, rock music on public address systems, and the wrong people running things can be harder spiritual trials than fasts and vigils. If forty days pass with our thinking we have kept a good Lent, we have kept a bad one. That would break the commandment against tempting God. To tempt God is to put His justice to the test by the ridiculous spiritual impertinence that authors of spiritual manuals delicately call "presumption." It is what provoked the biblical imprecations against meretricious rituals and abominable sacrifices. This is a point that may have eluded a Catholic archbishop in South Africa who, in an earnest effort to make worship more indigenous, recently proposed sacrificing cows for blood libations at Mass. I never expected to have to take up my pen against animal sacrifice, but new occasions teach new duties. The Eucharistic Sacrifice is different from all the other sacrifices of all the religions that have ever tried to appease Heaven. First, it is all-sufficient, so we need not turn the sacristy into a butcher shop. Second, it is rational and therefore inseparable from moral truth. In Romans, St. Paul declares the Eucharist to be an offering of spirit and mind, and Joseph Cardinal Ratzinger has identified intuitions of this in the ancient Dead Sea and Alexandrian Jewish communities. The moral dimension of the "reasonable sacrifice" (*logike latreia*) of which Lenten anticipation is a prophecy and an icon is the reason we call this sort of presumption a bad thing, like praying to God without having first incarnated that prayer in acts of charity or like receiving much Communion and confessing little. We may tempt God—that is the tawdriest privilege of a free will—but God is not mocked. Not for long. Presumption has its consequences. Look at the 360 degrees of desolation around us. Look at our parishes. Lent should mean more of both confession and Communion, spiritual reading, examination of conscience, benevolent acts, and prayer issuing in resolution.

He Spoke to Us (2016)

Thy Will Be Done

Pride complicates life, and humility simplifies it, and total humility attains spiritual perfection. St. Teresa of Calcutta had a formula for this: "Just give God permission." Once a soul "gives God permission" in confession and daily mortification of selfishness, God empowers the virtues to accomplish what He wants. The sublime consummation of this is in Our Lord's own obedience to His Father at the start of His holy agony: "Not my will but Thine be done" (Luke 22:42).

A Year with Fr. Rutler (2017)

Tiepolo in the Confessional

When Jesus describes the father running out to meet the son with compassion and joy in the parable of the Prodigal Son, you can already see the wounds in His hands and the light of the Resurrection dawning behind Him: "Your brother was dead and is alive again, and was lost and is found" (Luke 15:32). In my confessional I have an engraving of Tiepolo's painting of this scene. The actual scene is lived out every hour of every day in the confessionals of Catholicism.

Hints of Heaven (2014)

Tradition

If Pius IX said that he was tradition, "*La tradizione sono io*," we can give thanks for such audacious humility. Every schismatic has said one way or another, "I am the alternative to tradition!" The bishop of Rome does not invent tradition; he locates it.

A Crisis of Saints (1995)

The Transfiguration

The Transfiguration is celebrated on the sixth of August, but an account of it is also proclaimed as the liturgical Gospel in Lent, because it was a way in which the Lord prepared Peter, James, and John for the Crucifixion. These were the same apostles who would be with the Lord as He sweat blood the night before His death. Immediately after His Transfiguration, Christ would cure an epileptic suffering a violent seizure at the foot of the mountain: glory and agony within a few hours. The unearthly light that shone from Christ on the mountaintop strengthened the apostles for when they would watch the sky grow dark on Good Friday. Even so, the apostles still would not fully understand why Christ had to die: when Our Lord told them that He must go to Jerusalem and "be lifted up," Peter said He would not allow it. What the fisherman meant as a brave act of love, Jesus said was the work of the evil one using Peter: "Get behind me, Satan" (Matt. 16:23). Satan uses people in attempts to block God's plan, fooling and flattering them to use their power and talent to obscure the radiance of God. Sometimes he does this through individuals, and other times through political movements and false religions.

A Year with Fr. Rutler (2017)

The Tranquility of Order

The recent action of our government's executive branch to protect our borders and enforce national security is based on constitutional obligations (art. 1, sect. 10 and art. 4, sect. 4). It is a practical protection of the tranquility of order explained by St. Augustine when he saw the *tranquillitas ordinis* of Roman civilization threatened. St. Thomas Aquinas sanctioned border control. No mobs shouted in the marketplace two years ago when the Terrorist Travel Prevention Act restricted visa waivers for Iran, Iraq, Syria, Sudan, Somalia, Libya, and Yemen. The present ban continues that, and only for a stipulated ninety days, save for Syria. There is no "Muslim ban," as should be obvious from the fact that the restrictions do not apply to other countries with Muslim majorities, such as Egypt, Indonesia, Pakistan, Malaysia, Bangladesh, and Turkey. These are facts ignored by demagogues who speak of tears running down the face of the Statue of Liberty.

At issue is not immigration, but illegal immigration. It is certainly manipulative of reason to justify uncontrolled immigration by citing previous generations of immigrants to our shores, all of whom went through the legal process, mostly in the halls of Ellis Island. And it is close to blasphemy to invoke the Holy Family as antinomian refugees, for they went to Bethlehem in obedience to a civil decree requiring tax registration, and they violated no statutes when they sought protection in Egypt.

A Year with Fr. Rutler (2017)

Travel

Travel is nothing more than motion until it becomes a pilgrimage.

The Curé d'Ars Today (1988)

The Triumph of Holy Reason

The attention span of a man being crucified is limited.... Unremitting pain, asphyxiation, delirium, exposure, and dehydration do not ordinarily concentrate the mind. All the more remarkable, then, that one of the thieves on the cross with Our Lord during His Passion should have turned to the other unfaithful thief and asked: "Do you not fear God, since you are under the same sentence of condemnation? And we indeed justly; for we are receiving the due reward of our deeds; but this man has done nothing wrong" (Lk 23:41). Here was a triumph of holy reason.

The Seven Wonders of the World (1993)

Truth

In the sixth chapter of the book of Proverbs is a list of things abominable to God, and one of them is lying (v. 17). God is truth. His Word is truth. He is the truth itself. When He came into the world as Christ, He said it clearly: "I AM the way and the truth and the life." The way to Heaven depends on our obedience to the truth of God. And our obedience to the truth of God, in turn, bestows eternal life. Without the truth, we lose our way — and we die.

Grace and Truth (2019)

Truth and Theory

There is a school of philosophy called idealism. It doesn't mean reaching for the highest and best, but rather believing that something is true simply because it is your idea. The French have glorified Western civilization in many ways over the centuries, but since at least the time of Descartes, many French thinkers have placed more confidence in their pet theories than in demonstrable facts. It is said that a typical French philosopher will ask, "That may be true in practice, but how is it in theory?" For two thousand years, the world has been tempted to deal with Christ that way — to say that He did wonderful things but that the moral and spiritual theory behind His practice just doesn't work. The Trinity doesn't work. The whole idea of the Word Made Flesh doesn't work. Would it not be better to let Him be the humanitarian, the reformer, the social liberator and leave it at that? But Our Lord did not come into the world to be merely a humanitarian or a reformer or a social liberator. He came to reconcile earth and Heaven. That is why He said that He had accomplished the work His Father had given him to do: He has let the world see God.

Grace and Truth (2019)

The Truth, Not Truths, Will Set Us Free

Our Lord promises that the truth will set us free: not truths, but truth, and that truth is Himself. In Him is the explanation of Death, Judgment, Heaven, and Hell. All facts, physical and moral, issue from Him who "is before all things, and in him all things hold together" (Col. 1:17). The "holy grail" of physics, a Unified Theory of the Universe, may not be attainable; but Einstein's close friend John Wheeler, of Johns Hopkins and Princeton, predicted shortly before he died in 2008 that if it is found, the biggest surprise about it will be its simplicity. Jesus could not have expressed Himself more simply when he told Pontius Pilate: "Everyone who is of the truth hears my voice" (John 18:37). Pilate's life in a backwater of the empire was a dreary routine mired in cynicism. But even Pilate was amazed that Christ's own people had "handed Him over" to the government. By their own declaration when Pilate took a poll of them, they wanted "no king but Caesar." Each generation is tempted to hand Christ over to cynics. We do it when we barter our conscience for comfort and our freedom for frivolity.

He Spoke to Us (2016)

The Two Sons of the Parable

There were two sons who promised to help out in the vineyard.... One son tells his father flat out that he will not work for him (Matt. 20:1–16). He is no hypocrite, but that alone will not get him a day on the Calendar of Saints. A man may follow his conscience all the way to Heaven, but he may also follow it all the way to Hell. Publicans and harlots will go to Heaven before the self-righteous hypocrites, but not because of publicanism and harlotry. They repented and believed. The son is saved because eventually he does go to work. The second son makes florid promises and is a darling for it, but he does not mean what he says. Here is every dishonest politician on inauguration day, every spoiled youth making marriage vows with the ink still wet on a premarital agreement about dividing property. Here, too, is the sad fellow who became a priest to please his family or to hide some moral pathology. St. Ignatius knew his spiritual army needed men as brave as their intentions and so in the *Spiritual Exercises* he wrote, "One must not swear, neither by Creator nor by creature, unless it be with truth, necessity, and reverence."

Hints of Heaven (2014)

The Two Thieves and Forgiveness

Need we forgive the most despicable of people? Answer the question like a saint—for saints consider themselves the most despicable. (The fact that they are so wrong about themselves highlights that they are so right about everyone else.) Now answer the question like Christ, whose blood absolved us. I have no chart to convert His blood into modern dollars, but I do know it was poured out freely at great cost. It is ours for the asking, but *only at the price of everything that prevents our asking.* That was the dilemma of the two thieves crucified with Christ. Only one was generous enough to ask.

Hints of Heaven (2014)

Understanding the Curé d'Ars

Vianney did things thought to be impossible, and he did them with an innocent blatancy. Some may be hard for us to believe if we are not scientific enough to recognize the limits of science. Henry IV called James I the wisest fool in Europe for knowing what he did not know; it is a talent helpful in understanding the Curé d'Ars.

The Curé d'Ars Today (1988)

An Unheavenly Scene

Our Lord said ... that damnation awaits those who call themselves Christians but do not spread His grace. They are fixtures in an unheavenly scene: "waterless clouds, carried along by winds; fruitless trees in late autumn, twice dead, uprooted; wild waves of the sea, casting up the foam of their own shame; wandering stars for whom the nether gloom of darkness has been reserved for ever" (Jude 12–13).

Hints of Heaven (2014)

Unearthly Innocence

The Church is the shrewdest of all institutions and has outlived all others because she is born of an unearthly innocence.

Hints of Heaven (2014)

Universities and the Resurrection

The historic universities produced some of the most illustrious saints; they taught the ordering of the imagination along with the intellect and will in the search for God's truth. Supreme confidence in the humble use of the intellect moved Newman's vision of learning as fearless adventure, and this he unrolled sonorously in *The Idea of a University*: "The Catholic is sure, and nothing shall make him doubt, that if anything seems to be proved by astronomer, or geologist, or chronologist, or antiquarian, or ethnologist, in contradiction to the dogmas of faith, that point will eventually turn out, first not to be proved, or secondly, not contradictory, or thirdly, not contradictory to anything really revealed, but to something which had been confused with revelation." Universities have now become largely irrelevant to the integrity of the social order and, indeed, centers of social and intellectual confusion, by having lost the will to be what God wishes them to be. A recovery of their social function will have to begin with a consideration of the meaning of sanctity. And this in turn will require their affirming the resurrection of the dead as the hope of life and learning.

The Seven Wonders of the World (1993)

Vacations

Against my better judgment, and at the urging of numerous people with mixed motives, I took a vacation in July. A retired bishop had told me I should take one. I objected that I had no need to go away, since I love what I do and do not need a vacation from it. He replied that I may not need a vacation, but perhaps my parish does.

He Spoke to Us (2016)

G. K. Chesterton said that "travel narrows the mind."[35] By this he meant that we appreciate things foreign when they are far away, but when we travel and encounter them, we focus on how different we are from them. I pray that I may keep my anxious vow, frequently broken, never to fly again. As a theologian, I know that if God had wanted man to fly, he would not have given us the railroad. So that is all I have to say about the strange custom of going on vacations.

He Spoke to Us (2016)

The Varieties of Blindness

Physical blindness is a condition; moral blindness is a choice.

The Seven Wonders of the World (1993)

Vatican II and the Liturgy

At Vatican II the Church had called for a restoration of the noble simplicity of the Roman rite in areas where it had become obscured; but this was what Pius V wanted, too, in 1570. Pius XII had placed himself in that direction, as had Clement VIII in 1604 and, more incidentally, Urban VIII and Pius X. The paramount

---

[35] "What I Saw in America," in *Collected Works of G. K. Chesterton*, vol. 21 (San Francisco: Ignatius Press, 1990), 37.

liturgical conservative and ritual eclectic, John XXIII, took his course in the same line; he also had an affection for quaint customs, though his revival of items such as the golden straw at Communion was short-lived. But as the Missal of 1962 indicated, Pius XII and his successor had been intent on revisions and not fabrications. Noble simplicity is preciseness of intention, not bleakness of expression. It is not contradicted by authentic ritual developments, no more than the purity of doctrine is compromised by the development of doctrine over the centuries. But in the iconoclastic mood after the council, free rein was given to the spirit of historicism, which was precisely the romantic misrepresentation of the past condemned by Pius XII.

The Archbishop of Sens, Jean-Baptiste Languet de Gergy, had made the same point when he censured the Jansenist missal of Troyes in 1736. The problem with historicism is its ignorance of history as an organic economy. The method of constructing the Novus Ordo was like the careful research that went into reconstructing Williamsburg—academic and idealistic. And not a little dead. A liturgical enterprise like that creates a new form by archeological committees, the way Zeus made Venus from parts here and there. That serenely sterile creature was an amalgamation instead of a unity, a composition instead of a tradition. As a callow youth, and therefore an historicist myself, I asked a venerable college dean why he had not renovated the altar in his cathedral. He countered by asking me why the Christian Church is the only institution in the world which considers the word "primitive" good. It has taken me a good many years to recognize that this craggy Anglo-Saxon in his decanal gaiters shared Papa Pacelli's slant on historicism. Translated into the American political idiom, we might say of the liturgical decline what Henry Codman Potter said of the nation in 1889: "We have exchanged the Washingtonian dignity for the Jeffersonian simplicity, which in due time came to be only another name for the Jacksonian vulgarity."

A Crisis of Saints (1995)

A Very Small Package

A culture trapped in its own existence becomes no greater than itself. The old maxim perdures no matter how many times it is repeated: "A man wrapped up in himself becomes a very small package." More important than wrapping gifts in Advent is the obligation to unwrap the self: to confess to Christ the sins that belittle His image in man and to live life as He wants it, so that we might rejoice with Him forever and never be separated from Him.

He Spoke to Us (2016)

Vianney and the Blessed Mother

Vianney turned to the Blessed Mother as the one certain guide to the meaning of meaning; without her humble submission to the Divine Will as a guide, the mind cannot even know how intelligence is born. He carried that terrible beauty of submission back from his mother's grave like a trembling flame, a fragile light that flickered until it burst as a great brightness in the dark caverns of the Enlightenment.

The Curé d'Ars Today (1988)

Vianney and Sin

Those who watched Vianney grimace became afraid at least as much for him as for themselves. His exclamations could not be dismissed as generic moralizing; he gave the impression of a man calling for help for himself. Their sins offended moralists, but they hurt him. What might have passed for his oratorical massacre of the sinners of Ars was a massacre of his innocence by Ars. It was there on display, happening in the sunburned man with hollow cheeks and hair hanging this way and that. He could indeed have been a perfect madman, but he knew himself to be an imperfect priest; he saw his people's sins as a judgment against himself.

The Curé d'Ars Today (1988)

Virtue

Whether people lived a generation ago, a thousand years ago, or even if their names were Adam and Eve, they all shared the human condition. Over time, civilizations have learned that we have to live according to the divine design implanted in creation. When we do that, it is called virtue.

Grace and Truth (2019)

The Virtue of Hope

There are two sides to fatalism: pessimism, which expects the worst, and optimism, which presumes the best. "Whoever thinks he is standing secure should take care not to fall" (1 Cor. 10:12). In contrast to both is the virtue of hope, which trusts that God will not fail us if we do not fail Him. The Crucifixion of the world's one innocent man was the worst crime in history, but it was not a meaningless tragedy, because it brought good out of evil. Those who are "crucified with Christ" through daily trials are not tragic heroes, but saints. St. Basil says: "Here is man's greatness, here is man's glory and majesty: to know in truth what is great, to hold fast to it, and to seek glory from the Lord of glory."

A Year with Fr. Rutler (2017)

Vicissitudes

Times and the vicissitudes of the times change, but the Church remains the means by which the sanity of the saints guides civilization through the unbalanced perceptions of mistaken theories of man.

A Year with Fr. Rutler (2017)

The Vineyard and the Cross

Christ says bluntly, "Behold, we go up to Jerusalem" (Matt. 20:18). That is where the vineyard is, and in the vineyard is the Cross. Those who arrived at the end of the day missed the raw sun glistening on the Galilean lake and did not hear the leper cry with joy; nor did they glimpse Jesus transfigured on the Mount. For them, at day's end, there is only the Cross and the Cross and the Cross ... and then the Light.

Hints of Heaven (2014)

Vocations

Any young man called to the priesthood must be like St. Paul: "It is no longer I who live, but Christ who lives in me" (Gal. 2:20). This is true of all Christians. *Cupio dissolvi*—"I wish to disappear." Dioceses that understand this excel in vocations, and those that do not, fail.

A Year with Fr. Rutler (2017)

A Voice from Heaven

The Risen Christ was not a ghost, nor was He a superman. He said little of Heaven, except that it is entered by doing His will with love. What matters is that "the Word was made flesh and dwelt among us," and so He speaks to us with a voice from Heaven. It is the language that everyone understands without interpretation if one is willing to listen.

A Year with Fr. Rutler (2017)

The Voting Booth

Real Catholics could change the world by a personal response to the Resurrection that (1) sends them to the confessional and (2) sends them to the voting booth. The two go together. I am edified each day by the sincere confessions I hear. As your pastor I pray that the way you vote will be a worthy offering at the altar of God and not material for confession.

A Year with Fr. Rutler (2017)

The Warsaw Speech of President Trump

President Reagan was advised by his chief of staff Howard Baker and National Security Adviser Colin Powell not to tell Gorbachev to take down the Berlin Wall. They thought it was "extreme" and "unpresidential." Such commentators might have called the Funeral Oration of Pericles "bellicose" and Queen Elizabeth's speech at Tilbury "demagogic" and Washington's farewell address in Fraunces Tavern "lachrymose and exploitative." While not making rhetorical comparisons between the Warsaw speech and what Lincoln said at Gettysburg, for times change and with it their vernacular, I should point out that in 1863 the *Harrisburg Patriot and Union* mocked "the silly remarks of the President" and sniffed: "For the credit of the nation we are willing that the veil of oblivion shall be dropped over them and that they shall be no more repeated or thought of." President Trump's heavily criticized Warsaw Speech (July 6, 2017) mentioned three priests: Copernicus, John Paul II, and Michael Kozal. The latter was the bishop of Wloclawek who was martyred by the Nazis in Dachau along with 220 of his priests in 1943. After lengthy torture, the Nazi doctor Joseph Sneiss injected him with a dose of phenol "to make easier" his way to eternity. St. John Paul II beatified Bishop Kozal two days after Reagan's Berlin speech. Sneiss has his disciples now in much of Europe, and he would have a busy practice today on our own golden shores in California, Colorado, Oregon, Vermont, Washington, and the nation's very capital. At the heart of the Warsaw speech were these words: "We put faith and family, not government and bureaucracy, at the center of our lives."

Calm in Chaos (2018)

George Washington and Religious Liberty

The foundational documents of our nation ensured religious liberty, but the Founding Fathers were not the Apostolic Fathers. George Washington was granted to our nation by a singular providence, and in his wisdom, he knew that what the Founding Fathers had ensured could only be maintained by vigilance. In his Farewell Address in 1796, he asked: "Where is the security for property, for reputation, for life, if the sense of religious obligation desert the oaths which are the instruments of investigation in courts of justice? And let us with caution indulge the supposition that morality can be maintained without religion." That Father of our country may have been more utilitarian than any of the Fathers of the Church in his assessment of the economy of divine law and natural law and positive law, but his warning was clear.

He Spoke to Us (2016)

Isaac Watts

In the late seventeenth century in Southampton, England, there was a boy who was addicted to verse. As a boy, Isaac Watts watched a mouse by the fireplace and said, "The little mouse, for want of stairs, went up a rope to say his prayers." His father told him to cut it out. The family had had enough of his constant scansion. He replied, "Father, father, pity take, and I will no more verses make." He didn't keep his poetic promise. Instead, he became the father of English hymnody, writing hundreds upon hundreds of church songs. We still sing many of them: "Joy to the World," "O God, Our Help in Ages Past," "When I Survey the Wondrous Cross."

Grace and Truth (2019)

The Way

When I was a student in Rome, I frequently got lost in the streets that were anything but straight: they were astonishingly winding and crooked in the ancient quarter where I lived, and more than once I walked into a blind alley. Yet when I asked a local Roman for directions, the answer was invariably: *Va sempre diritto* (Keep going straight ahead). I must say it was not very helpful. But that is what Our Lord says to us each day of our lives. The difference is that He does not point the way; He *is* the way.

A Year with Fr. Rutler (2017)

A Wedding Feast, After All, for Miss Havisham

As a priest, I have witnessed the marriages of more than eight hundred couples. It is gratifying to hear from them on their anniversaries, and to baptize and even marry some of their new generation. Solid marriages are beacons and ballast for those whose understanding of family life may be dim and unsettled in our distressed culture. Some of the happiest weddings have been free of the extravagance that is the fashion of a meretricious society. Sometimes, a couple prayerfully decides to call the wedding off, and usually this is prudent, if it is the outcome of an awareness of the seriousness of the vows. The other day a couple in California called off their wedding, having already paid for a $35,000 reception. Rather than cancel, the family invited the homeless of Sacramento to share the feast. Young and old and abandoned showed up, and what could have been a dismal day — something like Miss Havisham's cobwebbed banquet table with its desiccated wedding cake — became bright for many.

A Year with Fr. Rutler (2017)

"Well Done, Good and Faithful Servant!"

Each one of us is engaged in ... spiritual warfare, and each one of us is being tested each day. There is no cause more just than that of Christ. And if we fight this spiritual warfare by fasting, by prayer, by joyfully living our daily routine according to the life of the virtues, then, by God's grace, we will hear the voice of Christ saying to us, "Well done, good and faithful servant; ... enter into the joy of your master" (Matt. 25:23).

Grace and Truth (2019)

Wesley and Vianney

John Wesley said the whole world was his parish; Vianney could say in a more authentic way that his parish was the whole world. He could prove it in the Catholic sense because he did not mean it in a parochial sense. The whole round world would come to the Curé d'Ars because the truest importance in the round world was held in his hands: so small that it would have to be feasted on to be felt and adored to be seen. Any priest is given the gift, but Vianney accepted the gift with a holy gluttony, so greedy that he convinced people this was all that mattered. The farthest he ever walked again was the distance home. "At the sight of a steeple you can say, What's in there? The body of Our Lord. Why is he there? Because a priest has passed by and said the Holy Mass."

The Curé d'Ars Today (1988)

Westward Ho!

There is a curious human urge to move west; it is a symbol of the desire to find new things and be young where there is no past; it was symbolized in myth by the glorious sun spirit, Phoebus Apollo, who fed ambrosia to his horses before dawn and rode them westward in a chariot of diamonds and chrysolite. But the very strange people one meets in parts of California, for instance, are a clue that the west can have a disastrous effect if you think you have reached it. To think that the farthest horizon is the final limit of all that exists is a flat way of looking at a round world. Materialistic people are spiritual flatlanders, and they will not easily understand their place in a round world; they think of the west as a physical direction, whereas the saints know of a metaphysical west that is a destiny. Looking for direction without a loftier destiny is devastating madness.

The Curé d'Ars Today (1988)

What Is Man?

"What is man, that thou art mindful of him? And the son of man, that thou visitest him?" (Ps. 8:4). The psalmist answers his own question: "Thou hast made him a little lower than the angels and crowned him with glory and honor" (Ps. 8:5). The

Letter to the Hebrews quotes this and declares, not by any archeological discovery or forensic evidence, but by the eyewitness of the apostles themselves: "We see Jesus, who for a little while was made lower than the angels, crowned with glory and honor because of the suffering of death, so that by the grace of God he might taste death for everyone" (Heb. 2:9).

A Year with Fr. Rutler (2017)

What St. Ignatius of Antioch Told the Ephesians

According to tradition, when Trajan was en route to Armenia, he stopped in Antioch, where the bishop Ignatius was brought before him. The emperor was perplexed that such a gentle man would not water down his Faith in order to cooperate with the state. Before arriving in Rome, where he was tossed to the lions, Ignatius wrote to the Christians in Ephesus: "Do not err, my brethren. Those that corrupt families shall not inherit the kingdom of God. If, then, those who do this as respects the flesh have suffered death, how much more shall this be the case with anyone who corrupts by wicked doctrine the faith of God, for which Jesus Christ was crucified! Such a one becoming defiled in this way, shall go away into everlasting fire, and so shall every one that hearkens unto him." St. Ignatius was second in succession to St. Peter as bishop of Antioch. He was a student of Christ's most beloved apostle, John. So what Ignatius wrote pulses with the authority Christ gave to Peter and the heart John could hear beating at the Last Supper.

A Year with Fr. Rutler (2017)

What to Say at the City Gates

If there have been no decent hymns written in the last generation, there is still reason to expect great ones in the next. Antiquity is not the justification of greatness; quality is. But if someone gushes that one's taste is as valid as another's, we have to reply with Catholic common sense what the Church has said in her finest moments at the city gates: *If you think that, you are a barbarian.*

The Stories of Hymns (2016)

The Wheat and the Chaff

Christ will "gather the wheat into his barn, but the chaff he will burn with unquenchable fire" (Luke 3:17, Douay-Rheims). St. Luke calls this "good news." Unquenchable fire hardly seems like good news, until you realize that Christ is separating good from evil and saving mankind from the degraded delusion that these categories are impressions without substance.

A Year with Fr. Rutler (2017)

Whistling in the Dark

I remember standing next to an elderly Jewish woman at a pro-life meeting. During an opening prayer, a group of pro-abortion activists began to blow whistles in order to drown out the prayer. They could not contradict the fact that we were there; they could not contradict the fact that we were praying; and they could not contradict the fact of God. They could only try to cover it up by blowing whistles. The elderly Jewish woman turned to me and said, "I've heard that sound before. I grew up in Germany, and

I can remember when the Nazis first started. They would send the Nazi Youth into the parks, and when anti-Fascist speakers mounted the podium and tried to be heard, the youth were instructed to blow whistles."

Grace and Truth (2019)

Wisdom Itself

I remember a political debate where participants were asked, "Who is your favorite philosopher?" It is quite amazing, in today's day and age, that most of them were able to come up with any answers at all. But to their credit, they did. Mostly their answers were ones you'd expect—Aristotle, Plato, and so on. But one piously said that his favorite philosopher was Jesus. Another replied with even greater rectitude that Jesus was not a philosopher: Jesus is not a lover of wisdom, but wisdom itself. He is the truth that has ordered the universe. Philosophy is a natural activity of the mind—the discerning of the basic hierarchy of principles by which we deduce what truth is. Theology, however, moves beyond philosophy by considering the source of truth itself.

Grace and Truth (2019)

The Wise Virgins of the Parable

It is not idle allegory to say that the wise virgins processing to meet the Bridegroom are the Church in eucharistic celebration. The celebrants are those who live day in and day out, knowing that the Truth will appear. This explains the palpable radiance a pastor sees in some very old people who beam at the prospect of seeing God face-to-face. They are not among those burned at the stake or gored by lions. But martyrdom is a bad half hour. Fidelity consists in living the daily routine — if not ground by beasts, then ground down by the daily grind for as long as the Bridegroom wills it — before the heavenly nuptials.

Hints of Heaven (2014)

Why Be a Christian?

The reason for being a Christian is to be a saint, for a saint is a human who is fully human according to the intention of Christ.

A Year with Fr. Rutler (2017)

Why Christ Spoke in Parables

Understanding Christ's parables belongs to the childlike. The humble of heart recognize the lessons of the parables as they play out in the course of history. They surface in both the mistakes and the courage of the Crusaders, in both the glorious architecture and the inhuman tortures of the High Middle Ages, in the zealous missionaries and the haughty degenerates of the Counter-Reformation, and in the witness of the martyrs at the hands of the maniacs of the twentieth century. The parabolic treasure is hidden in the concrete of Wall Street as truly as in a Galilean pasture. Every culture, advanced or backward, can understand a parable, because it offers a universally sought pearl. Mr. Caveman would have nodded some form of assent, as would the French heirs to Louis IX and Louis Pasteur.... Parables are often dismissed as too simple: because a child can understand them, adults must yawn through them. And yet Christ spoke in parables. That fact is infinitely interesting and eternally salvific. In the face of worldly-wise criticism, one recalls the story of the tourist in Florence who sniffed that he was not all that impressed with the Uffizi's collection. A guard replied in halting but intelligible English, "Here we do not judge the pictures; the pictures judge us."

Hints of Heaven (2014)

Why Do the Wrong People Travel?

I am persuaded more than ever before of the wisdom in Nöel Coward's song: "Why do the wrong people travel, travel, travel/ When the right people stay back home?" A higher authority is St. Paul, who traveled only of necessity and was beaten, shipwrecked, and stung by scorpions in the process. He said, "When you live in New York, you don't have to travel because you are already there." Or perhaps it was another one of those saints. But it is true.

He Spoke to Us (2016)

Why Forgive?

There is no reason to forgive anyone unless it is done with enough humility to inspire humility in the one who is forgiven.

Hints of Heaven (2014)

Why the Media Ignore Christian Martyrs

Much of the media are reluctant to report, let alone express outrage at, the beheading of Christian infants, the crucifixion of Christian teenagers, the practical genocide of Christian communities almost as old as Pentecost, and the destruction to date of many churches in the Middle East. Why is this moral obliviousness (a sanitized term for what Lenin called "useful idiocy") so widespread? Very simply, many disdain Judeo-Christian civilization and the moral demands that follow from man having been made in the image of God. Their operative philosophy is that "the enemy of my enemy is my friend."

A Year with Fr. Rutler (2017)

Why Satan Hates Babies

Satan never looks like Satan.... One special hatred of his always exposes him for what he is. Because Our Lord said that we must become like little children to inherit the Kingdom of Heaven, Satan hates babies. With great wisdom, the older *Rite for the Baptism of a Child* begins: "I exorcise you, unclean spirit, in the name of the Father and of the Son and of the Holy Spirit. Come forth, depart from this servant of God, for He commands you, accursed and damned spirit, He who walked upon the sea and extended His right hand to Peter as he was sinking."

A Year with Fr. Rutler (2017)

The Will

Nature works in cycles, and all animate creatures follow patterns, with the exception of you and me. Mankind has a free will that acts by choice rather than instinct. That is our glory and our peril. The right use of the will leads to bliss, and the wrong use leads to eternal separation from that glory, or to what is bluntly called damnation.

A Year with Fr. Rutler (2017)

Wolves and Sheep

Joseph Stalin was responsible for the deaths of around twenty million men, women, and children by massacres, torture, starvation, and execution. Figures diverse as Lord Beaverbrook, Dean Acheson, Averell Harriman, and George Marshall noticed his habit of doodling pictures of snarling wolves. Sixteen days before his death, he told an Indian ambassador, Shri Menon, "When a wolf shows his teeth, you know he is not laughing." In his paranoia he saw wolves all around him and said, "Peasants know how to handle wolves. They exterminate them." It is hard to explain such figures apart from evil as a palpable foe. There was no paranoia in Our Lord's counsel to His disciples: "I am sending you as sheep among wolves. So be wise as serpents and innocent as doves" (Matt. 10:16). In that menagerie of metaphors is the strategy of spiritual combat. Wisdom and innocence destroy foolishness and naïveté.

A Year with Fr. Rutler (2017)

Wolves in Shepherds' Clothing

At one party's convention, the name of God was excluded from its platform, and a woman who boasted of having aborted her child was applauded.[36] It is a grave sin, requiring sacramental confession and penance, to become an accomplice in objective evil by voting for anyone who encourages such evil, for that imperils the nation and destroys the soul. It is the duty of the clergy to make this clear and not to shrink, under the pretense of charity, from explaining the Church's censures against such evils as abortion. Wolves in sheep's clothing are dangerous, but worse are wolves in shepherds' clothing.

A Year with Fr. Rutler (2017)

Wonderland

Of the temptations to which Our Lord allowed Himself to be subjected, the most difficult to understand was the temptation to fly. Actually, wanting to fly is not all that peculiar, if by peculiar is meant unique or unusual. Everyone is tempted to fly. By that, I do

---

[36] The Democratic National Convention held in Philadelphia, July 25 to 28, 2016, nominated former First Lady Hillary Clinton, a vocal supporter of abortion and of the Planned Parenthood Federation, for president. The previous week in Cleveland, July 18 to 21, the Republican National Convention, by contrast, nominated New York entrepreneur Donald J. Trump, who had spoken against abortion during the campaign and vowed to nominate Supreme Court justices "in the mold of [pro-life] Justice Antonin Scalia." The Republican National Convention program also included numerous mentions of God by political speakers, as well as formal prayers.

not mean the impetus that drove Icarus and the Wright Brothers. No, Satan's flying is contempt for reality. Wanting everything my way is flying in the face of facts.... Our world, and certainly our nation, is suffering a crucible of temptations. In many ways we have already succumbed to them, which is why great saints have called ours a "Culture of Death." Attitudes and even sometimes laws have flown against reality: vice is freedom, decadence is dignity, killing unborn children is righteous, the unnatural is natural, maleness and femaleness are not facts but moods, and marriage is whatever the ego wants it to be.... The temptation to fly is the primeval sin of pride, living a lie, and pretending that the world made by God is the world reinvented by man. By refusing to fly, Jesus saved us from the degradation of acting like idiots in a world of nonsense. It was expressed well by Alice as she prepared to enter Wonderland: "If I had a world of my own, everything would be nonsense. Nothing would be what it is, because everything would be what it is isn't. And contrary wise, what is, it wouldn't be. And what it wouldn't be, it would. You see?" Tragically, there are those now who do see it that way and want the world to be Wonderland.

A Year with Fr. Rutler (2017)

The Wonders of the Eternal World

The Wonders of the Ancient World are now old in the way of dust: crumbled stones, fallen towers, sand-swept gardens, darkened lamps. The words of Christ from the Cross are alive and clearer each day.... "Heaven and earth will pass away, but my words will not pass away" (Matt. 34:35; Mark 13:31; Luke 21:33).

The Seven Wonders of the World (1993)

The World's Light Not the Light of the World

Society cannot be brightened by itself. Dark lies may be taught in the fluorescent light of high-tech classrooms. In cities, zones with the most neon signs tend to locate moral deeds darker than those in the back alleys. Abortion mills use halogen surgical lights the way all-night searchlights marked concentrations camps. The more the human intellect flashes lights in this world, the more the human will can blind itself to the Light of the World.

The Seven Wonder of the World (1993)

Worrying about the Future

Christ did make some predictions — the death of Judas, the destiny of Peter, and the destruction of the Temple — but He counseled against worrying about the future. His only prediction we need to know is fulfilled in every generation: "Heaven and earth will pass away but my words will never pass away" (Matt. 24:35).

A Year with Fr. Rutler (2017)

Worship

By kneeling in the face of affliction and saying Amen, suffering moves from humiliation to humility; as humiliation is the source of loneliness, humility is the strength of solitude, which cures it. Contemporary culture finds this no more plausible than did the proud sceptics dancing in the holly groves of post-Cartesian France. But the modern mind is in the process of realizing, to its bewilderment and agony, what the *philosophes* dismissed with mandarin disdain, and it is this: anything worth an Amen has been crucified. Man and woman were worth God's own Amen at creation; it took the crucifixion of the Holy One to bring the Amen back. The brutal reality of that moment was foolishness to the ancient philosophers, who were the prototypes of the later skeptics. They hungered for the *kalon*, by which they meant the noblest realization of interior beauty and goodness, but so long as it was an idea and not a divine presence in reality, it became a cliché of contentment and rectitude. Without the true sacrifice of Christ, the human race can only say Amen to superficial ideal-ism. And this, more than anything, lies at the heart of modern banality in worship; where the majesty of Christ's sacrifice is lost, and where the Amen of the Blessed Mother is obscured, the only object left to worship is worship itself.

The Curé d'Ars Today (1988)

The Worst of Times

Sinners in the Church's ranks sin most easily when times are easy, while martyrs, apologists, and doctors flourish best in the worst of times.

He Spoke to Us (2016)

Zacchaeus

Zacchaeus, that little man, is each one of us because we are so very little in proportion to the universe. "Make haste and come down, for I must stay at your house today" (Luke 19:5). The act of humility that saved Zacchaeus is the same act that saves us every time we open the door of the confessional. We want to see Jesus, and that is where we see Him. He is always passing by, but not seen by most people, in the Holy Mass, which may seem to be a routine unless we open our eyes to Him in the sacrament of reconciliation. It is only when we invite Him into our souls by confessing our sins that He invites us into His Heart. "Come down," He says, and we do come down. We come to the very depths of reality when we say, "Bless me, Father, for I have sinned." If it's difficult for us to identify our sins, it's simply because we're not looking closely enough. If only we could see our souls the way He does. It helps to make a good examination of conscience by scrutinizing our souls as thoroughly as we scrutinize what we can discern of others'. We are very good at spotting others' flaws, but that's pride. Humility turns that moral X-ray on our own intellect and will. When you invite a guest to your home, you take time to prepare the house. If Jesus were to come into your house at this very moment, what would you change? Christ is always knocking at the door, and if we open, He will come in. Now ask: "What is there in my soul that I would rearrange if I knew He were coming in right now?" And then: "Well, why haven't I rearranged it already?" Once we begin to do that, especially through the sacrament of confession, we will hear the voice of Christ, who stops and says to you, "Today, right now, I want to come into your soul."

Grace and Truth (2019)

Acknowledgments

Over the years, I have worked with many publishing houses, but I have rarely encountered the efficiency, grace, and dedication that I encountered in working with Sophia Institute Press. From the very start of the project, Charlie McKinney, the publisher of Sophia, showed me nothing but encouragement and support. Carley Cassella, assistant editor, was unflaggingly helpful, providing me with all of the electronic materials I needed and proving an ingenious aid whenever I ran into difficulties. Similarly, Dr. John Barger, the founder and senior editor of Sophia, was full of sympathy and good counsel when I shared with him how I thought the project should take shape. All writers are reliant on good editors, and I am blessed to have had the privilege of working with such a fine and discriminating editor as John. Nora Malone, Sophia's inspired copy editor, went through the typescript with a fine-tooth comb and found and corrected many blunders and oversights, for which I am wildly grateful. Others helped me as well, notably my dear friends Robert Crotty, Esq., and Father Carleton Jones, O.P., both of whom sensibly dissuaded me from introducing Madame de La Tour du Pin into the festivities. Anne White, Father Rutler's ablest editor, was a source of stalwart encouragement, as were my good friends Eugene and Jo Anne Sylva and Margaret Fernandez. Lastly, I am keenly indebted to another dear friend, Neil Merkl, Esq. the president of the Guild of Catholic Lawyers, who read the manuscript in typescript and made many shrewd, learned, and judicious suggestions.

Index

abortion, opposition to, xix,
26, 52, 71, 77, 78, 85, 101,
112, 113, 114, 116-17,
272-3
and baptism, 162-4
and Cardinal Raymond
Burke, 85
and Culture of Death,
xxiv, 50, 137, 154, 170,
238, 279
and "demographic winter,"
163
and dignity of human
person, 140
and dignity of life from
moment of conception,
77
and genetics, 158
and Hans von Balthasar,
166-7
and Hillary Clinton, 278
intrinsic evil of, 79
and invincible ignorance,
114

and justification of pro-life
as most important of
political issues, 175
and just-war criteria for
battle of life, 135-6
and Kermit Gosnell, 137
and Lord of Creation, 158
and George Edward Lynch
(1917-2003), auxiliary
bishop of Raleigh, 160
and Margaret Sanger, 100
and Mario Cuomo, 195-6
and misuse of reason, 138
and *Mit Brennender Sorge*
(1937), Pope Pius XI's
encyclical castigating
eugenicist rejection of
the natural law, 173
and mothers, 177
and partial birth abortion,
138
and *Permitting the Destruction of Life Unworthy of
Life* (1920) by Alfred

Hoche and Karl Binding, 138
and Planned Parenthood, 100
and Weimar Republic, 138
and what might have been if *Roe v. Wade* had never been passed, 163
absolution, 51
Act of Contrition, 41
Acton, Cardinal Charles Januarius Edward (1803-1847), 29
Acts of Apostles, 11, 60, 84, 88
Adoration, 5, 86, 172-3
Adam and Eve, 16, 49, 53
Adams, John, 4, 63
Adams, John Quincy, 4
Adoration, 86
Advent, xxiv-xxv, 5, 50, 86, 89, 129, 212, 242
and Light of Truth, 157-8
and memory, 176
and self-absorption, 262
advertising, power of, 121
aesthetics, 5
Aerts, Johannes, Dutch Apostolic Vicar and Sacred Heart Bishop in Makulu province of New Guinea, and martyrdom by Japanese in 1942, 151
African Church, 29

Agincourt, Battle of (1415), 199
Agony in the Garden, 58
Agnus Dei, 140
Albigensians, 221
Alfonso XIII, King of Spain, 44
Allberry, Charles Robert Cecil Augustine, heroic RAF pilot, 152-3
Allia River, Battle of (390 B.C.), 58-9
almsgiving, 7
Alton, Lord David, pro-life peer, 174
and recent rise of Catholic population in Great Britain and Commonwealth, 174-5
America, 28
American Civil War, 107
Amoris Laetitia, 8
and *Punch*, 187
and sycophancy, 187
anarchism, 23
Andritzki, Father Alois, and protest against Saxon sanatorium, which killed 16,000 lives adjudged "unworthy of life," 152
and beatification by Pope Benedict XVI, 152
Angelicum University, 41
angels, 9, 10, 61, 63

Index

Anscombe, Elizabeth, 9
antinomianism, xxiii, 254
apostasy, xxiii, xxvi, 112
Apostolic Faith, 10
apostles, 57-8, 110
appeasement, 67
architecture, 74
Aristotle, 42, 273
arrogance, 11
Ascension, 11
asceticism, 34
Ash Wednesday, 13, 146, 223
atheism, xx, 13, 85, 218
Auden, Wystan Hugh, 14, 18
Augustan Age, 51
Auschwitz,
    and martyrdoms, 150

Bach, 11, 18
Bacon, Sir Francis
    and "Knowledge is power,"
        199
Balthasar, Hans Urs von, 18
"banality in the pulpits," 37-8
"banality of evil" (Hannah
    Arendt), 70
"banality in worship," 281
baptism, 14, 15. 73, 107
barbarians, 15, 272
Barth, Karl, 18
Basset, S.J., Father Bernard, 17
Beatitudes, 21, 50
beauty, xxiii, xxiv, 18, 36, 50,
    130, 177, 208, 209, 234,
    281

and "terrible beauty of
    submission," 262
and the saints, 177
Beethoven, Ludwig von, 11
Belloc, Hilaire, xii, 87-88
Benedict XVI, Pope, 55, 56,
    104, 117, 123, 133, 152,
    186, 189, 219
and "the interior watchful-
    ness of the heart" that
    instills "holy meek-
    ness," 202
Benson, Robert Hugh, xii
Bernheim, Giles, Chief Rabbi
    of France, 117-18
Bernanos, George
    and lapsed Catholics, 210
Bernini, Gian Lorenzo, 11
Bible, xi, 19, 211,
Biffi, Cardinal Giacomo of
    Bologna, 212
bilocation, 41
blasphemy
and comparing refugees to
    Holy Family, 254
Blessed Sacrament, 83, 87,
    100, 109, 230
blindness, 42, 260
    and seeing, 42, 52
"bliss beyond time and space,"
    68
Body and Blood of Jesus
    Christ, 24
boredom, 10, 68

Bradford, William (1590-
1656), Governor of Plym-
outh Colony, 4
Buck, J. Stuart, 30
on liberal Protestant
theologian John Selby's
Spong's disdain for
African bishops, 30
Bruckner, Anton, 11
Buckley, Jr. William F., 25, 213
and conservatism, 213
Burke, Cardinal Raymond
on abortion, 85
"burlesque journalism," 31

Caesar, 25, 38, 144
Caffara, Cardinal Carlo
(1938-2017), one of Dubia
Cardinals, 133
Calvary, 8, 239
Calvinism, 7, 18
Calvinist Moral Tradition, 7
Canon Law
canon 915 of *Code of
Canon Law*, 85
capitalism, 65
capital punishment, 28-7, 79,
146-7
Caravaggio, Michelangelo
Merisi da, 153
Carnegie, Andrew 145
Casey, John Richard Conway
(1933-2006), 42
catechesis, xxiv
crisis of catechesis, 74
and spiritual warfare, 74

Catechism of Catholic Church,
xxiii
cathedrals of Middle Ages, 74
Cathedral of Notre Dame, 73,
74
Catholic Encyclopedia (1917),
xx, 24-25
Catholic journalists, 31
Catholic schools, 25-6
Catholic voting, 113
and Catholic "misrepresen-
tatives," 173
Cezanne, Paul, 11
Chanteloup, Emanuel Anatole
Raphael Chaptal de, Aux-
iliary Bishop of Paris, 151
charity, xxii, 53, 65, 66, 114,
222, 251, 278
"profound mystery of charity," 231
and public executioner,
146-7
timidity masquerading as
charity, 67
charity vs. envy, 66
Charles II, King of England,
33
definition of "gentleman,"
32-33
Charles Martel, "the Ham-
mer," ruler of the Franks,
103
Chateaubriand, François René,
Vicomte de, 86
Chesterton, Gilbert Keith, xii,
25, 98, 144

on art of journalism, 31

on billboard lights of
Times Square, 157

on desire and moral per-
missibility, 138-9

on St. Thomas More, 229

Choate School, 33-4

and President John F. Kennedy, 33-4

children, 15-16, 72-3, 109

and "confused children,"
177

and sacrifice of in society
worldwide, 166-7

childlikeness, not childishness,
16

China

and fondness for sterilizing
women, 115

Christ, Jesus, 7, 56, 191

authority of, 35

courtliness of, 33, 46

Fatherhood of, 80

gentleness of, 88

innocence of, 35

life of, not an allegory, 111

mockery of, 47

and Paradise, 191

perfection of, 194-5

pity of, 195

redemptive Power of, 166-7

teaching, how He passes
on, 48

wisdom of, 48

Christendom, xx, 146, 229

Christmas, 15, 35, 242

Christ the King, 122

Christ the Redeemer, 23

Christian civilization, 67, 106

Christina, Queen of Sweden, 60

church bells, 27

Churchill, Sir Winston Leon-
ard Spencer, 24

on appeasement, 67

on courage, 44

and Harry Lauder, 36-7

Church Militant, 37

Church reform, 210

Cicero, 214

and John Henry Newman,
214

civic integrity, how to secure
and safeguard, 15

civilization, xx, 11, 15, 27, 48,
78, 90, 209

and fatherhood, 80

Claret, St Anthony, Spanish
archbishop and mission-
ary, 213

and right judgment, 213

Clarke, Sir Edward

and forensic evidence for
Resurrection, 84

cliché, 51

climate change, 39

Clinton, Hillary Rodham,

and antagonism to "deep-
seated cultural codes,
religious beliefs, and
structural biases," 105

and fondness for abortion,
278

and Saint Hildegard of
Bingen, 105
and Saul Alinsky, 105
clubland, 71
cohabitation, 43, 164
and adultery, 164
and deprivation of grace,
164
and divorce, 164
and Eucharist, 164
and fornication, 43
Coleridge, Samuel Taylor
on history, 143
collectivism
collectivism and greed, 66
Commandments, 7, 8, 15, 18,
34
commencement addresses, 39
confession, xxiv, 13, 29, 39,
40, 41, 83, 106, 194, 242,
247
confirmation, 42
Confraternity of San
Giovanni, 29
Conley, James, Bishop of Lincoln, Nebraska
and "Land O' Lakes State-
ment" (1967), 141-2
conscience, 58, 71, 85, 134,
163, 173, 251, 256, 282
and Heaven and Hell, 257
and St. Thomas More, 229
contemptissima inertia, 51
contraception, 26, 52, 77

conversion, xii, xxii, xxiii,
xxiv, 5, 36, 60, 69, 83, 97,
114, 123, 181, 182, 194,
200, 204, 214, 227, 257,
and Father John Neuhaus,
183
Cook, Cardinal Terence,
and the author's mother,
73
Coolidge, Calvin, 28
Copernicus, Nicolas, 29
Corelli, Arcangelo, 5
Corinth, 43
bereft of sacramental sense,
43
contempt for sacredness of
life, 43
Corinthians vs. Galatians,
43
Corinth and New York
City, 43
Gnostic notions of super-
natural, 43
St. Paul and Corinth, 43-4
Corpus Christi, Feast of, 95
Council of Orange (529),
and affirmation of St Au-
gustine's theology, 127
Council of Trent (1545-63),
118, 127
courage, xvii, 6, 7, 49, 49, 94,
101, 104, 124, 136, 164,
208, 229, 240, 246, 274
and Churchill, 44
and sanctity, 45-6

and St. Thomas Aquinas,
44
and war, 44-5
Coward, Nöel
"Why Do the Young
People Travel?" (1951),
275
Creator, xv
crime, 29
crimes of Christians in eyes of
Romans, 51
Crosby, Bing, 78
Cross, the, xiii, xix, 7, 16-17,
23, 27, 47, 75, 82, 98, 151,
210, 279
wood of the Cross *medicina
mundi*—"medicine of
the world," 169
cruelty, 56
and sentimentality and
legalism, 199
Cuomo, Mario, politician
compared to incorruptible
St. Thomas More, 196
framer of "personally op-
posed, but ..." justification of abortion, 195-6
Culture of Death, xxiv, 50,
137, 154, 170, 238, 279
culture, xxi, 7, 59, 73, 91, 95,
119, 132, 142, 144, 146,
154, 165, 170, 183, 187,
191, 212, 226, 262, 268,
274, 280
and affluence, 98

"any crisis in culture is a
crisis in saints," 215
breakdown in culture, 244
and Caesar, 25
"culture of self-assertion,"
21
ecclesiastical culture, 64
and "hellishness," 95
and materialism, 250
and narcissism, 32
the Roman Catholic
Church as "guardian of
culture," 32, 170
and St. Louis IX, patron of
culture, 221-2
and salutary influence of
sacramental marriage
in "our distressed cul-
ture," 268
"where the Mother is
loved, there is a culture
of life," 170
custom, 60
cynicism, 5, 68

Dachau, 152, 266
damnation, 49, 241, 258
Da Vinci, Leonardo, 22
death, 3, 12
Declaration of Independence,
28
defense of Faith, 141
defense of Truth, xv, 6
and Cardinal Giacomo
Biffi, 212

Deism, 85, 126
De la Tour, 153
demagoguery, 78
desire and dogma, 53
Deus Absconditus, 54
devout life, xxii
Dewey, John, 100
Dickensian clerks, 55
"dictatorship of relativism," 56
dignity, 60
dignity of life from moment of
    conception, 77
discipline, 21
discipleship, 56
Diogenes the Cynic, 21
Divine Plan, 71
divorce, xix, 165
doctrinal Roman Catholic
    Faith, xxvi
dogma, 8, 53, 93, 95, 211, 259
Don Juan of Austria, (1545-
    1578), victorious admiral
    of Holy Alliance at Battle
    of Lepanto, 103-04
Doria, Andrea (1466-1560),
    Genoese admiral who
    fought against Ottoman
    Turks, 104
drugs, 58
dust, 13

earthly death vs. eternal death,
    3
earthly home, 54
Easter, 8, 15, 60

Easter Show at Radio City
    Music Hall, 19
Eastern Church, 5
ecstasy for Anglo-Saxons, 71
Eden, 118
edification, 36
education, 62
    and pogroms and holo-
        causts, 62
    education itself not re-
        demptive, 62
egotism, 60, 71
Einstein, Albert xvii, 6, 29
    realized intellectuals are
        not inveterately coura-
        geous in times of crisis,
        6
Eliot, Thomas Stearns
    and "The Journey of the
        Magi" (1927), 161
    and the saints, 161
Elizabeth, Queen of England,
    266
    and Tilbury speech after
        defeat of Armada, 266
Elizabeth II, Queen of Eng-
    land, 122
Elizabeth, Queen Mother of
    England
    and courage during Second
        World War, 45
emotion, 32, 85, 108, 127
    and truth, 76
enfranchisement of women, 18
English Reformation, the, 64

Enlightenment, 87, 242
envy, 65
    charity vs. envy, 66
Epiphany, the 66
equality, 28
Esau, 21
Esolen, Anthony
    and Bible, xi
    and conversion, xii
    and the Cross, xiii
    and "the far country of
        scholars," xii
    and "fire of love," xiii
    good shepherds and
        wolves, xiii
    Letters of St Paul, xi
    liberal biblical criticism, xi
    Mencken, H. L., xii
    and "the real world of
        grace, humility, and
        truth," xii
    and Rutler, G. W., xii,
        writer, xii, disciple of
        the Lord, "first-rate
        scholar," "wonder-
        ful teller of human
        stories," "youthfulness,"
        xiii
    and St John Vianney, Curé
        d'Ars, x, xii, "frolic
        youthfulness of," xiii
    Shaw, G.B., xii
    Virgin Mary, xi
eternal harmony, 61
Eternal Logos, 68

Eucharist, 7, 23, 95, 107, 109,
    209, 250-1
eulogizing, fulsome, 130
euphemism, 52, 68-9
euthanasia, 52, 77
    and Nazi doctor Joseph
        Sneiss, who injected
        the martyr Bishop
        Michael Kozal with
        phenol, after the Nazis
        tortured him, 266
evangelization, 69
evidence for miracles, 226
evidence for Resurrection, 84
evidence for the existence of
    God, 69
evil, xiii, 15, 35, 41, 58, 67,
    79, 89, 112, 113, 135, 149,
    168, 170, 184, 196, 198,
    200, 201, 219, 224, 234,
    239, 264, 272, 277
    "abortion a definitive
        moral evil," 85
    Adam and Eve and the
        "cleverness of evil," 16
    and capital punishment,
        146
    and the Cross, "the ulti-
        mate balance between
        good and evil," 235
    good and evil not abstrac-
        tions, 248
    and Hannah Arendt's "ba-
        nality of evil," 70
    material agents of evil,
        70-1

and mediocrity, 70
and Original Sin, 123
power of evil often under-
    estimated, 38
the reality of evil, 245
voting and objective evil,
    278
evil spirits, 35
excommunication, 71, 79, 85
    and *latae sententiae*, 79
existentialism, 22-3
Exodus, book of, 193

faint of heart, 77
faith and reason, xxii, 75, 96,
    142, 254
Fall of Man, 75, 127
    and Jansenism, 127
    and Lutheranism, 127
fall of Roman Empire, 51
falsehood, 108
false religions, 76
false witness, 77
fame, 78
family, xxiii, 29, 37, 51, 78, 79,
    103, 105, 117, 133, 186,
    196, 213, 221, 254, 257,
266, 268-9
fanaticism, 79
fantasy, 79
"fascination with emptiness,"
    22
fasting, 105, 223, 269
    compared with dieting, 80
fatherhood, 80, 180

and civilization, 80
"priesthood the sacrament
    of spiritual father-
    hood," 84
Fatherhood of God, 80
Fatima Prayer, 107
Faulhaber, Cardinal Michael
    von, Archbishop of Mu-
    nich, 134
    and National Socialism,
    134
    and the moral limits of
        State power, 134
Faust (1859), opera by Charles
    Gounod, 81
    and "the maternal scream,"
    81
federalizing of education, 25
fence sitting, 33
Fiat Lux, 53
Fillmore, President Millard
    and Father Matthew's
        pledge, 168
Finucane, Brendan Eamon
    Fergus "Paddy"
    youngest Wing-Com-
        mander in RAF history,
        153
    and death at 21 after
        shooting down 32 Ger-
        man flyers, 26 single-
        handedly, 153
firemen
    and confession, 3, 238
fire worship, 83

Index

First Amendment, 15
First Communion, 108-09
foibles of human race, 71
forgiveness, 20, 41, 51, 107,
 113, 182, 210, 226, 275
 and two thieves, 257
fornication, 43
 and cohabitation, 43
Founding Fathers, 15
Four Last Things, 86
Franklin, Benjamin, 64-5
 and epitaphical plagiarism,
 65
 and John Mason, 65
freedom, 24, 91, 118, 134, 135,
 142, 192, 193, 196, 256, 279
free will, 58, 127, 148, 251,
 277

Gaudete Sunday, 89, 131
gender, 53, 133
genetics, 158
genocide of Catholics, 103
Georg, Crown Prince of
 Saxony and later Jesuit,
 (1893-1943)
 and dubious drowning in
 Berlin after joining the
 priesthood, 153
George VI, King of England
 and courage during Second
 World War, 45
Gerlier, Cardinal Pierre-Marie
 of Lyons (1880-1965), 95,
 151

and collaborationist Vichy
 radio mockery of for his
 hiding Jews and resis-
 tance fighters, 151
German bishops, 30
ghosts, 90
Gibbon, Edward, xviii, 90-1
gift of awe, 91
gift of faith, 92
gift of light, 153
gift of motherhood, 92
gift of tears, 41
gifts of the Holy Spirit
 and their strengthening of
 intellect and will, 42, 154
Gilbert & Sullivan
 and *Iolanthe* (1883), 94
Gilson, Etienne, 74
 and architecture, 74
 and "Christianity and Philosophy" (1936), 74
 on Pascal, 231
 and the "understanding of
 what God has made,"
 or science, 231
"glamor of iniquity," 47
glory of God, 11, 14, 23
glory of Heaven, 15
God of Abraham, 10
God's Largesse, 93
God the Father, 7, 20
God the Judge, 10
God's Will, 251
Goethe, Johann Wolfgang
 von, 95-6

Good Friday, 107, 253

goodness, "the fruit of Christian life," 7, 10

good, true, and beautiful, the, 131

Gosnell, Kermit
    and media's silence during his murder trial for serial infanticide, 137

Gospel, 4, 94, 140

Gothic Revival, 73, 94-5

Gnosticism, 43, 80, 94-5. 137

grace, xiii, 11, 29, 79, 88, 92, 96, 112, 140, 202-3, 227

greed
    greed and collectivism, 66

grief therapy, 183-4

guardian angels, 9

guilt, 29

Guinness, Alec, 97
    and acting, 97
    and *Blessings in Disguise* (1986), 97
    and Passion and Resurrection of Christ the world's greatest drama, 97
    and truth, 97

hagiography, 20, 98

Hamel, Father Jacques, martyr, 166

happiness, 71, 98

Harding, President Warren G., 28

Harvard Crimson, 30

Haydn, Josef, 11

Heiner, Dennis Clinton Graham, 100-02

Heaven, 7, 9, 10, 12, 68, 73, 83, 89, 94, 96, 99, 102, 129, 130, 139
    and publicans and harlots, 257
    and sanctifying grace, 176
    ultimate reality, 207-8

heavenly destiny, 54

Hegel, 185
    Newman's *Development* is not Hegel's "dialectic," 186

heliocentricity, 30

Hell, 33, 49, 56, 86, 94, 95. 102, 107, 137, 151, 210, 212, 214, 229, 236, 239, 240, 256, 257

Henry V, king of England, 199

heresy, 103

Herod, Antipas (22 B.C.-A.D. 40), ruler of Palestine, 81-2

history, 6, 20, 32, 76, 103-04, 105
    "contempt for history," 38

Hitler, Adolf, 56
    and Winston Churchill and Harry Lauder, 17

holiness, 7, 20
    scorn for, 105

holy anger, 40

holy awe, 106

Holy Child, 66
Holy Communion, 29, 39
Holy Family, 254
holy fear, 91
holy innocence, 52
holy mountain, 50
Holy Spirit, xv, xxv, xxvi, 3,
    11, 22, 42, 83, 95, 106,
    108, 109-10, 148, 209
    and *Bayeux Tapestry*, 110
    as Comforter, 109-10
    and memory and the life of
        culture, 154
    and robes of Truth for jus-
        tices and priests, 201-2
    as teacher of virtue and
        right conduct, 154
Holy Week, 110, 189
    and reality, 111
holy reason, triumph of, 254
home, 61, 161
hope, 91, 154, 161, 169, 190,
    193,
    "hope and change," 112
    and pagans, 190
    and St Paul, 224
hot chocolate for the coddled
    young, 184
Hugo, Victor 73
    and Gothic Revival, 73
    and *The Hunchback of
        Notre Dame* (1831), 73
human condition
    in the modern age, 76
    and redemption, 185

tragedy of, 111
Humanae Vitae (1968), encyc-
    lical of Pope Paul VI, xx,
    115-16
human race, 96
human rights, 18
humility, 5, 80, 99, 116, 144-5
    and royalty, 140
    the gift of truth, 145
Humpty Dumpty, 56, 116-17
Hunyadi, János Corvinus (c.
    1387-1456), Hungarian
    crusader against Turks, 103
Husseini, Haj Mohammed
    Effendi Amin el, Grand
    Mufti of Jerusalem
    and Hitler and Final Solu-
        tion, 151
    and handing over 5,000
        Jewish children in
        Palestine for extermi-
        nation, 151
hymns, 119, 272
    and the Mass, 119-20

ideology, 64
ignorance, 120
illogic, 78
illusion, 53
imagination, 124-5
immigration, 253-4
"impatience with God's un-
    fathomable patience," 38
Imperial Rome, 63, 121
Incarnation of Truth, 71

incense, 121
incredulity, 46
indifferentism, sin of, 67, 79, 212
indulgences, 29, 113-14
infirmity, 34-5
information, luxury of, 121
innocence, 73, 109
intellect, 3, 6, 16, 20, 56, 96, 123, 124-5
intellect and will, 3, 282
    and how gifts of the Holy
        Spirit fortify, 42, 154
intrigue, 124-5
irrationality, 68
Ireland, 66-67
    and "adolescent rebellion"
        against Holy Mother
        Church, 67
    and Catholic education, 67
    and Druidism, 67
    and sodomy, 66-67
Isaiah,
    "Woe unto them that call
        evil good," 239
Islam, 4, 103-4

Jacob, 20-1
Jacobins, 117
Jaki, Stanley, Hungarian-
    born Benedictine priest,
    physicist, philosopher and
    theologian, 125
James, William 62
    on education, 62

Jansen, Cornelius, Bishop of
    Ypres and Father of Jansen-
    ism, 126
Jansenism, 65, 126-8
jargon, 128
Jefferson, President Thomas,
    and fondness for confis-
        catory principles of
        French Jacobins, 117
    and Koran, 63
Jena-Auerstedt (1806), Battle
    of, 142
"Jerusalem the Golden"
    (hymn), 128-9
John XXIII, Pope, 82-3, 98
Johnson, Samuel, 130
joy
    compared with happiness,
        130-1
Judas, 23
judgment, 122, 125
    and insanity, 122, 125
    and taste, 131
Judgment Day
    and Catholic politicians,
        131
judgment of Christ, 71
judgment of God, 132-33
Julian the Apostate, 14
Julian of Norwich, 33
justice, 53, 62, 134-5
just-war criteria, 135-36
Jutland, Battle of, 17

Kant, Immanuel, 94

Kasper, Cardinal Walter, 29
   conviction that Catholics
      cannot swing heroic
      virtue, 104-05
   disdain for African bish-
      ops, 29-30
   and "Pope Francis's Revo-
      lution of Tenderness
      and Love" (2015),
      104-5
   and "servile fear of those
      who underestimate
      their potential for holi-
      ness," 165
   and soft spot for sodomy, 29
Katyn Forest, 197
Kempis, Thomas à, 31
Kengor, Paul
   and St John Paul II's 1976
      speech in Philadelphia
      re: "final confronta-
      tion," 132
Kennedy, President John Fran-
      cis, 33-4
   and Roman Catholic
      Faith, 136
   and Justice Brennan, 136-7
Knox, Monsignor Ronald, 143
   and *Enthusiasm* (1950), 65
knowledge,
   and Francis Bacon's
      "Knowledge is power,"
      199
   and qualification that
      "knowledge of truth

is key to right use of
      power," 199
Kolbe, Maximilian, martyr,
      150
   and canonization by Pope
      John Paul II, 150
Koran, the, 63-64
   and Thomas Jefferson and
      John Adams, 63
Kowalski, Josef, Salesian Fa-
      ther martyred at Auschwitz
      for refusing to trample on a
      rosary, 150
   and beatified by Pope John
      Paul II, 150
Kozal, Michael, Bishop of
      Wlocklawek and martyr
   and Nazi doctor Josef
      Sneiss who euthanized
      him with phenol after
      torture, 266
   and beatification by Pope
      John Paul II, 266
Kronstadt, Father John, East-
      ern Orthodox Priest, 229

"Land O' Lakes Statement"
      (1967), 142
   and Bishop James Conley,
      141-2
   and John Henry Newman,
      142-3
   and Yalta Conference
      (1945), 143

La Rochefoucauld, François, 6th Duc de, xvi
Latin Doctors of the Church and recognition that praise, not sterile speculation, should be the issue of thought, 143-44
Lauder, Harry, music hall entertainer, 36-37
Lazarus, 40
law of gravity, 53
Lee, Robert E., 145
legalism, 199
Lenin, Vladimir, 155, 156, 276 and shrine for erected by Sidney and Beatrice Webb, 155
Lent, xvi, 5, 30, 63, 112, 147-8, 245 and John Chrysostom, 148 and small disciplines of, 148 and spiritual discipline, 245
Lepanto, Battle of, 17-18, and Feast of Rosary 104 and St. Pius V, 104
Lepidus, 51
Lewis, Clive Staples and hymns, 119
Leyte Gulf, Battle of 17
Liberal Protestantism, 8
Liberalism, 66 contrasted with liberality, 66

liberty, 19, 28, 136, 142, 180, 187, 232, 267
lies, 76, 191
life of mind, 62
Light, the, 14, 83 and O. Henry, 189
Light of Christ, 157
Light of Heaven, 14, 26
Light of Truth, 157-8
Light of World, 21, 107, 156, 203, 280
Lincoln, President Abraham career 45-6 courage, 45-6 "Father Abraham to an afflicted people," 81 Gettysburg Address, 205, 266 resilience, 45-6 self-effacement, 205
literacy, 31
littleness, 9, 26
Liturgy, 36, 80, 83, 89, 119, 120, 147, 220, 229, 252, 260, 261 and Vatican II, 260-2
liturgical calendar, 82
Living Word, 56
Livy, 59, 214
logic, 56, 68
Lord of Creation, 158 and genetics, 158
Lord of Truth, 54
love, xiii, xix, 158-9
love of God, xii, 40, 44, 161, 171, 120-11

Lustiger, Cardinal Jean-Marie
   and Youth World Day
      (1997), 159
   and "the French being
      French," 159
Luther, Martin
   and St. Thomas Aquinas,
      165
Lynch, George Edward (1917-
   2003), auxiliary bishop of
   Raleigh
   and Declaration of In-
      dependence (1776),
      159-60
   and heroic pro-life witness,
      159-161
   and Cardinal John
      O'Connor's view that
      he merits canonization,
      160

Madison, James, 117
Magi, the, 66, 161
magnetism of Christ's Church,
   even for Satan, 218
Mardi Gras, 13
Marmion, Abbott Columba,
   98
marriage, xix, 18, 78, 118, 133,
   164-5
   and cohabitation, 164
   and counterfeit marriage,
      78
   exaltation of family, 51
   indissolubility of marriage,
      44, 51

marriages as "beacons and
      ballast" for "a distressed
      culture," 268
   and weddings, 268
   "a status symbol rather
      than an essential core
      of society," 165
martyrs and martyrdom, xxiv,
   77, 103, 152, 166, 220,
   266, 274, 276, 281
   and Edward Gibbon, 90-91
   and Wise Virgins, 273-4
Marxism, 15
Mason, John, millenarian
   preacher (1646?-1694)
   and Benjamin Franklin, 65
   and Ronald Knox's *Enthu-
      siasm* (1950)
Mass, the, 63
Matthew, Father Theobald,
   Irish temperance crusader,
   167-8
Mead, Margaret, 155
   and refusal to acknowledge
      Fall of Man, 156
Mearns, Thomas Hughes
   (1875-1965), poet and
   educator, 90
media,
   misuse of, 169
   refusal to acknowledge
      Christian martyrdom,
      276
mediocrity, 38, 62
meekness, 11, 21-22
memory, 73, 76

and Advent, 176
and Old Testament proph-
ets attuned to source of
all memory, 155
and the life of culture,
154-5
Mencken, Henry Louis, xii, 28
Merman, Ethel, 57
Merton, Thomas
and *The Seven Storey
Mountain* (1948), 63
Mickiewicz, Adam
and play about Poland's
national suffering,
"Christ of Nations,"
197
Milton, John 56, 94
miracles, 38, 118, 168, 181,
184, 188, 228, 232
and Adoration, 172-73
and rejection of evidence
for, 226
Miss Havisham, 269
Mit Brennender Sorge (1937)
prophetic encyclical
castigating rejection of
natural law and deifica-
tion of State, 173
modern age, 3
and Job, 174
and philosophical errors
of, xv
and rejection of evidence
for miracles, 226
modernity, 94,

and deficient understand-
ing, 174
Modernists, 143
Mona Lisa, 22
Montaigne, Michel de, 232
Monteverdi, 11
moral strength, the foundation
of, 21
Mother of Fair Love, 168-9
Mother of God, 177
motherhood, 81
mothers, 16, 21
"every mother a prophet of
life," 177
Mother Saints, 178
Moulay Ismail Ibn Sharif (c.
1646-1727), Sultan of
Alaouite Dynasty, 4
Mount Zion, 10
mountaineering, 57-8
mourning, 180
Mozart, 11, 18
Murmansk Run
and the author's father,
180
and the "clarion voice of a
great generation," 180
music, 18
the music of worship, 181
mustard seed, 26, 149, 181
Mystical Body of Christ, 182
and evangelization, 182
not to be confused with
ecclesiastical bureau-
cracies, 182

Napoleon, 182

National Socialism, 15

nationhood, 20-1

Naturalism, xx

natural law, 7, 139, 151

    and divine law, defiance of which led to tragedy of WWII, 151

    and *Mit Brennender Sorge* (1937), Pius XI's encyclical against deification of state, 173

nature and grace, xxii, 161-2, 227

Nazis, 6

    and master race, 173

    and *Mit Brennender Sorge* (1937), Pope Pius XI's encyclical contra deification of state, 173

Neo-Paganism, 183

Neuhaus, Father John, 31, 183

New York, 19, 27

New York Post, 69

New York Times, 31

Nietzsche, Friedrich, 21

    and madness, 122

    and power, 21

    and right judgment, 122

    and "slave mentality," 21

nihilism, 23

nobility contrasted with safety, 220

nocturne, 50

nostalgia, 37, 89

Obama, President Barak Hussein, 63

obesity, 98

O'Connor, Flannery

    on sentimentality, 82

    "The Church and the Fiction Writer" (1957), 82

O'Connor, Cardinal John

    and George Edward Lynch, auxiliary bishop of Raleigh, 160

Octavian, 51

O. Henry, pen name of William Sydney Porter, 189

Old Testament Prophets, 155

    and the source of all memory, 155

Olivers, Thomas, hymn writer, 199

    "Praise to the Living God," 199

oratory, 28

Ordinary Time, 11, 189-90

Original Sin, 41

origin of Great War, 94-5

Orwell, George 146

Our Lady of Lourdes, 42

Palestrina, Giovanni, 11, 219

Palm Sunday, 89

pantheism, xx, 39

parables, 41, 97, 139-40, 149, 191, 273-4, 274-5

Paradise, 191

parish life, xxiii, 5, 35, 37, 192, 194
  parish contrasted to university for purposes of education, 62
Paris, 39
Pascal, Blaise
  and "humbling of reason," 231
  and "the profound mystery of charity," 231
Passion, the, 71, 89
peacock, 66
penitence, 5
Pentecost Sunday, 95
perception, 54
Pericles
  and Funeral Oration, 266
persecution of Catholics, 103, 188
pews, the case against, 196-7
pilgrimage, 254
  and travel, 254
Pius IX, Pope 98
  and Canute, 247
  Syllabus of Errors (1864), 246-7
  and tradition, 252
Pius X, Pope, 82
  and "Oath against Modernism" (1910), 74
Pius XI, Pope
  "The family is more sacred than the state, and men are begotten not for the earth and for time, but for heaven and eternity," 79
  and Mit Brennender Sorge (1937), encyclical castigating denial of natural law and deification of State, 173
Pius XII, Pope
  and Humani Generis (1950), 123
Pilate, Pontius, 35
Piwowarczk, Father Jan
  and Karol Wojtyla, 150
Planned Parenthood
  and Catholic politicians, 85
  and Margaret Sanger, 100
Plato, 86, 273
Pliny, 214
policemen, 3
political power, 38
politics, 62
Pompey, Gnaeus Pompeius Magus, Roman soldier and statesman, 48
pop psychology, 32
popular sovereignty, 28
Porter, Cole
  "Down in the Depths on the Nineteenth Floor," 57
power, 54, 199
  and Francis Bacon, 199

"power of holy meekness, which inherits the earth," 202

practical god of Romans, 54

prayer, 15, 63, 89, 98, 114, 119, 120, 144, 148, 200, 217, 225, 241, 244, 251, 267, 269, 272, 278
  and Fatima, 107
  and morning prayer, 176-7
  and Order of Malta, 141

preaching, 200

presumption, 250-1

Preysing, Johann Konrad von, Bishop of Berlin
  and contention that the world's woes during World War II were "the result of human contempt for natural and divine law," 152

pride, 5, 192-4, 201

priesthood, xxiv, 3, 22, 202

Prince of Lies, 47, 49, 54, 55, 78, 207-8

Proclamation of Christ to non-Christians, 203

Prodigal Son, 205

prodigies and prodigals, 204

progress, 205

prophecy, 205
  and Abraham Lincoln, 205
  and John the Baptist, 205
  and Mary, the Mother of God, 205

"protocol of all moral confusion," 76

Prometheus, god of fire, 83

Protestantism, 206

Psalms, xi, 54, 270-1

public penance
  for the defacement of altars, 206

public thinkers, 206

Punch, 187

purity, 50

Quintilian, 214

Rachel, 73

rationalism, xx-xxii, 87
  and definition of "rationalist," 207

reality, 53, 91, 108
  heaven ultimate reality, 207-8
  reality of the saints, 208

Real Presence, 208-9

redefining reality, 26

redemption, xxii

reform, 215
  and the crisis of culture, 215

refugees
  and Holy Family, 254

regret, 210-11

relativism, 215

relativity, 30

religion and science, 211

religious liberty, 15

remembrance, 11
renunciation, 105
repentance, 29
resilience, 75
Resurrection, 60-1, 63
    and Sir Edward Clarke's
        examination of evi-
        dence for, 84
    and universities, renewal
        of, 259
Revelation, book of, 10, 16
reverence for dead, 113-14
Richard the Lionhearted, 103
right judgment, 213
rights of man, 28
right to life, 78
ritual, 8
Roeder, Felix, 151
Roman Catholic Church, xviii,
    24-5, 27, 2, 76, 83, 89
    artistic patrimony of, 37
    and indigenous cultures,
        121
    and indissolubility of mar-
        riage, 24
    Mother of Western Cul-
        ture, 36
    and Spirit of the Age, 244
    unearthly innocence, 258
Roosevelt, President Franklin
    Delano, 197
    and complaint regarding
        Poland during Yalta
        Conference, 197
    and Katyn Forest atrocity,
        197

Roosevelt, President Theo-
    dore, 54, 216-17
    admiration for St. John
        Fisher, St. Thomas
        More, and Cardinal
        Gibbons, 216
    Prayer by John Henry
        Newman read at
        funeral, a favorite of
        Roosevelt's son, Quen-
        tin, 217
Rosary, 101, 107
Rothschild, house of, 151
Rubinstein, Anton
    and "Kamennoi Ostrow"
        at Radio City Music
        Easter Show, 19
rulers, 217
Russian proverb, 218
Rutler, Father George William
    and abortion trade, xix
    and Advent, xxiv-xxv
    and "adventure of sin and
        grace," xiii
    and Albert Einstein, xvii
    as aphorist, xvi
    and apostasy and antino-
        mianism, xxiii
    and "building up the
        kingdom of God," xii,
        xviii-xix
    and civilization of Chris-
        tendom, xx
    and Confession, xxiv
    and conversion, xxiii

and crisis of catechesis, xxiv, xxvi
and Culture of Death, xxiv
and defense of the unborn, xix
and divorce, xix
and doctrinal Roman Catholic Faith, xxvi
and edification of souls, xviii
education, xxi
and eternity, xix
and French Revolution, xx, 86
and anti-clericalism of, 86
good shepherd, xxiii-xxiv
and history, xix
and *Humanae Vitae* (1968), xx
and human love, xix
job description of missionary, xxv-xxvi
and Lent, xvi
and "love of God and devotion to his Church," xii, xxii
and marriage, xix
missionary, xxv-xxvi
and *Oxford University Sermons* (1843), xv
and parish, life of, xxiii
pastoral vocation, xxv
and perfectionism, xvi
personification of good faithful dutiful

evangelizing parish priest, xxiii-xxiv
and *philosophes*, xx
prescience, xx
priest and good shepherd, xii, xiii
pro-lifer, xix-xx
and rationalism, xx-xxii
and reality and illusion, xxii
and relativism, xvi
and Roman Catholic Tradition, xxv
and *Redemptoris Missio* (1990), xxv-xxvi
and saints, xxi
and St. Augustine, xxii-xxiii
and St. John Henry Newman, xv
and St. John Paul II, xx, xxv-xxvi
and St. John Vianney, Curé d'Ars, "model of all priests," xii, xx-xxii
and sanctity of life, xx
and salvation of souls, xxiii
scope of learning, xii,
and slave trade, xix
solicitude for spiritual well-being of readers, xix
teacher, xv, xviii, xxv, xxvi
thought, "consistent, coherent ... and prophetic," xix,

and unity of, xix
wit and wisdom, xv, xxvi
wolves, xiii

sacramental sense, 43
    alien to Corinthians and
        New Yorkers, 43
sacred music, 219-220
    and Newman's idea of the
        "continuity of type"
        in the development of
        doctrine, 219
    and Pope Benedict XVI,
        219-220
sacrifice, 21
"safe spaces"
    and college students trau-
        matized by President
        Donald Trump, 183-4
saints, xxi, 13, 20, 24-25, 38,
    49, 61, 63, 79, 91, 113,
    120, 207, 208, 226, 274
    and beauty, 177
    and current cultural recep-
        tion, 226-7
    and joy of sanctity, 230
    and "metaphysical west,"
        270
    "sacraments of the sacra-
        ments," 218
    and sanity, 264
St. Ambrose, 143
St. Anthony
    and opposition to Al-
        bigensian Cathars

in southern France
"whose misunder-
standing of creation
denigrated marriage
and family life while
promoting abortion,
sodomy, and assisted
suicide," 221
St. Augustine, xxii-xxiii, 67
    and Council of Orange
        (529), 127
    and doctrine of grace, 126
    and Jansenism, 126
    and praise, 143
    and selective quoting, e.g.,
        "Love God and do
        whatever you please,
        *for the soul trained in
        love to God will do noth-
        ing to offend the One
        who is Beloved.*" [italics
        added], 134-5
St. Basil, 14, 264
St. Benedict, 147-8
St. Bernadette Soubirous, 41,
    198
    and Ronald Knox, 198
St. Bernard of Clairvaux, 181
St. Catherine of Siena, 29
St. Dorothy, 208
St Francis de Sales
    and Pope Benedict XVI,
        103-04
    and Cardinal Kasper,
        103-04

St. George, 208
St. Gregory Nazianzen, 14
    and baptism, 14
    and the Trinity, 14
St. Gregory the Great, 143
St. Ignatius Loyola, 17
    and prayer, 120
    and *Spiritual Exercises*, 120,
        257
St. Ignatius of Antioch
    and warning against cor-
        rupting the Faith of
        God with "wicked
        doctrine," 271
St. Jerome, 143
St. John, 7, 11, 16, 20, 23, 35,
    39, 108, 111, 193, 205, 256
    and memory, 176
St. John of Capistrano, 103
St. John Climacus, 242
St. John Damascene, 181
St. John Henry Cardinal New-
    man, xv, 17, 25
    and distortion of his idea
        of doctrinal develop-
        ment, which, *pace*
        Modernists, is no
        "training manual for
        the alteration of tradi-
        tion," 185-6
    "Ex umbris et imaginibus
        in veritatem" (epi-
        taph), 72
    and fondness for Roman
        authors, 214

and "Land O' Lakes State-
    ment" (1967), 142-3
and motto from St. Francis
    de Sales, "Heart speaks
    to heart," 230
Oxford University Sermons
    (1843), xv
and "passion and pride,"
    192-4
and relationship to truth,
    72
and San Giorgio in Vela-
    bro, 160
and *The Idea of a University*
    (1873), 192-4
and "whole work of God,"
    xv
wisdom, defines xv
St. John Paul II, xxi
    and *Centesimus Annus*
        (1991), 198
    and final confrontation
        between Church and
        anti-Church, Gospel
        vs. anti-Gospel, xx,
        132-33
    and *Redemptoris Missio*
        (1990), xxv-xxvi
    and Yalta Conference, 197
St. John Vianney, Curé d'Ars,
    xii, xx-xxii, xxii, 7, 41,
    126, 188-89, 208
    and Blessed Mother, 262
    blessing of the sick, 22
    courtliness, 46

and demonic possession,
201
and Eucharist, 269-70
"first and last a parish
priest," 83
and battle between good
and evil, 200-1
and the Mass, 270
and metaphysics, 171-2
"Not all the saints started
well, but they finished
well," favorite saying,
75
and party labels, 141
and priesthood, 202
in the pulpit, 162, 200
refutation of old deists and
new counterparts, 8
"The saints are like many
mirrors in which Christ
contemplates himself,"
23-4
and sin, 263
understanding the Curé
d'Ars, 258
St. Katharine Drexel, 96
St. Louis IX, 103, 221-22
St. Luke, xxvii, 48, 84, 88,
233, 273
"pioneer historian," 84
St. Mark, 188
St. Matthew, xxvii, 9, 11, 35,
130, 139, 161, 211
St. Maximilian Kolbe, 150,
208

St. Mother Teresa of Calcutta,
215-16, 251
and the author's mother,
73, 178
St. Nicholas, 208
St. Patrick, 223-24
and Druidism, 67
St. Paul, xi, xxvi, 17, 23, 34-5,
56, 60, 75, 89, 224
his conversion, how it
opened his eyes and
heart to true nature of
love, 123-4
his "ineffable joy," 214
his preaching of "a highly
developed, Trinitarian
theology" to "raucous"
Corinthians, 43-44
and secularism, 235-6
St. Peter, 49, 50, 60-1, 74, 88,
130
St. Philip Neri, 224-5
St. Pio of Pietrelcina (Padre
Pio), 9
St. Pius V, 104
St. Thérèse of Lisieux, 208
St. Thomas Aquinas, 8, 190
on courage, 44
and Martin Luther, 165
and prevention of "pseudo-
philosophical hum-
bug," 165
St. Thomas Becket, 82
St. Thomas More, 228-9
and G. K. Chesterton, 229

and conscience, 229,
St. Timothy
  and zeal for souls, 202-3
St. Vincent de Palotti, 29
Sanger, Margaret, eugenicist,
  100, 156
  and popularizing of Nazi
    eugenics, 156
salvation
  mysteries of, 216
  unmerited, 122
salvation history, 35
salvation of souls, xxiii, 54, 69
sanctity,
source of, 113
Sanctus, 63, 230
Sandreau, Abbe, authority on
  exorcism
  and *The Mystical State*, 200
  and "price of holiness,"
    200
  and St. John Vianney, 200
Satan, 15, 35, 47, 54, 93, 102,
  108, 133, 161, 164, 166,
  182, 185, 198, 218, 240,
  244, 245, 247, 253, 276,
  279
scandal, 38
Schönborn, Cardinal
  Christoph
  and distortion of John
    Henry Newman's idea
    of development of
    Christian doctrine,
    185-6

science, xx, 11, 18, 19, 43, 80,
  126, 127, 163, 211, 225,
  231, 232
  and limits of, 258
secularism, 234
secular humanism, 234-5
security, 91
self, 86
self-assertion, 21
self-destruction, 86
selfishness, 40
Seneca, 89, 214
senescence
  and Queen Elizabeth II,
    175
September 11, 2001 (9/11), 3,
  14, 71, 238
Scepticism, xx
sceptics, 39
science, xx, 18
schools, 19
secular humanism, seeds of
  modern, 88
seeing, 42
  and blindness 42
sentimentality, 56, 76, 81, 199,
  236
separation of Church and
  State, 236-7
September 11, 2001, 237-8
Sermon on the Mount, 21,
  238-9
serpents, 239
seven gifts of the Holy Spirit,
  42, 154, 239-40

servility to selfishness, 91

sin, xxii, xxiv, 3, 20, 40m 123,
    241
    and damnation, 241
    formal cooperation with
        grave sin (abortion), 85

sinners, 20

Sirach
    "God gives no one permis-
        sion to sin," 135

Shakespeare, William, 35, 130

Shaw, George Bernard, xii
    on Hell, 86

simplicity, 240-1

slave trade, xix, 4

sloth, 37

snowfall in New York City, 27

Sobieski, John III, King of
    Poland, 104

Socrates, 233-4

social illusion, 32

social engineering, 79

socialism, 65
    contrasted with capital-
        ism, 65
    and rich and poor, 65

social order, 116-18

social policy, 78

sodomy, 221
    and counterfeit marriage, 78

solemnity
    and serenity, 243

song, 243

Spain, 5

Spanish heroes, 37

spin doctors, 243-4

spirit of the age, the, 244

spiritual discipline, 244-5

spiritual warfare, 245-6, 269
    and need to be equipped
        with Catholic ord-
        nance, 74

stoics, 89

Spong, John Selby, 29

Stalin, Joseph, 56, 68-9
    and show trials, 56
    and wolves, 277

Stapp, Henry Pierce, physicist,
    171-2

State, the
    and the law, 134

Suetonius, 63, 75-6

Sulieman I, Ottoman sultan,
    106

Summa Theologica, 8, 165

sycophany, 187

Tacitus, 214

Taylor, President Zachary
    Taylor
    and Father Matthew, 168

tears, 247

Temple in Jerusalem, 63

temptation
    and Culture of Death,
        278-9
    and Holy Mother Church,
        247-8

tepidity, 7, 8

Terence, 214

terrorism, 39, 68, 90, 248-9
Thanksgiving, 15, 249
Thatcher, Margaret, 90
theodicy, 70
theology, xi
therapy, 19,
therapy vs. salvation, 32
Tiberius, 32, 75-6
Tiepolo
    and confessional, 252
    and painting of Prodigal
        Son, 252
Titus, Flavius Sabinus Vespa-
    sianus, Roman emperor, 48
timidity, 49
Trafalgar, Battle of, 17
tradition, 37, 252
Transfiguration, 57-58, 130,
    151, 252-3
    and SS Peter, James, and
        John 57
tranquility of order, 116
travel, 254, 275
    and pilgrimage, 254
Trinity, 14, 69, 82, 86, 95, 126
    and St. Gregory Nazian-
        zen, 14
    and triune economy, 66
Truman, President Harry, 102
Trump, President Donald J.
    and family, 266
    and Warsaw Speech (6 July
        2017), 266
Truth, xv, xxii, 6, 75, 76, 103,
    108, 255
    and emotion, 76
    and power, 199
    robes of Truth of Holy
        Spirit for justices and
        priests, 201-2
    and sentimentality, 76, 81
    and spin doctors, 243-4
    and theory, 255-6

Ungenitus (1713), Pope Clem-
    ent XI's papal bull con-
    demning Jansenism, 126
Universal Church, 5
Universal Theory of the Uni-
    verse, 241
unreality, intolerable cruelty
    of, 138
    and terrorism, 248-9
unseen world, 28
unsought mortifications, 250
Urban IV, Pope, 95, 199

vacations, 259-60
vandalism, 145-6, 189
    and Rodin's *Thinker*, 189
Vatican II, 260-2
    and the Liturgy, 260-2
vice, 58
Vichy, 151
    collaborationist Vichy
        radio mocked Cardinal
        Gerlier of Lyons for
        hiding Jews
    and resistance fighters 151
vineyard, the 264

Virgin Mary, xi, 15-17, 21, 41
and Francisco de Zurbarán,
Virgin Mary as a Child
(1658-1660), 179-80
Mother of Fair Love, 168-9
Mother of God, 177
and "terrible beauty of
submission," 262
"where the Mother is
loved, there is a culture
of life," 170
virtue, 3, 263
heroic virtue, 98
and hope, 263-4
natural virtue, 90, 138
Vivaldi, Antonio, 11
vocations, 263, 265

Washington, President
George, 15, 80-1, 107, 145,
and religious liberty, 267
Watts, Isaac, father of English
hymnody, 267-8
Way of Perfection, the 76, 268
Webb, Beatrice and Sidney,
155
and reverence for Vladimir
Lenin and his new
world order, 155-6
and purveying of lies, 155
and workers' earthly paradise, 156
Wedding at Cana, 118
weddings

extravagant weddings
indicative of a meretri-
cious social order, 268
and Miss Havisham, 269
Western civilization, 62
Western culture, 36
Whately, Richard, 98
wheat and chaff, 273
Wheeler, John, physicist, 256
will, 3, 277
and damnation, 277
wisdom, xv, 91, 273
Wise Virgins, 273-4
Word Made Flesh, 23, 35, 265
works of darkness, 106
World War I, 94-5
World War II, 6
lessons learned by author
of *Powers and Principalities* (2013), 149-53
world, the, 9, 41
and "euphemism for reli-
gion and politics," 93
saints and atheists and, 13
worldly importance, 9
wolves in shepherd's clothing,
278
worrying about the future, 280
worship, 5, 280-1
worst of times
and apologists, doctors and
martyrs, 281
Wurlitzer, 19

Yalta Conference (1945)
and "Land O' Lakes State-
ment" (1967), 143
Yeats, William Butler, xvi
youth
illustrious young of history
compared to pampered
charges of progressive
academy, 183-4

zeal, 140
Zacchaeus, 232-3,
and humility 281-2
Zechariah, 181
Zurbarán, Francisco de, *Virgin
Mary as a Child* (1658-
1660), 179-80

About the Author

Father George Rutler has long been a pastor of parishes in the heart of New York City. He holds academic degrees from the United States and Europe and is the author of many books. He has broadcast programs on EWTN since 1978.

About the Editor

Edward Short is the author of *Newman and History*, *Newman and His Contemporaries*, and *Newman and His Family*. He lives in New York with his wife and two young children.

Sophia Institute

Sophia Institute is a nonprofit institution that seeks to nurture the spiritual, moral, and cultural life of souls and to spread the Gospel of Christ in conformity with the authentic teachings of the Roman Catholic Church.

Sophia Institute Press fulfills this mission by offering translations, reprints, and new publications that afford readers a rich source of the enduring wisdom of mankind.

Sophia Institute also operates the popular online resource CatholicExchange.com. *Catholic Exchange* provides world news from a Catholic perspective as well as daily devotionals and articles that will help readers to grow in holiness and live a life consistent with the teachings of the Church.

In 2013, Sophia Institute launched Sophia Institute for Teachers to renew and rebuild Catholic culture through service to Catholic education. With the goal of nurturing the spiritual, moral, and cultural life of souls, and an abiding respect for the role and work of teachers, we strive to provide materials and programs that are at once enlightening to the mind and ennobling to the heart; faithful and complete, as well as useful and practical.

Sophia Institute gratefully recognizes the Solidarity Association for preserving and encouraging the growth of our apostolate over the course of many years. Without their generous and timely support, this book would not be in your hands.

www.SophiaInstitute.com
www.CatholicExchange.com
www.SophiaInstituteforTeachers.org